TELEVISION
AND THE PUBLIC SPHERE

The Media, Culture & Society Series

Editors: John Corner, Nicholas Garnham, Paddy Scannell, Philip Schlesinger, Colin Sparks, Nancy Wood

Media, Culture and Society
A Critical Reader
edited by
Richard Collins, James Curran, Nicholas Garnham, Paddy Scannell, Philip Schlesinger and Colin Sparks

Capitalism and Communication
Global Culture and the Economics of Information
Nicholas Garnham, edited by Fred Inglis

Media, State and Nation
Political Violence and Collective Identities
Philip Schlesinger

Broadcast Talk
edited by
Paddy Scannell

Journalism and Popular Culture
edited by
Peter Dahlgren and Colin Sparks

Media, Crisis and Democracy
edited by
Marc Raboy and Bernard Dagenais

Culture and Power
A Media, Culture & Society Reader
edited by
Paddy Scannell, Philip Schlesinger and Colin Sparks

Interpreting Audiences
The Ethnography of Media Consumption
Shaun Moores

Feminist Media Studies
Liesbet van Zoonen

TELEVISION
AND THE PUBLIC SPHERE

Citizenship, Democracy and the Media

Peter Dahlgren

SAGE Publications
London • Thousand Oaks • New Delhi

First published 1996. Reprinted 1997, 2000

SAGE Publications Ltd
6 Bonhill Street
London EC2A 4PU

SAGE Publications Inc
2455 Teller Road
Thousand Oaks, California 91320

SAGE Publications India Pvt Ltd
32, M-Block Market
Greater Kailash – I
New Delhi 110 048

British Library Cataloguing in Publication data

A catalogue record for this book is
available from the British Library

ISBN 0 8039 8922-9
ISBN 0 8039 8923-7 (pbk)

Library of Congress record available

Typeset by M Rules

*For my mother
and the memory of my father*

Contents

Preface

One of my earliest memories of television journalism was watching the coverage of the J.F. Kennedy assassination and its aftermath. Aside from the solemnity of the occasion, I recall how strongly I was gripped by the idea that not only was I watching this with my parents at home, but I was also watching it with millions of other people at the same time. Unbeknown to me at the time, I had stepped into the public sphere. Habermas' *Structural Transformation of the Public Sphere* had appeared in German the previous year, but it would be many years before I encountered the full Swedish (1984) and English (1989) translations. But even prior to the availibility of those texts, I had become intrigued by the role of the media in modern societies and their relation to the functioning of democracy. The emergence of the critical paradigm invited a sceptical turn in such reflection, and with the translations of Habermas' book, an overarching critical framework was made available. The concept of the public sphere, as the historically conditioned social space where information, ideas and debate can circulate in society, and where political opinion can be formed, became a central, organizing motive. This framework cast the public sphere as a sociological concept as well as an inspirational vision of something better yet to be attained.

Despite the impressive scope of Habermas' book, questions remained. Literature from a variety of fields addressed some of the issues, often raising still new questions. With the translation of Habermas' *Theory of Communicative Action* (1984, 1987), yet another major step had been taken in theoretical clarification of communicative processes and the social order. However, again issues arose, and it seemed that a whole industry of secondary literature emerged, interpreting, summarizing and criticizing Habermas' project. I encountered yet other studies, though not directly engaging with Habermas, charting trajectories relevant for examining the relationships between the public sphere, the media and democracy. There was – and is – still much to learn.

One of the basic difficulties with the notion of a public sphere is that once one begins to unpack it and examine how the various theoretical and empirical components fit together, it becomes very convoluted. All things are connected (as both Hegel and Buddha would affirm from their respective notions of Enlightenment), and in the case of the public sphere, it becomes difficult to see not only all the interfaces but also the boundaries which demarcate the phenomenon from its environment.

This book is an essayistic effort to explore some of the connections and boundaries of the public sphere, partly empirically but largely theoretically. It is chiefly a project of clarification, an attempt to 'sort things out' at the conceptual level, with the intention of providing a clearer platform for future empirical work. It is in part an encounter with Habermas, because his work is so obviously central here, even if I find difficulties with it. I also draw from a variety of literature within social, cultural and political theory, as well as media studies. I have found inspiration in various strands of feminist theory. I try to highlight some of the more significant debates around key points of contention. While I strive to steer my own course through all this material, it will be evident that in many cases there are no easy answers. I would be misleading the reader if I implied that he or she should anticipate full resolution on all the issues. Indeed, much of the discussion pivots on an encounter between the critical tradition and what I see as the more constructive versions of postmodern theorizing – and much of the message of the latter is that we need to heighten our tolerance for ambiguity.

Television figures prominently in this study since it has become, for better or worse, the major institution of the public sphere in modern society. I examine television from the horizon of the public sphere and the public sphere is illuminated, in part, with television in mind. I try to elucidate the limits and possibilities – the conditions – for their relationship. Television is evolving rapidly, technologically and structurally. My horizon here incorporates the dominant, 'mainstream' public service and commercial television (which I see as now including cable and satellite television as well broadcasting). While some of the newer developments such as the links to computers and telecommunication are of significance and will no doubt continue to grow in their import, I will leave such developments for a future treatment. The concrete examples from television which I use are drawn largely from Sweden and, to some extent, the USA, since it is with these that I am most familiar. However, these illustrations are largely of a generic nature and it is my assumption that any reader familiar with Western television culture will recognize the type of programming to which I am referring in each instance.

Given that television and other media institutions and their output are vital to the public sphere, the pursuit of progressive media policy remains of utmost importance. Yet to understand the public sphere, we must see the limits of the role that especially television can play, even under the very best of circumstances. Hence, while Chapters 2 and 3 are devoted to discussions of television, the ensuing chapters take up other topics. Social structure, for example, broadly understood, of course plays a major role in defining the character of the public sphere. Also, one of the recurring themes in the text is that we must understand the public sphere in terms of sociocultural interaction among citizens.

Sociocultural interaction has to do not only with encounters in which people act out their roles as citizens and discuss social and political issues. It also has to do with the more fundamental construction of social reality at the intersubjective level. Society is in part generated, maintained and altered in our ongoing interactions, in a complex interplay with structural and historical factors. Norms, collective frames of reference, even our identities, ultimately derive from sociocultural interaction. In short, it is via such interaction, and the practices it embodies, that we generate our culture. This dimension of interaction constitutes an irreducible component of the public sphere. Not all interaction is a manifestation of the public sphere, but the point is that the functioning of the public sphere is greatly dependent upon the nature of sociocultural interaction. That is why the democratization of civil society – which is a way of conceptualizing the terrain of interaction – is of vital importance for the public sphere.

Each chapter in the book approaches a certain set of issues and it is my aim that the organization and sequence of the chapters will foster the gradual unfolding of an overall perspective. There are a number of cross-referencing notes scattered throughout the text, concerning topics touched upon but postponed for fuller treatment further on. This is particularly evident in the first chapter, where many topics are introduced to convey an overview of the discussions to come. Some themes, such as the notion of rationality and the tensions around it, appear in several contexts, but I have done my best to avoid repetition.

Chapter 1 situates the theme of the public sphere in the larger problematics of contemporary democracy, centring on the relationship between state and civil society. I provide a cursory treatment of Habermas' by now rather familiar concept of the public sphere, and go on to discuss some of the critical response to it. The issues which emerge – and to which I return in later chapters – can be organized into four themes; these provide a conceptual framework of four dimensions of the public sphere: social structure, media institutions, media representations, and sociocultural interaction.

In Chapter 2, I focus my attention on television as a medium, reviewing the literature on television research and on what is sometimes loosely called 'television theory'. I approach television as an industry, as audio-visual texts, and as sociocultural experience. The industry side includes its political economy, its organization, as well as professional practices. In discussing television as audio-visual text, I emphasize among other things the contingency of meaning, and the significance of its mimetic quality. Also I take up the tension between television as popular culture and public knowledge. Television as sociocultural experience takes us into its ubiquity, its reception, its pleasures, and how its mythic, narrative mode of representation resonates in everyday life. As an institution of the public sphere, television certainly has its liabilities, but we must not ignore its assets.

I turn in Chapter 3 to a discussion of television journalism, which I organize around the theme of its increasing popularization. The notion of the popular becomes an entry port to a discussion of a number of television journalism's contemporary formats, including talk shows and tele-tabloids. The 'force field' between information and story is examined, and I also probe the possibilities of the dialogic dimension in television journalism and its relation to moral sensibility. Popular television journalism includes both promises and pitfalls, but it may not always be evident which is which.

Chapter 4 represents a shifting of gears, as I attempt to sketch some of the contours of the social and epistemological contingencies of modernity. It is my contention that any serious thinking about the public sphere must come to terms with the dominant dynamics of the historical present, including the multilayered relationship between 'public' and 'private'. In this chapter I thus take up some key aspects of modernization – economic, political, technical and cultural – but I also emphasize the importance of recognizing our current epistemic situation. Our knowledge is expanding exponentially, yet the grounds for knowing seem increasingly unsteady. At the same time, we as individuals, groups and societies have made reflexivity a key feature of modernity. These developments impinge on the conditions of the public sphere.

Much of Chapter 5 is an engagement with elements of Habermas' theory of communicative action. I underscore both its importance and its limitations, highlighting what I see to be unnecessary restrictions engendered by his rather austere notion of rationality. By exploring the arational, by opening up the discussion to versions of the unconscious and its link to signifying practices – the imaginary and the emancipatory – I indicate a somewhat different theoretical route to communication and intersubjectivity.

Chapter 6 explores two key themes: civil society and citizenship. As the setting for the interactional dimension of the public sphere, civil society also provides an analytic opening for recontextualizing television reception. I take up recent attempts to theorize civil society and to link it to Habermas' framework, noting both gains and limititations in this effort. The struggle for a viable public sphere must also go via civil society, institutionally securing it and culturally filling it with democratic values. Citizenship has returned to the agenda with a vengeance, and it is apparent that changing historical circumstances are altering its definitions and implications. While political theory and philosophy have much to tell us on this score, so do theories of identity, especially as developed within feminism. Citizenship becomes – or rather, must become – an integrated element of the self if a democratic culture is to thrive. Citizenship has to do with belonging and participating, and again we see how the public sphere is inexorably intertwined with social structural and interactional dimensions.

There is neither a full summary nor firm conclusions in Chapter 7, but I do synoptically review some of the main points from the previous chapters and probe some of their implications. In particular, I take up the role of television journalism and explore some of the political horizons of civil society. I also offer some reflections which point to media policy, arguing that we need a 'polyphonic' public sphere which consists of what I call a common domain and an adversary domain.

I feel I have incurred massive debts in putting together this book. I would like to express my gratitude to the Humanities Faculty of Stockholm University for a part-time research grant which made the work possible. I began my research in earnest while a visiting scholar at the Department of Film and Media Studies, University of Stirling, during the autumn semester of 1992 and am very grateful for the opportunity. I especially wish to thank Philip Schlesinger for his hospitality and advice. My colleagues and doctoral students at the Department of Journalism, Media and Communication have provided a supportive intellectual environment where these ideas could grow.

In particular Johan Fornäs, with whom I recently taught a course on Modern Critical Theory, has offered many helpful insights.

For helpful conversations at various stages of the project I wish to thank John Corner and Marc Raboy. Louis Quéré provided helpful feedback in the context of the annual summer course of the European Doctoral Network in Communication at the University of Stendhal – Grenoble 3. Simon Frith and Michael Schudson read early drafts; Klaus Bruhn Jensen read several chapters; Veronica Stoehrel and Johan Fornäs read the whole manuscript. My appreciation goes out to them all. They are, of course, all absolved of responsibility for shortcomings in the text.

I am also grateful for encouragement from the Media, Culture and Society Series editors Paddy Scannell and Colin Sparks, and particularly to Sage editor Stephen Barr for his guidance and patience.

Finally, warm thanks to Karin, Max and Finn, for tolerance during all the evenings and weekends when work on this project intruded on our private sphere.

PART I
INITIAL HORIZONS

1
Mediating democracy

In today's world, democracy remains precarious and vulnerable. We can point to many factors which contribute to this, among the more obvious being declining economies and their political fall-out, an environment threatened by the fundamental premises of our civilization, a chaotic international system where the status of the nation-state is increasingly problematical, and where the distinction between the military and criminal use of organized violence is often blurred. Many in the West who cheered the collapse of the Soviet system saw the triumph of both capitalism and liberal democracy. At this historical juncture, global capitalism clearly has no serious competitor. However, what this means for the well being of humanity and for the planet is arguable. What it means for democracy is also problematic. If the tension between democracy and capitalism has long been with us, in the contemporary situation the threats to democratic development cannot be seen as emanating exclusively from the logic of the market.

While private corporations function beyond popular democratic control, many allegedly democratic regimes bypass both their electorates and representative assemblies. Even with the most noble of intentions, the process of government has become paralysingly difficult. Many decisions which governments face require a degree of knowledge or even expertise far beyond the grasp of most citizens. In many countries, citizens, in turn, are increasingly withdrawing from the official political arena, leaving its management to 'the political class', which Hobsbawm (1994) describes as 'a special-interest group of professional politicians, journalists, lobbyists and others whose occupations ranked at the bottom of the scale of trustworthiness in sociological inquiries.' Such depoliticization includes on the one hand the affluent, who have the private means and influence to pursue and satisfy their interests, and on the other, those among the majority who increasingly feel they have nothing to gain from participating in a game they view as rigged against them.

Some of the forces undermining democracy are explicit, active and obvious, while others are more implicit or passive. Some antidemocratic forces may be unwitting: the consequences of human intentionality cannot always be predicted. Yet, though one may in darker moments wonder if democracy in the future will be seen as a temporary parenthesis in the history of civilization, we also find continual as well as new and unexpected manifestations of democracy's power to inspire. Not least as a far-reaching and compelling issue on the contemporary societal agenda, democracy is very much alive. It remains an historical accomplishment, continuously needing to be regenerated. We cannot take it for granted or assume that it will live its own life, yet rumours of its death are premature. Drawing lessons from the revolutions of 1989, Hobsbawm (1994) in a paraphrase quips 'the 20th century showed that one can rule against all the people for some of the time, some of the people all of the time, but not all the people all of the time.'

For better or worse, democracy is also one of our most pervasive and all-purpose hurrah words. The powerful publicly extoll it, the vast majority support it; few people will publicly admit to being against it. The invocation of democracy can serve as a ritual of collective belonging, joining people from virtually all social sectors in a common cause. It would seem that this allegiance to democracy creates such an all-encompassing 'us' that one is hard put to point to a 'them' – an 'other' who stands opposed to it. The only catch, of course, is that democracy can mean quite different things to different people; the vision it embodies is far from unitary. Moreover, as societal and political conditions change, so too can the definitions of democracy – criteria found to be too ambitious can be modified.

The health of democracy in the course of the twentieth century has more and more been linked to the health of systems of communication, though of course democracy cannot be reduced to issues of the media. However, the dynamics of democracy are intimately linked to the practices of communication, and societal communication increasingly takes place within the mass media. In particular, it is television which has gained a prominent position within the political systems of the modern world. Concern for democracy automatically necessitates a concern about television, to which I turn in the two following chapters.

In this chapter, I begin with reflections on democracy as a model and as an ideal, based on some of the more recent literature. Thereafter, I briefly take up Habermas' much discussed theory and model of the public sphere. It is now well over three decades old, yet continues to inspire thinking about the relationship between the media and democracy. Then I review some of the major issues which have arisen in the criticisms levelled against it, thematizing the major points of contention. I will be returning to a number of these themes later in the book. Much of the debate around the public sphere has taken the form of media policy discussions. This is of the utmost importance and must continue. However, accompanying this frame must be a broader understanding of the social structural and sociocultural dimensions of the public sphere, and how these condition its possibilities and limits.

Desiring democracy

The concept of democracy has an evocative rhetoric which embodies so many of our desires for the good society. Yet, as with many objects of desire, closer inspection can generate complication. Citing Dunn, Arnason (1990) speaks of two basic directions in democratic theory today: one which is 'dismally ideological', representing a conservative functionalization, and another which is 'fairly blatantly Utopian', which he sees as a romantic radicalism. This polarity certainly captures some of the theoretic tension: in the first case, for example, in mainstream political science we have a declining level of ambition regarding the criteria for democracy, where necessity becomes virtue. Thus, democracy is no longer seen as a system expressing the will of the people, but rather one which offers consumer choice in the rotation of élites. That this system seems to lead to declining levels of citizen participation is even hailed as an attribute of its success, in that it enhances its stability (Simonds, 1989, develops this view). Moreover, there is a closure at work, whereby the concept of democracy becomes identical with the current political systems of liberal capitalist societies. The Utopian antithesis, of course, is easily revealed to rest on a cheerful mixture of wishful thinking and sociological near-sightedness.

Rather than choosing between the two extremes, we would do well, carefully and flexibly, to situate ourselves between them. If we reject the identity logic that says what we now see is by definition the realization of democracy, we can still judiciously retain and expand upon that which is worth saving within the present arrangements. Indeed, looking further to the philosophical tradition of liberal democracy, many on the left (for example, Held, 1993; Keane, 1988a; Mouffe, 1992b) emphasize the importance of preserving many of its ideals, the argument being that their implementation in practice would result in truly radical consequences. Thus, the left too can see in the tradition of liberal democracy important elements for setting limits on state power and for generally handling conflicts of interest and social antagonisms. Democratic procedures become a way to organize and mediate the varying competing interests, projects, and values within plural societies, while at the same time the perceived limits of the liberal tradition are identified and contested.

In addition, if the Utopian version at times loses contact with the problems of social reality, the importance of a vision – of a horizon – should not be undervalued. I will return to the theme of Utopian horizons later, but regarding the romantic view of democracy, I would just say that it is often associated with what is called its direct or participatory version. As a model for the political systems of advanced industrial societies it cannot, of course, be taken seriously. Even the small worlds of university democracy require mechanisms of representation: is there any faculty member prepared to sit on *all* the committees which are of relevance to him or her? Oscar Wilde once quipped that the problem with socialism is that it would take up too many free evenings; the same can be said for democracy in general.

Ideally we should have a blend of direct and representational mechanisms, as Held (1989) argues. Not only do elements of direct democracy, which involve face-to-face relations, enhance the responsiveness of the system itself, but – assuming they are sufficiently widespread – they also provide 'training grounds' for anchoring democracy in the experiences of lived reality. This sociocultural dimension, which encompasses values and a sense of identity as a citizen, is important both for the vitality of democracy as a system and the dynamics of the public sphere.

There are other difficulties as we probe deeper into democracy. Chaney (1993:115) takes up the built-in tension which appears when intellectuals talk about 'the people'. The rhetoric of political mobilization, whereby intellectuals incorporate themselves with the people, structures a dubious collective self-consciousness, for the people also remain to some extent an 'Other', an object of ethnographic curiosity. Simonds (1989) goes further, suggesting that when the people do make progressive political choices, they are lauded for their clear-sightedness and commitment; but when they manifest reactionary tendencies, they are portrayed by intellectuals as being duped by ideology, manipulated by the media, and seduced by politicians. In other words, the people are deemed free agents only when they happen to choose correctly, and are seen as victims, tools of sinister powers, when they veer towards reactionary politics. Now of course 'the people' manifest the philosophical ping-pong of free will versus determinism as much and as little as anybody else, including intellectuals. The problem is that the rhetoric of democracy, which celebrates the formation of popular will and the power of the people, must also live with the insight that the majority may not always choose the enlightened path. A system which is fundamentally democratic may be deemed good on that formal criterion, but there is no guarantee that the decisions arrived at will be an expression of the 'good society'. There is always the ominous dark side of democracy; it does not ensure peace and light. In Eastern Europe today, for example, as many xenophobic and populist policies win acclaim, there must be a good number of former dissident intellectuals who feel disappointed by 'the people' whose liberty they struggled to achieve.

It is just this kind of democracy, without guarantees and without foundations, that Keane (1991) writes about. This agnostic view can be seen as a largely procedural version of democracy. It is not assumed that democracy is infallible: bad decisions cannot be precluded, but rather what is crucial is that any decision taken can, in principle, be reversed. Also, while democracy is generally understood to provide mechanisms for arriving at agreements, perhaps more importantly it must also offer mechanisms for handling disagreements, which in turn may warrant reversals of previous decisions. Democracy requires systems of rules and commitments to abide by them, but beyond that does not *per se* ensure that any particular set of values will prevail.

A similar agnosticism is reflected in Mouffe's (1993) arguments that we must free ourselves from the thought that we will ever reach a point in history characterized by pervasive social harmony. Expanding on themes she and Laclau developed earlier (Laclau and Mouffe, 1985), she asserts that there is no end to the political, no juncture awaiting us which will not be characterized by conflicts and antagonisms. In a similar vein, we will never arrive at a fully realized democracy, a millenium where everyone participates in will formation and where unanimity prevails (Mouffe, 1992a:Introduction). This is because social interests, as well as individual and collective identities, are relational and contextual; they are never static. New situations give rise to new interests and identities, new constellations of cooperation and antagonism. The varied conflicts emerging in the aftermath of the collapse of communism give ample evidence of this.

The challenge of such a perspective requires a sober balancing act, to acknowledge the Sysiphus-like character of our condition and *still* not give up on a moral vision. As Garnham (1992) pointedly comments in his evaluation of Habermas' notion of the public sphere, what we have here is not Utopianism but, on the contrary, a tragic view of life. Such a view understands and comes to terms with human limitations, the vicissitudes of history, and the misplaced hubris of certain strands of modern thought. It tries to generate 'a garden', knowing that it is in perpetual struggle with a wilderness which can encroach both from within and without. In regard to democracy more generally, Mouffe says that we should not dream about the disappearance of political conflict, but rather that political adversaries can meet each other in dialogue and not view each other as enemies to be liquidated. Like Keane and Held, Mouffe takes a procedural view of democracy, emphasizing the need for a common democratic culture expressed through loyalty to democratic values. Again, this is something which cannot be a trait of the system or a feature of structure; it must be anchored in the microworlds of people's everyday values and experience.

In western society, a fixation of the formal political system as the exclusive centre of politics continues to exist and continues to frame the common understanding of democracy. Yet, as Beck (1992), Eder (1993) and others point out, there is a growing loss of power by centralized political systems; changes in social structure are bringing about new forms of political culture. An unravelling of centralized systems politics correlates with transitions whereby many formerly non-political topics become, if not politicized, at least 'sub-political' or 'quasi-political'. The obvious manifestations of this, but not the only ones, are contemporary social movements, such as those of various feminist and ecological orientations. These developments tie in with another important yet difficult polarity with regard to democracy that many theorists (for example, Held, 1989; Keane, 1988a; Cohen and Arato, 1992) have recently taken up, namely the relationship between the state and civil society, with particular emphasis on the status and position of civil society.

The concept of civil society is a contested one among contemporary theorists. Tester (1992), for example, sees civil society essentially as an incoherent expression of the antinomies of modernism: while it served to kindle people's imaginations for a while, the idea of civil society disassembles with the failing self-confidence of modernity. In Tester's acerbic words, civil society today can feed our imagination only 'to the extent that it can continue to provide easy and comforting answers to easy and irrelevant questions' (Tester 1992:176). Walzer (1992), on the other hand, sees civil society as an absolutely essential 'space of uncoerced human association and also the set of relational networks – formed for the sake of family, faith, interest and ideology – that fill this space' (Walzer 1992:89). It is this line of thinking, further developed by Cohen and Arato (1992), which I find fruitful and to which I will return later in the book. For Walzer, civil society must serve as a buffer against single-minded and reductionistic visions of the good life, including political community, economic production, market activity and nationalism. Against their singularity, civil society stands as 'the realm of fragmentation and struggle but also of concrete and authentic solidarities' (Walzer 1992:97). It is the domain of association which exists basically for the sake of sociability, rather than for any goal of social formation.

An interesting aspect of Walzer's formulation is that he sees a paradox in civil society's relation to the state and to politics generally. He warns against seeing civil society in exclusively apolitical terms, yet civil society must not be reduced to the interaction of citizens within the state: 'Only a democratic state can create a democratic civil society; only a democratic civil society can sustain a democratic state' (Walzer 1992:104). Thus, citizens' political power is necessary, but not sufficient; there must be a viable social dimension beyond the political. While Walzer sees this as a paradox which he feels unable fully to resolve, one can also see this as an important theoretical step: treating the boundary between the political and the sociocultural in a fluid manner, seeing it as permeable and contestable, may well prove to be a crucial feature of democracy's future.

It is the interplay between the state and civil society which both Held (1989) and Keane (1988a) emphasize. Each side, as Walzer suggests, is a precondition for the democratization of the other. This necessitates what Held calls the need for a 'double democratization'; our democratic desire requires a dual focus – a struggle on two fronts. Civil society is not to be reduced to a political arena, yet its democratization is a political project. It does not derive from or express any natural 'authentic humanity' and can certainly function in many repressive ways. It may well tend to hinder the conditions for political reflection and participation. If the state is too weak, it cannot foster democratization of civil society. If it is too strong, it becomes too interventionist; without a viable civil society, the state becomes too all-encompassing. The democratization of civil society has to do with the development of a democratic culture or mentality within the context of everyday life. Yet in the face of the state, civil society remains relatively powerless. The concept of civil society highlights among other things the inseparable links between the sociocultural and the political. A rigid distinction between them, writes Hohendahl (1992:108), 'will necessarily constrain our understanding of those concerns that come under the category of the good life'.

At the level of theory, civil society has a particular relationship to the public sphere. In brief, civil society constitutes the sociocultural preconditions for a viable public sphere. The two categories are inseparable, but not identical: much of civil society, such as the whole realm of family relations, has little to do with the public sphere directly. Also, the public sphere encompasses the media, which are not easily situated within civil society. I will take up the concept of civil society and its relationship to the public sphere in more detail in Chapter 6. For now I want to turn my attention directly to the public sphere.

The public sphere as historical narrative

Notions of what is termed the public sphere, or public space, which thematize the role of interaction among citizens in the political process, can be traced back to the ancient Greeks. Notions of what is 'public' are of course premised on conceptions of what constitutes the 'private'. The public/private polarity has several overlapping historical strands, as I take up in Chapter 4. In recent modern political thought, however, the idea of 'public' in relation to the processes of democracy has been given ambitious formulations in the work of many writers; among the most prominent are Dewey (1954/1923), Arendt (1958), and Habermas (1989/1962). The concept is by no means identical in these three authors; they work out of different traditions and their approaches vary. The functions and problematics of the mass media, for example, are explicitly central to Dewey and Habermas, but not to Arendt. There are similarities and differences in their political, sociological and historical horizons, but it is Habermas' version which is the most fruitful, despite a number of serious difficulties. Thus, my focus here will be on his concept of the public sphere and the response it has evoked. Specifically, my emphasis will be on his notion of the political public sphere, rather than the more broad cultural public sphere, where literature and the arts circulate. In a later chapter I will also consider some of his ideas regarding communicative rationality, which can be seen to extend and modify his earlier thinking on the public sphere. While I will focus on Habermas, the three authors can be and have been fruitfully compared; a recent effort in this regard, with an hermeneutic perspective on citizenship, is found in Alejandro (1993).

In this section I will first briefly summarize Habermas' (1989/1962) theory of the public sphere. This will only be a compressed synopsis; a comprehensive overview of this topic, containing many commentaries, is found in Calhoun (1992). From there I will review the major criticisms that have been levelled against it. Finally, I will present a scheme of four dimensions as a conceptual aid approaching the public sphere analytically.

In ideal terms, Habermas conceptualizes the public sphere as that realm of social life where the exchange of information and views on questions of common concern can take place so that public opinion can be formed. The public sphere 'takes place' when citizens, exercising the rights of assembly and association, gather as public bodies to discuss issues of the day, specifically those of political concern. Since the scale of modern society does not allow more than relatively small numbers of citizens to be physically co-present, the mass media have become the chief institutions of the public sphere. Yet Habermas' concept of the public sphere insists on the analytic centrality of reasoned, critical discourse. The public sphere exists, in other words, in the active reasoning of the public. It is via such discourse that public opinion is generated, which in turn is to shape the policies of the state and the development of society as a whole.

Of course this is not how society today actually operates. Habermas tells a story; it is a rather melancholic historical narrative in two acts. In the first act he portrays a fledgling bourgeois public sphere emerging under liberal capitalism in the eighteenth century. This 'category' of the public sphere is historically specific to the societal arrangements of Britain, France and Germany in this period. Prior to this, in the Middle Ages, there was no social space which could be called 'public' in contrast to 'private'; powerful feudal lords (as well as the Church) may have displayed themselves and their power to the populace, but this did not in any way constitute a public sphere in Habermas' sense. With the demise of feudalism, and the growth of national states, parliaments, commerce, the middle classes and, not least, printing, a public sphere began to take root in certain societies of Western Europe. This public sphere consisted of certain segments of the educated, propertied strata (almost exclusively male), and operated via such media as intellectual journals, pamphlets and newspapers, as well as in such settings as salons, coffee houses and clubs. This exchange of factual information, ongoing discussion and often heated debate was a new phenomenon, to which Habermas attributes much significance.

The second act traces the decline of the bourgeois public sphere in the context of advanced industrial capitalism and the social welfare state of mass democracy. With mass democracy, the public loses its exclusivity: its socio-discursive coherence comes apart as many less educated citizens enter the scene. The state, to handle the growing contradictions of capitalism, becomes more interventionist; the boundaries between public and private, both in political economic terms and in cultural terms, begin to dissipate. Large organizations and interest groups become key political partners with the state, resulting in a 'refeudalization' of politics which greatly displaces the role of the public. The increasing prevalence of the mass media, especially where the commercial logic transforms much of public communication into PR, advertising and entertainment, erodes the critical functions of the public. The public becomes fragmented, losing its social coherence. It becomes reduced to a group of spectators whose acclaim is to be periodically mobilized, but whose intrusion in fundamental political questions is to be minimized.

The story of the decline of the public sphere is still very much with us, continuously being replayed in updated versions by researchers and commentators. On the other hand, the gloomy portrayal of the modern public sphere's demise has been rejected in more optimistic corners as overstating the case. From yet other corners, Habermas' affirmative historical picture of the rise of the bourgeois public sphere has been contested. Some may even question the utility of the notion of the public sphere itself. However, I find the concept still to be a valid and helpful one. It points to those institutional constellations of the media and other fora for information and opinion – and the social practices around them – which are relevant for political life. That these institutional constellations and practices may be anaemic does not *per se* mean they are irrelevant.

The political public sphere constitutes a space – a discursive, institutional, topographical space – where people in their roles as citizens have access to what can be metaphorically called societal dialogues, which deal with questions of common concern: in other words, with politics in the broadest sense. This space, and the conditions for communication within it, are essential for democracy. This nexus of institutions and practices is an expression of public culture – visible and accessible sets of societal meanings and practices – and at the same time presupposes a public culture. One could say that a functioning public sphere is the fulfilment of the communicational requirements of a viable democracy. And like the concept of democracy, to use the notion of the public sphere does not suggest that what we see today is its consummate embodiment. Again, we would be advised to try to position ourselves between 'dismally ideological' and 'blatantly Utopian' views.

Habermas' intellectual roots lie with the Frankfurt School, and his theses about the public sphere became inspirational for much critical media research. But as Peters (1993) points out, his basic understanding of democracy and the public sphere are not totally remote from the Anglo-American liberal tradition and its notion of the marketplace of ideas. The liberal discourses (that is, the 'classic', not 'neo-liberal' ones) on media and democracy normally do not use the category 'public sphere', but they nonetheless underscore the citizens' need for useful and relevant journalism. With access to reliable information from a variety of perspectives, and a diversity of opinions on current affairs, citizens will arrive at their own views on important issues and thus prepare themselves for political participation. Both the public sphere and the marketplace of ideas can be seen as normative and very idealized pictures, easily contrasted with current realities.

But there are differences as well. Habermas situates the bourgeois public sphere within the history of capitalism, the rise of the interventionist state, and the emergence of the culture industries, emphasizing not least the difficult conditions which democracy requires and how the modern media can obstruct those conditions. Thus, we should not lose sight of the fact that the public sphere retains an anchoring in critical theory, and to use the term incorporates the media within a critical perspective on democracy (see, for example, Dahlgren and Sparks, 1991). If the shortcomings of the marketplace of ideas at best tends to generate calls for reforms in the conditions and operations of journalism, the disparity between the model and reality of the public sphere goes further. It evokes wide-ranging critical reflection on social structure, the concentration of power, cultural practices, and the dynamics of the political process.

Many have written on the inspirational quality of Habermas' text, lauding the weight he gives to the modern media, the historical perspective on their evolution, and, not least, his emphatic reminder of the twin dangers of state power and corporate control over the logic of their operations. Criticisms from many angles have also been forthcoming; many have pointed to the ambiguous status of the entire concept of the public sphere in Habermas' book, arguing that it appears both as a normative ideal to be strived for and as a manifestation of actual historical circumstances in early bourgeois Europe. In other words, how are we to view those social features in the late eighteenth and early nineteenth centuries whereby a relatively small group of economically and politically privileged men communicated with each other within the context of a small, budding press and the settings of salons, coffee houses and exclusive societies? Was this a genuine public sphere or merely an exercise in bourgeois self-delusion? Should we see this only as an emancipatory space or should we also see it in terms of Foucault's perspective, as Verstraeten (1994) suggests: he makes the point that we can also look at the public sphere's social disciplining and exclusionary functions which stand in contrast to its liberatory aspects.

However, if we allow that the public sphere was not merely an ideological misconception but contained at least the germ of something new and progressive (which Habermas argues for by contrasting the bourgeois public sphere with previous historical versions of what constituted publicness), it was in any case very much grounded in a notion of small-scale print media and rational, conversational interaction among a small sector of, at that time, much smaller populations. Where does that leave us in the age of massive-scale societies and electronic media? If the public sphere today is so dominated by the mass media, what does this suggest for the viability of the larger analytical category of civil society? If we do not simply equate the public sphere with the mass media, there remain many questions for democracy about the nature and extent of face-to-face communication.

Feminists have criticized not only the actual exclusion of women in the bourgeois public sphere, but also Habermas' failure to make a critical point of this in his evaluation. Such feminist encounters with Habermas' work (see especially Fraser, 1987, 1992) merge with the larger critical feminist projects illuminating the gender partiality within the public/private distinction of liberal theory and within political philosophy more generally; at bottom this project has to do with reconstructing the concept of democracy in the light of feminist analysis (see Pateman, 1987, 1988, 1992; Nicholson, 1992; Phillips, 1991, 1993; Bock and James, 1992; Jónasdóttir, 1991; Brown, 1988; Elshtain, 1993). Feminist as well as other writers have taken up the overly rationalistic view of human communication in Habermas' work. This rationalist quality of Habermas' understanding of discourse becomes more explicit and central in his later work, particularly in his major theoretical contribution from the early 1980s, *The Theory of Communicative Action* (1984, 1987), which I take up in Chapter 5. It is understandable that critics take into account the perspectives from this later study, and commentaries on Habermas' view of communication often connect the two phases of his work.

Habermas (1992a) responded to these and many other criticisms of his

Structural Transformation of the Public Sphere (1989/1962) in the context of a conference. He expressed appreciation for the interest and critical insights of the contributors, while reminding them that the book came out in the early 1960s. He self-critically assured his colleagues that were he to write the book today, he would make many changes, yet felt justified in asserting its continued usefulness, despite its limitations. It is hard not to agree. If the concept of the public sphere is one which hovers between philosophical and historical groundings, as one of the conference contributors (Hohendahl, 1992) suggested, we can perhaps turn this into a strength. We can take the idea – the vision of a public sphere – as inspirational, yet accept that there is no single universal model which is possible or even suitable for all historical circumstances. The task becomes to try to devise new forms and strategies. If modesty must prevail on our social and historical analyses, we should allow ourselves to be ambitious and expansive in our conceptual and normative thinking.

Four dimensions

As we can already see, critical encounters with Habermas' conception of the public sphere have come from a variety of directions. I cannot attend to all the issues here; for example, one question to which many have pointed has to do with his historical interpretation which ignores alternative public spheres which functioned parallel with the bourgeois one. But by synthesizing a number of key points in the commentaries – I make particular use of texts by Garnham (1992), Peters (1993), Fraser (1992), Thompson (1990) – we can conveniently sort the critical themes and questions into four areas: media institutions, media representation, social structure and sociocultural interaction. This in turn offers us a framework for conceptualizing four analytic dimensions of the public sphere. Each dimension serves as an entry port to sets of issues about the public sphere, both theoretical and conceptual questions as well as empirical and evaluative ones about its actual functioning. No one dimension stands on its own; all four interlock with each other and constitute reciprocal conditions for one another.

The dimension of media institutions, their organization, financing, regulation, and the dimension of media representation, chiefly in regard to journalistic coverage, are the two which generally receive most attention. Both figure at the centre of considerable policy debate. The dimension of social structure points to the broader horizon of factors which constitute the historical conditions and institutional milieu of the public sphere. These structural elements from the broader institutional arrangements of society include social stratification, power alignments, and, not least, the state. Economic, political and legal aspects are included here. Also, the nature and quality of the entire educational system, and its place in the social order, becomes relevant in this regard. This is a topic I cannot pursue here, but the role of education in shaping the analytic and communicative competencies of the citizenry is crucial for the character of the public sphere, despite the inevitable ideological dimensions of schooling. Finally, sociocultural interaction refers to non-mediated face-to-face encounters between citizens, to relevant aspects of subjectivity and identity processes, and also to the interface of media and citizens, that is, the processes of reception. Civil society composes the space for much of the public sphere beyond the media; without attention to this interactionist dimension of the public sphere, the whole conceptual foundation of democracy is undermined.

The dimension of social structural factors defines not least the 'political ecology' of the media, setting boundaries for the media's institutional and organizational profile, as well as for the nature of the information and forms of representation and expression which may circulate. Obviously the social structural dimension also impacts on the patterns of sociocultural interaction. Thus, social structure complexly constitutes a set of conditions for the public sphere which can also be charted via the three other dimensions. Social structure is no doubt the dimension which is conceptually the most difficult to deal with, since it is potentially so vast. In fact, at some point in the analysis, social structure must be put in brackets if we are not to not lose our specific focus on the public sphere. However, its role must not be lost from view. That the public sphere cannot be seen as a space operating in isolation from all other social, political and economic domains, as if it were a self-contained entity, is one of Habermas' central points. To understand the public sphere under any specific historical circumstances requires taking into account the larger societal figurations which both comprise its space and constitute the preconditions for its functioning.

A society where democratic tendencies are weak and the structural features of society are highly inegalitarian is not going to give rise to healthy institutional structures for the public sphere. Such structural features translate into mechanisms whereby the basic patterns of power and social hierarchy detrimentally shape the character of the public sphere. These mechanisms operate by institutionally *delimiting* the public sphere as such; for instance, the state, together with vested interests, can pursue media policies which hinder the flow of relevant information and constrict the range of opinion. Alternatively, such mechanisms may operate *through* the public sphere to hinder democratic development, for example 'news plants', disinformation, trivialization. Further, power and social hierarchy can shape the public sphere at the level of interaction, impacting on the sites and settings where such contact takes place.

Media institutions

Policy issues around media institutions and their output are of course the most tangible and immediate expression of political attention to the public sphere. Such policy issues include the organization, financing, and legal frameworks of the media. The legal frameworks encompass not only questions of ownership, control, procedures for licensing, rules for access, and so on, but also the freedoms and the constraints on communication. The public sphere's entwinement with the state and with society's overall political situation comes most clearly to the fore in the case of broadcasting. Such policy is shaped to a great extent by forces and actors located within the state and the economy; progressive policy efforts attempt to steer this influence in democratically productive directions, and also aim to enhance the influence of the public itself in shaping broadcasting (Raboy, 1994).

Habermas' image of the public sphere lurks beneath the surface of many progressive interventions into media policy issues (see Raboy, 1991; Raboy, 1994); however, all such efforts do not have to depend on his conceptualizations. The loosely defined movement for democratic communication and information (see, for example, Splichal and Wasko, 1993), which has been active at local levels as well as in the international debates over the New World Information Order during the past two decades, emphasizes a similar vision of the public sphere, even if its vocabulary differs somewhat. As Wasko and Mosco put it:

> Thus the concept of democractic communications is two-fold . . .:
> 1. *democratization* of media and information technologies, or participatory and alternative media forms and democratic uses of information technologies; and
> 2. *democratization through* media and information technologies, or media strategies of various social movements and groups devoted to progressive issues and social change. (1992:7)

In Europe, the most explicit appropriation of Habermas' public sphere concept has been within the British debates where it has been utilized as a platform from which to defend public service broadcasting. There was a strong effort from the left to associate public service broadcasting with the realization of the public sphere, and to portray commercial broadcasting and the market model of financing as a serious threat to it (Garnham, 1983; Scannell, 1989; R. Collins, 1993). However, critiques of public service broadcasting were also forthcoming, even from the left. Across Western Europe, these institutions were perceived as paternalistic in their programme output, they tended to ignore the growing pluralistic and multicultural character of their own societies, and they were generally stagnant and in need of creative renewal.

However, in the 1980s the ideological bathwater was accompanied by the critical baby when the political climate began to support policies which strived to subvert the very principles and goals of public service. The commitment to serve and represent the interests of *all* the citizenry was increasingly displaced by policies that aimed to introduce and/or expand the commercial broadcasting sector. For the most part this has not enhanced the development of democracy. While there is of course much variation among the different countries, it can be said that, generally, the increased commercialization of television has not augmented the diversity of programming, whether judged in terms of form or content. On the contrary, programming has tended to follow the classic logic of homogenization and has been aimed at the large, general market, with the output of all channels becoming increasingly standardized (see, for example, Achille and Bueno, 1994 for a discussion of these trends).

In Sweden, for example, the public service channels still retain programmes aimed at specialized groups within society, but they also feel they must compete with the commercial channels. They do this by using some programming which is largely identical to the broadly popular fare of the commercial channels, thereby further reducing the overall diversity available. The immediate policy danger is that, with increased homogenization, the public will begin asking why they should pay a licence fee for channels that provide an output not significantly different from that of those which are supported by advertising. The long-term dilemma is that the remaining diversity becomes replaced by mere repetitive abundance, and that abundance will be low on programming which strengthens the public sphere.

The ideational reconstruction of public broadcasting as a goal is at present greatly hampered by the prevailing political climate which puts the tradition of the social democratic welfare state on the defensive and believes that social policy issues are best resolved by market forces. However, there are further practical difficulties ahead, aside from the political climate. The economics of public service are highly problematic in a period where costs continue to rise rapidly, and where a political ceiling seems to have been reached on the size of licence fees. Along with the need for the internal institutional renewal mentioned above, there is also the problem that public service broadcasting is so strongly linked to the nation-state. As a political unit, the nation-state is by no means on its death bed, but the growth of transnational economic and financial flows, coupled with migration and other forms of globalization, have contributed to eroding much of its former sphere of power. As many have noted, the nation-state is in some ways both too small and too large a unit to deal effectively with many of the newer historical realities.

Technological innovation in transnational television cannot be ignored: how should public service television position itself *vis-à-vis* the growth of satellite channels? There have been calls taking the public service model into the international arena and developing a pan-European public sphere based on non-commercial broadcasting (for example, Venturelli, 1993). However, the historical, sociological and political obstacles to a European public sphere based on public service television are not to be underestimated, as Schlesinger (1994) and Hjarvard (1993) clearly demonstrate. Not least is the question of what is the political entity to which the viewers of European television would be the polity? The European Union is hardly a political institution where popular will is invited and mediated to a responsive decision-making body. Transplanting the public sphere to a global context also involves enormous financial as well as regulatory considerations. Porter (1993), for example, takes up some of the complicated legal issues surrounding the rights of viewers which are involved in transfrontier television.

We should recall that the traditional arguments in support of public service broadcasting were premised in part on the airwaves being a scarce resource, and thus requiring state regulation. This logic becomes somewhat eclipsed in the new media environment, where technologies are not dependent on a space in the spectrum. Also, traditional media like the press must be incorporated into policy thinking which aims at enhancing the public sphere. Public service broadcasting still must play a central role, but the ideal of the public sphere requires a broader perspective which can encompass the entire media landscape (see Curran, 1991, for an ambitious attempt in this direction). Thus, the state has less to say about broadcasting specifically, as it allows television and radio to be run by private concerns, but must instead tackle the overall structural media situation, such as issues of concentration and cross ownership. In a sense, what is needed is re-regulation, to counteract the negative aspects of market forces and to optimize the positive role they can play.

Media representation

The dimension of representation directs our attention to media output. It is concerned with what the media portray, how topics are presented, the modes of discourse at work, and the character of debates and discussion. In empirical terms the concern is largely with journalism, as it is broadly understood – news reporting is but one of several journalistic genres. Representation has to do with both the informational and extra-informational aspects of media output, such as the symbolic and rhetorical. Moreover, as I take up in a later chapter, all the non-journalistic media output takes on relevance as a semiotic environment of the journalistic material, as well as of our everyday lives more generally. Analysing what comes out of the media has been the dominant focus of media research through the decades, and the wide-ranging variety of methodological tools and analytic constructs mobilized for this purpose is generally familiar to researchers.

The dimension of representation in the public sphere points to such basic questions as *what* should be selected for portrayal and *how* should it be presented. The answers to these basic questions, which lie at the core of the journalistic profession, can only have rather broad, guide-line formulations; new events, ongoing developments and historical circumstances demand that the answers always remain tentative. The criteria relating to media representations should only have an 'until further notice' character, since they must respond to an ever-changing social reality. Ideally, within journalism, self-monitoring and self-reflection would always be simmering just below the surface, ready to be actualized. We know from the sociology of newswork, however, that the organizational practices of journalism – like all other bureaucratic structures – tend to deflect such problematization and strive to 'routinize the unexpected' (see Tuchman, 1978).

All media representation potentially can become an object of critical analysis – from whatever perspective one is working from. Research which shares the organizational frames of reference of journalism can focus on the quality of coverage of particular issues, invoking such criteria as objectivity and bias. Though in academic quarters these seem to be increasingly eclipsed by newer analytical strategies (see Hackett, 1984), fundamental issues of truth and accuracy can never become wholly irrelevant. The media themselves can be manipulated by powerful and organized sources, which can result in distortions and disinformation. (Ericson, et al., 1989). Alternatively, from a critique of ideology perspective there is much to be said about media representation; from Baudrillardian theory one can explore the theme of simulacra, and so on. For television analysis in particular, there are now a number of methodological trajectories (see Allen, 1992).

Also, we should bear in mind that television representation is not just constructed portrayals, visual stories about what is happening in the world. As Scannell (1991) reminds us, television's representations consist to a great extent of talk. This talk is public talk, usually taking place in a studio. It consists of people talking among themselves, but its 'communicative intentionality' is such that it is aimed at the television audience beyond the studio. Indeed, it seems at present that 'talk television' is expanding, no doubt partly in response to economic factors (it is a relatively inexpensive format), and figures prominently in the growing popularization of television journalism, a theme I will return to in Chapter 3.

From the standpoint of the public sphere, there is a need for continual monitoring of what goes on in the media, analysing specific cases and routine representations, while at the same time it is important not to lose sight of the larger, more theoretical issues. Some of the theoretical issues around communication and subjectivity will be dealt with in Chapter 5; here I will just mention a few of the topics around representation which have elicited debate. Perhaps most central is the question of whether representation via the media is in itself at all compatible with the notion of a public sphere. Peters (1993) takes this up as a difficulty in Habermas, whose public sphere model is very wedded to the notion of face-to-face interaction. Despite the centrality of the early press to Habermas' understanding of the bourgeois public sphere, he reveals a distrust of mediated representation, a sense that it is an obstacle to discursive rationality and communicative authenticity. We can safely assume that the mass media are not about to fade from the scene – and in fact they continue to grow – and that just as representation in democracy is unavoidable, so is representation in communication. Neither by itself necessarily means the demise of civilization, even though both generate special problems. The question is how we can make best use of representation for democratic purposes.

Other commentaries on Habermas have taken up the issue of the desirability and feasibility of shared discourse rules in media representations, that is, the tension between universalistic and particularistic communicative logics. Should there be one overarching mode of discursive reason, one key code of communicative logic which is to prevail above all others, or is a multiplicity of different, but equal modes to be fostered? This may seem like a rather academic issue, but in the context of multicultural and multilingual societies, where identity politics are gaining in importance, it raises very concrete questions not only about modes of media discourse but also flows into policy issues in culture and education, as well as the criteria for citizenship (see Taylor, 1992).

A related but perhaps even more pointed issue has to do with rational/analytic versus affective/aesthetic modes of communication, a topic which takes on particular relevance with regard to television. There is often a questionable assumption at work, whereby politics is analytically associated with rationality, and entertainment is seen exclusively as pertaining to emotionality. Controversial questions arise: Can television communicate in a 'rational' manner (however that may be defined)? Should it always strive to? Does it inevitably portray even the most serious issues of public concern largely in terms of emotionality? Is the 'entertainment bias' in television so strong that it unavoidably trivializes everything it touches, as some diatribes claim (for example, Postman, 1985)? And even if we assume that there are 'good journalistic programmes' (again, however this may be defined) on television, can they really be very meaningful if they are surrounded by programming and advertising whose chief aims are to capture and hold our attention by providing escapist pleasure? In other words, would a few oases of rationality make much difference in a media culture, the chief characteristics of which are arational?

Social structures

Returning to Habermas' model, commentators have raised a number of theoretical questions to do with the public sphere's structural dimension. A fundamental one, which Garnham (1992) emphasizes, has to do with scale and boundaries. He makes the indisputable point that there must a coherence, a goodness of fit, between political entities and the scale and boundaries of the public sphere. The difficulties of attaining this in the modern world via policy strategies should be obvious. However, it is precisely this evolution of political realities which must be incorporated into policy considerations: how to structure a public sphere which is congruent with the processes of political decision making and the consequences of the decisions taken. In terms of democratic theory, Held (1993) discusses how, currently, global realities are increasingly problematizing traditional conceptions of political boundaries and entities, and the challenge that this implies for how we are to view the structures and processes of democracy. Held and many other commentators note especially the processes of globalization, whereby some of the traditional structures, functions and *raisons d'être* of the nation-state are being eclipsed by transnational processes, regional developments and local decentralization.

Another issue has to do with fitting the public sphere to the complex social structures of modern society. In short, is it better with a centralized or a pluralistic model of the public sphere? Can everyone be accommodated within one and the same public sphere, or is such a goal oppressive? Can factors such as class, gender and race, and their cultural correlates, be disregarded? Such differences begin with the fundamental features of social structure. These are not easily bridged by media discourses. Or should precisely such bridging be seen as a goal of a centralized public sphere? It is alleged that arguing for a 'one size fits all' public sphere subordinates minorities to the discursive and social power of dominant groups. The counter argument is that political decisions taken within a political entity objectively can affect everyone within it, regardless of their subjective positions, and to construct separatist public sphere enclaves is to foster discursive ghettos which are detrimental to democracy.

Now, few would argue that everyone should or even can always participate in the same societal conversation, and it may be in part a semantic question whether one argues for a single large pluralistic public sphere which connects many smaller discrete arenas or whether one posits that a multiplicity of many smaller public spheres is what constitutes the public sphere as a whole. However, the two formulations may well capture differing emphases or perspectives, and the tension between the whole and the parts remains a central policy problematic. Public spheres must arise partly out of necessity, in response to particular circumstances. Media institutions are, in theory, accessible to constructive policy intervention – if, of course, the political interest can be mobilized. Social structure, however, reflects the slowly shifting complexities of a societal totality which increasingly defies both coherent conceptualization and decisive steering. If the public sphere generally, like democracy, is viewed as a political accomplishment, it will be understood that its boundaries, even its forms, must remain at some level open and contestable.

Interaction: social bonds and social construction

If we think in terms of the 'space' in which 'public sphering' gets done, we can readily see that while the media constitute much of this space (as discursive, semiotic space), the space of the public sphere is – and must be – larger than that of media representations. It must also include sociocultural interaction. This dimension takes us into the realm of people's encounters and discussions with each other, with their collective sense-making and their cultural practices. The processes and setting of media reception are also a part of this dimension of interaction: the interface between media and its audiences. Reception studies are normally cast in terms of people making sense of the output, however, I would also underscore the importance of basic functions such as comprehension and recall (see Höijer, 1992). Beaud (1994) problematizes the whole idea of a televisual public sphere, given the apparent amnesia among viewers which he sees deriving from televisual discourse.

Even if television in many cases is a totally individual affair, the experiences gained from viewing are carried over into social interaction. And where viewing is a social activity, done together with others, talk about the programming can take place simultaneously with the transmission as well as directly afterwards. Thus, while most viewing still takes place in the home, which is traditionally seen as a private space, this domestic site of 'mediated publicness' is where talk about public matters may begin – hence my assertion that reception is often a first step of interaction. (I will pick up the theme of reception again in Chapter 6.) Finally, interaction has to do not only with what gets said between people, but also the processes of intersubjectivity and identity which arise in this interaction, and which in turn shape a sense of belonging and a capacity for participation in society.

While reception analysis is prominently on the media research agenda, interaction is the dimension of the public sphere which has often been given somewhat short shrift in terms of theoretical attention. Mediacentric perceptions tend at times to ignore the issue of what takes place between citizens. It is useful to compare Habermas with a liberal American writer such as Dewey (1954/1923), whose thinking on the distinction between audience and public is echoed in the influencial work of the Chicago School of sociology (McIntyre, 1987). Both Habermas and Dewey argue that a 'public' should be conceptualized as something other than just a media audience.

A public, according Habermas and Dewey, exists as discursive interactional processes; atomized individuals, consuming media in their homes, do not comprise a public, nor do they tend to contribute much to the democratization of civil society. There are of course strong interests in society which have a stake in defining 'the public' in terms of aggregate statistics of individual behaviour and opinion; such approaches certainly do have their uses from the standpoints of marketing, the official political system, and not least from that of media institutions themselves. However, from the standpoints of democracy, it is imperative not to lose sight of the classic idea that democracy resides, ultimately, with citizens who engage in talk with each other.

The theme of interaction is hardly a new one: the early sociological formulations about the processes and effects of mass communication underscored the 'two step flow' and the notion of intermediary 'opinion leaders' (see Katz and Lazarsfeld, 1955). Obviously not all social interaction can be treated as manifestations of a well-functioning public sphere; there must be a focus on politics and current affairs – a quality of publicness attained by people interacting in their roles as citizens. Even if we find it harder these days to mark boundaries and maintain distinctions, the public sphere must have politics as its chief horizon, even if we allow that this category is always potentially in tension with the prepolitical and the cultural.

For convenience, we can specifiy three areas of analytic concern within the interactional dimension of the public sphere: discursive, spatial, and communal. The discursive has to do with the nature of the talk which circulates between citizens. (This category would also include non-verbal forms of interpersonal communication.) There are many topics which can be raised in regard to the discursive aspects of interaction; perhaps most relevant for the public sphere is the question of discursive resources and repertoires: what are the ways of meaning-making at work within given sectors of the populace and what bearing do they have on political competence? This evokes in part the discussion above on universalistic versus particularistic discourse rules in media representations; regardless of possible inherent suppressive aspects of the dominant modes of political communication, if one does not have access to them or at least to their translatable equivalence, one is excluded from the processes of democratic participation.

The spatial refers to the sites and settings of social interaction. Where do people meet as citizens? What factors foster or hinder their interaction in these spaces? The nature of urban/suburban architecture, the fear of crime, home media technology and other factors become relevant in this regard. Such themes take us into several subfields of sociology, urban anthropology, as well as social geography. The spatial is seldom separable from the discursive: both together serve to define contexts and occasions. Thus, in terms of the media, Sennett (1977) sees them as reinforcing the retreat to domestic space and contributing to the decline of public culture. That much public space and interaction is dedicated to consumer practices and discourses becomes significant for the public sphere, since the role of citizen is displaced by that of the consumer; the cultural assumptions surrounding shopping malls, for example, do not make them prime settings for the public sphere.

Space is of course conceptual as well as strictly topographical. Certainly the newer electronic interactive media offer a new version of social space. The experimental electronic town meetings on cable systems have been one manifestation of this newer space. Another manifestion is the public network which is set up as an ever-present citizen resource: The Public Electronic Network (PEN) in Santa Monica, California, is the first such publicly funded electronic network, and initial evaluation suggests that one of its advantages may be that it facilitates interaction between people who would not normally have much contact with each other when they share the same physical space (van Tassel, 1994). Still more dramatic is the expansion of the Internet, with its data bases, e-mail, electronic bulletin boards and other forms of virtual reality. This cyberspace, the most placeless of spaces, can be put to many uses which can contribute to the public sphere, and no doubt its relevance will continue to grow. However, the battles for political control and economic exploitation of the Internet are already well under way. (For an American introduction to the Internet, written in a popular style which also takes up the issues of citizenship and the public sphere, see Rheingold, 1994.) However, despite all the possible democratic uses and advantages of virtual reality, I would still argue that a democratic public sphere, and a democratic social order more generally, cannot exist exclusively in cyberspace: there must be face-to-face interaction as well.

The communal aspect refers to the nature of the social bonds between citizens. Sennett (1977) has argued that in the modern era, the 'ideology of intimacy', has contributed to the demise of public culture: public space becomes dead space because we have the expectation that the most desirable or valid form of relations between people is one of closeness. Yet the stranger is (increasingly) perceived as a possible threat. This tendency undercuts the opportunities for people to meet as citizens and exchange views. The nature of what the social bond should be between citizens has been a point of contention within political philosophy, but it is clear that some minimal form of collective identity, what Vico (quoted in Shotter, 1993a:54) calls the *sensus communis*, is required. Even if it is de-emphasized, no democratic order will work without some shared sense of commonality among its members. Talk both manifests and presupposes some kinds of social bond between citizens.

I would make one final but important theoretic point regarding the dimension of interaction: talk is constructive. It is the foundation of the social order of everyday life, as the various social interactionist theorists have argued (Shotter, 1993a, offers a vigorous argument of the thesis of social construction via conversation). Interaction has traditionally been seen as fundamental to human existence, and rightly so. Even our identities, our 'selves', emerge via social interaction (see Burkitt, 1991). Through talk, the social world is linguistically constructed and maintained, albeit in dialectical interplay with the more structural features of society. Interaction is what makes the category of subjectivity come socially alive: subjectivity becomes a moment – a partial element – of what are fundamentally processes of intersubjectivity.

Talk can generate the unforeseen. From a constructivist perspective, talk represents the ongoing production of the social world, the perpetual making, circulating and remaking of meaning. It is not simply the expression of fixed inner subjective states, but rather the mutual creation of intersubjectivity, whose outcome is never fully predetermined. Our minds are not like computers, with the same inert data available for retrieval in any circumstance. The common notion of opinion as simply something existing in people, to be captured by multiple choice questions, is indeed misguided, for it ignores the dynamics whereby meaning circulates, is acted upon, and revised, to result in political interpretation and will formation (see Herbst, 1993, for a recent overview of popular perspectives on the concept of public opinion; Price, 1992, discusses the evolution and some of the current difficulties of the concept; and Steiner, 1994, presents three authors who take fresh critical looks at public opinion). We must view our inner realities as always partially potential: they become actualized through concrete interaction with other people. While our subjectivities tend to follow patterns, they can never be seen as predetermined.

Thus in terms of the public sphere, there must be interaction to permit and foster the *processes* of political sense-making. The centrality of social interaction through talk, and the concept of the public as discursive interaction which takes place in particular settings, must inform any theorizing about the public sphere (see also Lenart, 1994, for an update on the social science approach to social interaction as a factor between the individual and media impact).

Subjectivity, identity, interaction

Sociocultural interaction has many facets, and I have mentioned that I see subjectivity and identity as two important aspects. At a common sense level, subjectivity has to do with what goes on in people's heads and this is of obvious relevance for the public sphere: opinions and attitudes, values and norms, knowledge and information, frames of reference and schemes of relevance, world views, and so on, are all pertinent. These and related notions, which can be expressed in a variety of vocabularies from different traditions, are central features in the processes by which citizens participate in the communicative dynamics of democracy.

At another level, we may consider the general forms of collective subjectivity that prevail within various groups and classes in society at certain times. Certain world views, frames of reference, ideological understandings, and so on are sufficiently widespread and deeply embedded in various sectors of the population that they constitute important cultural patterns for those collectivities. Such forms of mass subjectivity may well be linked to contemporary trends in media output. More specifically, we might find that certain media discourses foster or hinder certain subject positions, and that these textual subject positions, inscribed in media discourses, actually do have some correlation with social subjects. Thus, the discourses of advertising, which permeate the semiotic environment of the public sphere, encourage consumption and invite a consumerist subject position, which certainly manifests itself in a general way in social subjectivity. Ours is a consumer culture, even if most advertising campaigns do not attain the intended success and even if many people are cynical about commercialism; the commodification of everyday practices and social relations is beyond dispute (see Willis, 1991, for an interesting analysis of the interface of advertising discourses and daily life).

Even the nature of the mass mediated public sphere itself can be examined from the standpoint of what forms of subjectivity it fosters. People do not simply emerge out of their private spheres as fully-fashioned individuals – as wholly competent citizens – and then leap into the public sphere. The media, not least those elements directly relevant to the public sphere, contribute to the shaping of subjectivity. The issue of ideology is always hovering in the wings, awaiting its cue.

The work of Negt and Kluge (1993/1972) can be seen in this light. Their book is more than just a commentary on Habermas; it represents a full-scale theoretical alternative. The very title of their book, *The Public Sphere and Experience*, defines a central dynamic. The original German word, *Erfahrung*, does not resonate with full equivalence in the English term 'experience'; the latter carries with it – among other things – empiricist associations, as Hansen (1993) points out in a text which also appears as a foreword to the English translation of Negt and Kluge's book. She writes that '*Erfahrung* is seen as the matrix that mediates individual perception and social horizons of meaning' (Hansen, 1993:188). Now, while the Marxism of Negt and Kluge remains within the older analytic framework of a philosophy of consciousness, and while nuances inevitably get skewed in translation, I would suggest that the term 'subjectivity' corresponds at least in part with the dimension that they emphasize. Thus, the public sphere, and the media more generally, can be understood in terms of their role in the organization of collective and individual subjectivity.

In addition, subjectivity also includes a particular aspect which is of importance for the public sphere, namely that of identity. Our sense of who we are, to ourselves and to others, takes on relevance for the public sphere because it shapes the way in which we participate, and may well determine if we participate or not. Specifically, this has to do with the nature of our identity as citizens, and what this means in the practical circumstances of political discussion and activity. For active participants in the public sphere, how, for example, do they balance their identities as citizens, which implies some sort of universality and commitment to the common good, to a 'civic culture', with the particular identities which emerge from pursuing specific interests? Or, from a different angle, the public sphere is not just a 'marketplace of ideas' or an 'information exchange depot', but also a major societal mechanism for the production and circulation of culture, which frames and gives meaning to our identities. How do the identities thus fostered relate to the vision of democracy?

More pointedly, if we link the pervasive commodification of public culture with the notion of citizenship as an identity, we see how, at the level of political ideology, forces on the right have been defining citizenship precisely in consumerist terms. I would suggest that one of the chief ideological tensions today is situated in this force field; what is at stake is whether people's identities as citizens can largely be reduced to and framed in consumer terms or whether some sense of the political – beyond market logics – can be retained in people's conceptions of citizenship.

These brief glimpses of the four dimensions of the public sphere should suggest something of the vast array of issues involved. If Habermas' theoretical step in conceptualizing the public sphere was an immensely valuable step, no one, not even Habermas himself, would argue that we should remain fully within those initial formulations. We must see the public sphere partly as an ideal we aim for a direction charted. It always remains (in the best of cases) a political accomplishment, ever in need of renewal, and we should avoid clutching an historically frozen model. It is an historically contingent space, negotiated and contested, situated at the interface of an array of vectors. It is structured by macrosocietal factors and shaped by the mass media, especially television. Yet, as I will underscore in later chapters, it is also socioculturally constructed by the discursive practices of civil society.

In the following chapter I will take up television, which is arguably the dominant media institution of the modern public sphere. I will be looking at structural, representational and sociocultural aspects of television, an approach which parallels that of the dimensions of the public sphere more generally. In Chapter 3 I turn more specifically to television journalism.

2

Prismatic television

All sorts of questions can be – and have been – asked of television, and many sorts of answers have been given, from a wide variety of perspectives and with the use of many different methodologies. Television is also inserted into a number of different popular and professional discourses, which thematize it in different ways, for example, as a news medium, as entertainment, as a great time waster, as a babysitter gone out of control, as a source of everyday chit-chat, and as a cause of negative social effects. Even if we remain relatively undaunted in the face of multiplying analytic and popular perspectives, the very polymorphous quality of the object itself makes it elusive. The closer we try to get to it, the more it seems to slip out of our conceptual grasp. Trying to get an analytic hold on television, an overview of its institutional features, its economic dynamics, its programming output – even in a small country such as Sweden – is to risk perpetual frustration. Heath (1990:267) says that, 'television is a somewhat difficult object, unstable, all over the place, tending derisively to escape anything we can say about it'. Yet we still can – and must – say *something* about it, realizing of course that whatever we do say is incomplete and selective.

In this chapter, I approach the multifarious reality of television in order to conceptually bring it within the framework of my discussion of the public sphere, though without claiming to exhaust all possible aspects of the medium. While all television output can be said to contribute to public culture (regardless of how we may evaluate the contributions), only some of television's output is a direct manifestation of the political public sphere. This programming, comprising a variety of genres and formats, of which news programmes are but one (albeit prototypical) case, I simply and loosely term 'journalism'. However, television's other programming is not irrelevant for journalism. Among other things, the other programming functions intertextually with journalism, helps define a semiotic environment in which journalism must operate, and contributes to viewers' horizons of expectation with regard to journalism as a televisual experience. Television journalism is at bottom *television*, and is thus conditioned by the specific features of the medium. In this chapter I will take up television generally; in the following chapter I turn my attention to television journalism, with the accent on its popularization.

Three angles of vision

Television is many things and can be theorized from a variety of positions. For instance, television can be treated as a 'teletechnological system', as

Silverstone (1994) insightfully demonstrates. Mainstream television's particular technology has certain implications for how it is used and consumed in its domestic settings – not least how it interfaces with other technologies in the home, such as video, teletext, telecommunications, computers and computer games, resulting in an integrated technological media ecology (see for example, Moreley and Silverstone, 1990; Silverstone, et al., 1992; and d'Agostino and Tafler, 1995). However, for ease of exposition, I will limit my discussion here to three sides of what could be treated as a televisual prism: television is simultaneously an industry, sets of audio-visual texts, and a sociocultural experience.

We can look at it from these different angles, each of which refracts our understanding of it in slightly different ways. I find the familiar figure of the prism useful here because not only does it suggest that television is many-sided and each side refracts our understanding in a particular way, but also because it implies the difficulties of seeing all the sides at the same time. As we turn our attention to one side of the prism, the others vanish from our view (even if we are able at some point, through conscious effort, to develop a degree of multiperspectivalism). Television cannot be reduced to any one or even two of these angles, but instead remains a composite and complex configuration. The understandings of television derived from the respective sides of the prism remain complementary. This prismatic view has obvious parallels with the multidimensional approach to the public sphere in the previous chapter. The industry of television – its political economy – is central to the media institutional dimension of the public sphere, and the television industry itself is obviously shaped by structural features of society; the audio-visual texts of television, or at least the journalistic ones, are key elements of the public sphere's representational dimension; television as a sociocultural experience correlates directly with the dimension of sociocultural interaction.

In the scope of this presentation I will not be surveying the whole field of television research. However, in my discussion I will be making use of some of the literature which I find helpful. In actually doing research on television it is often difficult analytically to juggle with all three angles on the medium simultaneously, yet the methodological challenge would seem to be to develop an approach, which, while emphasizing one angle, never lets the other two totally disappear even if they must recede into the background. To be cognizant of the dynamics of their mutual reciprocity will help avoid reductionist conclusions in television research.

This prismatic view can of course only be an analytical starting point for understanding television in relation to the public sphere. It guides the formulation of questions but does not, by itself, offer ready-made answers. However, the further we pursue the prism's respective sides, the more television's role – its potential and limitations – as a feature of the public sphere comes into focus.

Industry: organization, professionalism, political economy

What appears on television is of course the net outcome not only of a long chain of decisions and practical production stages, but also of larger institutional circumstances. In a word, television must be understood as an industry, regardless of whether its economic foundation is commercial or public service licence fees. Television as an industry can in turn be seen as the intersection of forces stemming from its organizational structures and dynamics, and the sets of professional frameworks operative among people in the television industry, and, of course, its political economy.

The level of organization is conditioned, but not totally determined, by the larger horizons of political economy. The sociology of television's organization takes up topics such as contextual imperatives, the nature and the evolution of work routines, and the conditions of production in terms of technology and schedule. This is an important sociology, with a good number of classic contributions (such as Elliott, 1972; Gitlin, 1985; and Hart, 1988. Within the specific area of television journalism, Tuchman, 1978; Schlesinger, 1987; and Gans, 1979, are among the standard texts. On the organizational perspective on news production in general and its relationship to political economy and culturological angles on production, see Schudson, 1991). In more recent years, this area has been somewhat ignored. The television industry has been in dramatic transformation over the past decade, and consequently organizational parameters may well present a rather frustrating object of research. One can only hope that undaunted researchers will soon return to probing the organizational side of the industry; the work of the Swedish media economist Björkegren (1994) seems promising in this regard, with his attempts to chart the differences in the industrial logic and decision-making processes between public service and commercial television companies in the present turbulent period. While it is television as a text and sociocultural experience which audiences encounter, analyses of these dimensions can only be enhanced by a deeper understanding of organizational structures and dynamics. And, alternatively, such analyses become weak in the long run if not informed by organizational perspectives.

Though all people working in television may be labelled 'professionals' in the sense that they get paid for what they do, professionalism has understandably been most studied in regard to television journalism, where there exists an explicit and self-conscious professional identity. Sociological opinion varies as to what extent professionalism within television journalism should be seen as an independent 'variable'. The more sceptically inclined (for example, Golding and Elliott, 1979) treat it as a case of transforming necessity into virtue: in simplified terms, political economy and organizational imperatives are seen as stringently delimiting the range of freedom, and the profession in essence defines that which they *must* do as that which they *should* be doing, allowing for occasional lapses which they will self-criticize. Others (for example, Hall, 1974) see some of the canonized practices of professionalism, such as the formal deference to 'objectivity', as actually serving as a conduit between power élites and the people, though its position is ultimately contradictory and unstable. Certainly such perspectives capture something fundamental about the significance of professionalism, but there are still other sociologically interesting aspects to pursue.

As a socially constructed and institutionally anchored framework, professionalism can provide specific clues to the dynamics of journalism. For one thing, professionalism not only addresses the standards and ethics of performance, it also structures the professional reward system, operating as a control mechanism (Soloski, 1989). Moreover, professionalism is not all of a piece, and national differences can be telling (see Kepplinger and Köcher, 1990). Both the codified and the tacit understandings among journalists can vary between countries, between media (print, television, radio), between media markets (for example, upscale, transnational, local), and across time. The profession of journalism itself is changing, with increased blurring of distinctions between itself and public relations, advertising, copy editing, press releases and so on (see Charon, 1994). Its distinction from the profession of history remains somewhat complicated (Lavoinne, 1994). More and more we see a cadre of modern 'media professionals', where journalism is experienced as only a part of one's professional identity, a role which may at times, but not necessarily, be at odds with other components.

At the subjective level, this heterogeneity of professional values can generate problems for journalists where they experience a dichotomy: professionalism as loyalty to their particular media organization versus loyalty to the ideals of journalism. Moreover, Swedish research (for example, Weibull, 1991) shows that there is considerable diversity among journalists as to how they experience and interpret professional roles and ethics. Many journalists perceive the organizational imperatives as hindering the realization of professional ideals. These insights are important, because they underscore that most journalists operate under considerable constraints, despite the popular image of the hero-journalist, and these constraints can be understood in terms of organizational factors. Thus, while traditional issues having to do with journalism's professional identity – for example, its general 'pursuit of respectibility' (Ruellan, 1993) – become amplified in the context of television journalism as an industrial product, these issues find no singular resolution. The ideological domestication of professionalism cannot simply be assumed; it remains a potentially contested terrain, yet one which at least some journalists still find critically enabling.

Turning now to the political economic perspective on the media generally; this approach was given great impetus by the path-breaking work of the late Dallas Smythe (1994) and of Herbert Schiller, who continues to probe the political economy of the media and information industries, often stressing the transnational dimension (see Schiller, 1991, for a recent contribution). Political economy has its origins in the Marxian tradition, though its utility today depends, as with many disciplines, on its capacity to think innovatively in relation to its traditions and to be rigorous in its use of empirical materials, rather than recycling old truths. The ownership, the control, and the regulation of television all have to do with its political economy, which in turn is integrated within the overall political economy of society. This, in turn, also mirrors the ever-increasing transnational character of economic relations in the modern world.

The political economy of television largely addresses issues having to do with the institutional logics of financing and economic control. I say 'largely' because, as Golding and Murdock (1991) explain in their concise overview of this perspective, a political economy of the media treats these institutions as 'cultural industries', which means that there is a need to 'focus on the interplay between the symbolic and economic dimensions of public communication' (1991:15). The media operate much like other industries, yet they are different in that the goods they produce 'play a pivotal role in organizing the images and discourses through which people make sense of the world' (1991:15). Thus, by definition, the symbolic output of the media as well as the relevant features of the audiences must be kept within the horizons of this perspective. The links to a vision of the public sphere are apparent:

> This general ideal of a communication system as a public cultural space that is open, diverse, and accessible, provides the basic yardstick against which critical political economy measures the performance of existing systems and formulates alternatives. (Golding and Murdock, 1991:22)

Therefore, rather than theoretically departing from a concept of sovereign individuals, 'critical political economy starts with sets of social relations and the play of power' (1991:18). These sets of social relations include the socio-cultural, material and political hierarchies among the audiences: a political economy of the media is concerned with the differential accessibility of various forms of media output within the population, since such differentiation is at base detrimental to the notion of citizenship and democracy. Elsewhere, Golding and Murdock (Golding, 1990; Murdock and Golding, 1989; Murdock, 1990; Murdock, 1992) have used this perspective to demonstrate how the inequality of citizen access to mediated culture and information is detrimental to democracy. From a different angle, Lodziak (1986) makes a similar point when he argues that the power of television cannot be understood exclusively via the ideology of the text, but must be seen in a larger context which elucidates audience members' social positions and relations of power within the social totality. Golding and Murdock rightly criticize certain strands within Cultural Studies for excluding and/or denigrating the dimension of political economy, but from this one should not conclude that political economic questions are the only ones worth asking, only that they absolutely must not be ignored. (I examine the relationship between Cultural Studies and media research in Dahlgren, forthcoming.)

Trying to answer the question of the relative weight to be accorded political economic and other kinds of factors would take us smack into a replay of the older debates regarding the position of historical materialism and which factors are determinate 'in the last instance'. I do not think any contribution I could make on that theme would make much impact on the traditional alignments in those debates, so here I will merely offer my own rule of thumb: it is not so much a question of ascertaining 'last instances' or seeking out ultimate causes, but rather of approaching complex phenomena such as television in a manner which takes into account their embedded and figurational character. Television as a whole resides in a multiple network of interdependent factors which both constrain and enable it as a phenomenon. The general methodological orientation should not be to try to extract one factor as the basic one – the relative weight of different factors may well vary in different circumstances – but instead to try to illuminate the interrelationship of the different factors, those of a political economic nature and others.

Under the commodity logic of the commercial system, the audience becomes the product, delivered to the advertisers, as many critics have pointed out; the programming is – at base – the 'filler' between the advertisements. This logic can help to explain why certain kinds of programmes are aired rather than others: broad appeal and the avoidance of serious controversy are two generally operative criteria. The consequences of commodity logic can be partly understood with the help of basic communication theory. As many introductory texts in communication explain, in Roman Jakobson's model of communication there are six 'functions' of communication, one of which is the phatic. This is the function which aims at keeping communication going; in a telephone conversation, it would include phrases such as 'Are you still there?', 'Can you hear me all right?', 'Don't hang up!'. Now, the explicit logic of commercial television, and increasingly the implicit logic within public service television, is that of phatic communication: don't hang up – or, in television terms, stay tuned! In other words, the point of the programming is to generate as many spectators as possible (and preferably of suitable discretionary income level) and to keep them watching/consuming as long as possible. The primacy of the phatic function is the key to television as 'spectacle'. To return to the telephone metaphor: clearly, if I am speaking with somebody for whom it is absolutely vital that I stay on the phone as long as possible, this imperative will have great impact on that person's conversational strategy with me. It would not account for everything that is said or all my experiences of what is said, but it would be a blunder to discount this phatic motivation if we were trying to analyse the conversation.

Analyses of the commodity logic, as well as of ownership and control, of commercial television represent the road most often travelled in the political economy of this medium. However, how does it look when we shift our attention to the European public service model? Under the public service model, the commercial logic was initially counteracted via a guaranteed funding based on taxation. Without the pressures of having to generate advertising revenue and always maximize the size of the audience, public service television was in principle free to pursue programme policies which derived from normative considerations of how best to serve the public interest. Its vulnerability was chiefly at the political level: the state and powerful interests could apply political pressure, many times with considerable success. At its worst, such pressures could implicitly threaten television with a reduction of its funding in order to whip it into line, as happened in Sweden in the early 1970s, when the power structure responded strongly to what it perceived as excessive left-wing perspectives in current affairs programming. The consequent 'big chill' had a debilitating impact on independent, critical journalism for over a decade.

However, even within the public television system one can find elements of the commercial logic at work. In Sweden, the second public service television channel was introduced in 1969, and very quickly the two channels used audience research results as a symbolic currency, competing with each other for higher ratings and scheduling their programmes competitively. Ratings could not be ignored in the evaluation of public service performance. Constructively addressing even this type of dilemma may not be entirely beyond the institutional regeneration of the public service system, but when public service broadcasting is rather suddenly cast in a competitive situation with commercial broadcasting, as happened in several countries in the 1980s, the premises for public service are dramatically altered. As deregulation proceeded through the 1980s, and as many Western European public service corporations ended up competing with both domestic and transnational commercial channels, they too began to feel the need to go, at least partially, the route of commodity logic; and audience ratings become increasingly important in the construction of programme strategies and schedules (see Ang, 1991, for a discussion of this development).

The fundamental logic of audience maintenance in analysis of the output is one pillar of the political economy perspective on television. However, television as an industry is multiply embedded: it is part of the 'news media' and hence is amenable to political economic analyses which grasp the news media as a coherent, transmedia sector. The importance of television in ideological terms is of course also paramount, and political economic analysis of, for example, US commercial television (Kellner, 1990) and US public service broadcasting (Hoynes, 1994) demonstrates the ultimate inseparability of the economic and ideological interests in television as an industry.

Television is also changing: it is increasingly a transnational satellite enterprise run by conglomerate corporations, and political economic analysis must take this into account (see R. Collins, 1992). At the same time, while one can chart a global trajectory in the post-war period where television played an important role in solidifying the position of the United States, this is changing. Schwoch (1993) shows how, within the framework of a world systems perspective, the new global situation after the fall of communism alters even the position of television within the geopolitics of culture. Moreover, the growing interface between television and telecommunications and computers requires us to broaden our horizons and see the articulations with technologies of surveillance and control (see Mulgan, 1991; Gandy, 1993). The institutional embeddedness of television, its growing links with other communication technologies, the conditions of its ownership and control, and the overall transformation of transnational media markets are all having their impact on television.

Mimetic televisual texts

Let us now shift the prism and look at a second side of television, namely its output. The actual process of signification in television (and all media) is doubly contingent. First, this contingency derives from the now familiar polysemic quality of all communication, of all texts: meaning is seldom fully unequivocal and tends to spill over the neat boundaries we may construct to contain it. In recent years, however, there has been a tendency within media research scholarship to exaggerate the polysemic character of television discourses. This populist proclivity is understandable as a reaction to some earlier strands of research which overemphasized the unilateral power of media messages. Yet, this excessive underscoring of the multivalence of televisual texts ignores the repetitive and formulaic nature of most television output, the relative stability of most social frames of perception, and the cultural familiarity with televisual discourses and genres – all of which contribute to delimit, though by no means ever eliminate, polysemic meaning.

Secondly, the contingency of meaning resides only partially within the text itself. It is only in its encounter with a public that the meaning in the programming becomes fully actualized, that the text 'comes alive', as it were. Indeed, Fiske (1987), following Barthes and others in literary theory, makes the distinction between programmes, as identifiable products or 'works', and 'texts'. He suggests that television output only becomes 'texts' in its encounter with audiences, where it is worked upon and given meaning. Thus, both the text itself and the processes of reception contribute to the contingency and – within limits – the instability of meaning.

Yet this double contingency of meaning within the audio-visual text does not make the text itself irrelevant from the standpoint of research, only somewhat complicated to deal with. There are today a variety of interpretive strategies for analysing the televisual text (see Allen, 1992, for an excellent collection which provides introductions to several such traditions as well as extensive references), with no one tradition in a privileged position. Each one works within a set of assumptions and methods, and has its partiality of vision. Yet, even if we cannot specify with full certitude all the possible meanings a televisual text may offer its audiences, we can still elucidate tendencies and likelihoods, specifying the different registers and discursive strategies at work. The domains of meaning which are relevant for media research are overwhelmingly social, not idiosyncratic, so the play of difference in regard to interpretive horizons should be cast in sociocultural, not individual terms. Thus, with a degree of modesty in our analytic view of the text, we can treat it as a form of 'raw material' in the process of meaning-making, awaiting interface with its publics. The characteristics of this raw material – even if our rendering of them must ultimately be tentative – are of great importance for the final 'product', or, more accurately, for the ongoing construction and circulation of meaning in which televisual texts participate.

The analysis of reception still cannot give us the 'final word' on a televisual text. The data gathered by such research – people's accounts of their meaning constructions from television – must in turn be interpreted and given a discursive representation by the researcher. And those who read such texts – themselves television viewers – will have to draw their own conclusions. All of this is not say that we therefore go spinning into a maelstrom of hopeless relativism. It is precisely such either-or thinking, an expression of the 'Cartesian anxiety' (Bernstein, 1983), which we need to transcend. Rather, a degree of epistemological modesty is called for. All our analyses of social reality, media related or otherwise, can only be interpretations. We struggle to make them as good, as accurate and as compelling as possible, but there is no privileged path out of the hermeneutic human condition.

At a general level, television communicates with various sets of codes. Fiske (1987) makes a useful distinction between three sets of codes. 'Natural codes' derive from the lived social world of our culture, and are manifested in the familiar patterns such those of dress, speech, conduct, setting and decor. 'Technical codes', which are a product of the television medium's modes of operation, are found in such conventions as those of camerawork, editing and lighting, which provide strong clues as to how we should see that which is presented. 'Ideological codes' are the resultant dimensions of televisual discourses which serve to organize collective perceptions in ways which have consequences for the social order as a whole, for example, codes which define, advocate and legitimize varieties of social position. I prefer to call this last category 'integrative codes', retaining the notion of ideology as a critical term and thereby not defining all cultural patterns a priori as contributing to social relations of domination. The ideological character of any forms of discourse is a relative quality and needs to be derived via a critical hermeneutic analysis of the discourse in its social context (Thompson, 1990).

Thus, integrative codes may well contain ideological dimensions – of class, race, gender, technocracy, and so on – but these must be analytically ascertained and specified. These codes also offer what Berger and Luckmann (1967) term 'symbolic universes', preconceptual frameworks which served to synthesize the disparate experiences of everyday life into larger, tacit ideational frameworks and provide them with fuller, overarching coherence and existential meaning. In any case, these three sets of codes – natural, technical and integrative – provide a conceptual starting point elucidating the ways in which television communicates. In particular they can help us to illuminate a very central feature of televisual texts, namely their 'realism'. This term, though familiar, is highly problematic. On the one hand, it is tied up with (literally) ancient debates on the nature of reality and the possibilities of objective representation of that reality. On the other hand, it is also closely wedded to traditions within the study of the novel and of film. In television, it becomes hard to point to any output which is not 'realistic' in some way: a children's cartoon about robots from outer space or a situation comedy both manifest degrees of realism within the confines of their genres. Indeed, Corner (1992) argues that within television studies, realism consists of a 'collection of begged questions' and that the general state of theorizing around it is a 'mess'. I agree, and, though my reflections here may not tidy up the situation, it still seems unavoidable that we must grapple with the issues involved and some of Corner's points are very helpful in this regard.

One of Corner's key arguments is that discussions of realism in television have been encumbered with lingering attempts to pop the bubble of 'illusion'. This trajectory is problematic, in his view, because it positions itself against the notion of the 'real', a notion which is difficult to pin down, since we can only know it through the lenses of our cultural constructions. So, for starters, at this level the argument about realism is not that it is inevitably illusory. Televisual texts may create depictions which are erroneous or misleading, but this is a different issue; it is not the same as saying 'television is by definition illusory because it utilizes realist representations'. I join with Corner in rejecting this latter position, not only on the grounds of the shifty nature of the instrument which is to undercut realism (namely, the real), but also because we must accept that all representation involves construction; there can be no immediacy with the real – at least not outside the pristine confines of mysticism.

Rather, the point about realism which has been so compelling in television studies is that it is used to explain the pleasures and popularity of the medium. Corner argues that this line of argument tends to collapse the distinction between what is basically two versions of the realism argument: the first where realism is the quality of being *like* the real, the second where it is the quality of being *about* the real. He suggests that there is a line of thought which sees the seductive character of the first version – the natural and technical codes providing an aesthetic of verisimilitude – as ushering the viewer into the second version, now trapped within erroneous understandings or knowledge. The pleasure and popularity which we assume derive from verisimilitude – although this assumption is not theoretically and empirically fully secure – need not automatically lead to illusion. It can, but we need not inject any determinism here. In fictional programming, it is verisimilitude and plausibility which are the keys. Corner then correctly points out that in non-diegematic programming, that is journalism, it is a question of the *veracity* of reference which is central, which in turn is carried by the veracity of image and speech.

Veracity, of course, is crucial, not least in relation to the public sphere. Some theoretically advanced investigations of the televisual text at times give the cavalier impression that the factual level of accounts is too mundane to be of much concern (Barry, 1993, discusses this unfortunate neglect of the problem of truthfulness). Even though the norms and practices of journalism are indeed highly problematical, a developed indifference to all issues of informational accuracy is a very misguided attitude. As Barry posits, there is no reason why critical attention to such themes as the ideological dimensions of the journalistic strategies of objectivity and impartiality must allow the question of veracity to remain a blind spot. Meaning and the range of interpretations among viewers are important, but so is the factual accuracy of the material from which viewers make sense.

To raise the issue of veracity does not imply that one can claim infallible or unproblematic access to the real, or that the discursive construction of social reality is somehow bypassed. But it does suggest that we can, within the limits of circumstances, make distinctions, weigh evidence, and make judgements about the proximity to the truth displayed by a given piece of information. Moreover, as Barry suggests, we need to study more the circumstances and factors which impinge on audiences' capacities to question the veracity of televisual texts – by comparing them with their own experiences or with other sources of information.

Viewers may at times question the veracity of television journalism, but the issue of the *actual* veracity of any non-fictional text is not *per se* dependent upon viewer subjectivity. It is a separate, analytic issue, whereas the pleasures of verisimilitude – that television is like the real – relate directly to subjectivity. Moreover, I would also argue that the pleasures of this verisimilitude spill over even into non-fiction television: we can find it pleasurable that television is both *like* the real and is *about* the real, without a priori slipping in any argument about there being an overall illusory mechanism at work or that veracity is by definition lacking in non-fiction television. With regard to television news, Stam (1983) discusses the idea of epistemophilia, the love of knowledge. There may be deception, there may be untruthfulness, and these may even be discursively systematic in the service of power. But such features are not by definition a part of television's essential ontology, whereas I will hazard to say that the pleasure of verisimilitude – in fiction, non-fiction, and entertainment programming – comes pretty close to it.

To avoid entanglements with these older debates and to clarify my position – which emphasizes the pleasure of verisimilitude, rejects the blanket argument of illusion, and posits that veracity is, at bottom, an empirical and not a subjective issue – I will use the less theoretically-laden term 'mimetic'. Television mimes reality and this is a key to understanding the pleasure it provides. This pleasure could be psychoanalytically theorized around what are termed primary processes, though I will not pursue that here. Suffice it to say that this pleasure of experiencing television can be understood in terms of the processes of its interaction with the audiences – the 'work' done by viewers.

Wilson (1993), who uses the concept of veridical (and by now we must be running out of synonyms!) speaks of the audience's horizons of expectations in regard to television. These are the multiplicity of dispositions audiences have which derive from prolonged cultural experience with the medium. The veridical effect is the sense that television provides transparent access to the world. This is understood as a product of, on the one hand, assumptions which are based on the audiences' perceptional frameworks and, on the other hand, the programmes' conformity to those assumptions (Wilson, 1993:113). Again, this seeming transparency of television is of course illusory, a fact which *can* have ideological implications, but Wilson also does not simply dismiss all television as inherently ideological. Rather, he suggests that the veridical effect is always historical in that the rules, or codes, are always evolving, and this is an important point.

The veridical effect in television would seem to run parallel to what many have said about the classic realist film. Here, however, Barker (1988) reminds us of the by now familiar notions of the segmented televisual text, which is at the heart of its famous 'flow' character (see Williams, 1974) and distinguishes television output from the more autonomous works of realist film. This segmentation – typified by disjuncture and rupture – fosters a cumulative decoding on the part of the audience: viewers need to pull together a broad and continuing discursive history. Moreover, the segmented nature of televisual discourse invites a variety of shifting subject positions in the viewer, involving interpretive work in a manner different from that required for the realist film (see also Hartley, 1992b).

Televisual texts make use of a variety of representational forms, but Barker argues that these are arranged hierarchically, with verisimilitude at the top, as culturally dominant. Citing Fiske and Hartley, Barker (1988:44) says that verisimilitude 'is the mode in which our particular culture prefers its ritual condensations to be cast'. In a manner which parallels Fiske's discussion of codes, Barker explains how this verisimilitude is achieved through a combination of specific codes which we associate with the depiction of reality. Thus, news and documentary programmes, for example, use particular types of camera work, editing, sound, and so on in their portrayals of reality. We come to associate these codes with the reporting of reality; they operate this way in our horizons of expectation. They are so familiar to us that we do not see them for the most part; we see *with* them. These codes are used in fiction programmes as well, to provide the quality of liveness, the 'reality effect', and Barker uses the police series *Hill Street Blues* as a paradigmatic example of the blend of natural and technical/vérité codes. Television's verisimilitude is the result of an ongoing process of negotiation between audiences and texts, within the boundaries established by the television medium and the general culture.

The constructivist move provides a measure of relativism in regard to evaluating representations of reality, but does not by any means alleviate the traditional issues of power; it only recasts them in a somewhat more subtle form. Thus, the traditional concern with ideology becomes refigured such that the critique of ideology can no longer claim the status of objective truth against the untruths which it accuses, since it too is socially situated. Its own constructed status becomes reflexively apparent, as well as its own potential entanglements with power. Thus, there can be no guarantee that the position from which ideology critique derives is itself beyond ideological implication; there is no privileged platform which would make self-reflection superfluous in this regard. Instead, ideology critique is seen, more modestly but more effectively, as an interpretive effort which tries to demonstrate the links between specific modes of representation and concrete forms of social domination, as Thompson (1990) and Barrett (1991) suggest. Critical hermeneutic analysis, as Best and Kellner argue (1987), needs to be able to fathom such links.

Within contemporary debates about television, any assertion of the mimetic quality of its discourses encounters arguments about cultural postmodernism, which in some cases have incorporated television as its exemplary flagship (see J. Collins, 1992, for an accessible example of such discussions). Observers have developed an inventory of postmodern characteristics in televisual discourses which, among other things, can be seen as undermining the mimetic: for example, irony, intertextuality, eclecticism, multi-subject positions, and 'hyperconsciousness'. This latter term refers to a form of self-disclosure or self-reflexivity which becomes paramount in the media: an acknowledgement of, and commentary in the media about, the media's status as constructed artifice. Television programmes seemingly reveal their own production processes or are about themselves as media phenomena, resulting in what Olson (1987) calls 'meta-television'. The postmodernist line of reasoning is also that television is dispersing into many forms/genres/structures; television as a whole is *not* a whole: it is untotalizable. Meaning is seen either as gushing surplus, spilling out beyond all efforts to grasp it, or, in the Baudrillard (1983) version, as denied, dispersed, absent. Baudrillard, moreover, argues for the concept of simulacra: television and other media no longer reflect an external reality. They bear no relation to any external reality, but have their own pure simulacra. In these and other ways, it is argued that television undercuts its alleged mimetic character.

Much has been written on these themes and I will make only a few brief points within the framework of my own discussion here. First, from the standpoint of television production, an industry perspective can go a long way in explaining the seemingly routine subversion of convention and the mingling and mutations of genres. Caughie (1991) argues that most of these innovations are derived from American commercial television, rather than European public service broadcasting. This is because the market logic requires ever-increasing product differentiation in the struggle to gain the fragmenting large mass audience: the formulaic repetition of television is balanced by incremental difference in an intense competition for niche positions. Thus, the mimetic is not eradicated, but its codes are updated.

Secondly, aesthetically-inspired enthusiasm has coloured sociological analysis. Abercrombie et al. (1992) explicitly make this point in the face of postmodern claims: realism (they prefer the traditional term) as a cultural form is alive and well – though by no means unchanged in the present situation – not least because audience reception is still largely geared to respond to it. They cite three basic parameters of realism (1992:119): it offers a window on the world, it employs a narrative which has rationally ordered connections between events and characters, and it conceals authorship and disguises the production process of the text. If we apply these parameters to contemporary television, for example, they still capture the fundamental logics at work, despite evolving conventions.

The mimetic still prevails, but it is not left unchanged by these developments. The research task is to be alert to the newer discursive dynamics of reality portrayal. The polysemic character of televisual texts and the instability of their meaning are no doubt amplified by the postmodern trends. However, the elucidation of meaning within the text does not cease to be

important. As Hartley (1992a) argues, in affirming the contingency of meaning, there is both an excess of meaningfulness in televisual texts – they
semiotically seep out and transgress boundaries – and, at the same time,
there is a contradictory valence at work (from television and the from the
power élite) to contain and control ideological drift; this latter tendency proceeds via a number of strategies, which include exclusion, marginalization,
and scandal (1992a:38). And finally, for all the talk (and text) about diversity
and eclecticism in television, I have yet to see mainstream television in any
country fulfil its potential for diversity. The points of view available, the topics and perspectives presented, and the modes of cultural expression given
voice, seem for the most part no less suppressed than they were before the
postmodern celebration. Television has yet to realize its democratic promise.

Two worlds?

In the above discussion I have no doubt slipped into talking about 'television
in general', an enterprise I warned about at the outset of the chapter – which
shows that following one's own advice is not always easy. But at some point
one does have to make distinctions in the programme output. Thus, one
stumbles head-on into the notion of genre. Genre is a problematic concept; it
refers to strategies of production, formal elements of programmes, as well as
the disposition of audience expectation (see Feuer, 1992). Generic classifica-
tion is always impermanent, since genres are constantly evolving. Yet genre
analysis does help us to get a handle on the modes of address and possible
subject positions built into specific televisual texts (for example, does the
televisual discourse treat us as citizens or consumers?). Corner (1991) says
that genre analysis also directs our attention to the degree of referentiality of
the text – that is, to what extent it makes claim to refer to some external reality – and to whether the text is propositional in its discursive devices or more
associative and symbolic.

With the tools of genre analysis one can make the basic distinction between
fiction and non-fiction programming, as Corner suggests. This distinction is
also culturally compelling: we want to be able to tell the difference between
programming which claims to represent reality and that which signals that it
does not. This separation is manifested in everyday discourses about television, as well as in television studies, both of programming and audiences.
Corner nicely captures the distinction with his terms 'the public knowledge
project' and 'the popular culture project'. Our interest in television tends to
lean towards an emphasis *either* on information, news, current events – the
representations of reality – *or* a focus on fiction and entertainment. The analytic separation here goes further than just which type of programming comes
under scrutiny. It also has to do with the epistemological assumptions used
and the questions asked. Moreover, there is a gender factor at work, which I
will return to shortly.

The study of news and current affairs programming would at first glance
seem to correlate with a concern for the public sphere. The public knowledge

project aims to elucidate what kinds of information about the world are transmitted, retained, understood and interpreted. This research and political interest must be distinguished from the interest in television as popular culture, though insights from such studies may well have relevance for understanding how current affairs programming is constructed and received by viewers. The popular culture project emphasizes the enjoyment provided by and derived from the media. My inquiry here is that even if the separation is both empirically plausible and conceptually necessary, it is at the same time problematic on a number of levels. This is not to say that the distinction collapses. Rather, probing the boundary a bit more may help us better to understand television's conditions – its limits and possibilities – as an institution of the public sphere.

At the most obvious level, we can empirically note the increasing porousness of the classic information/entertainment distinction itself, as the programming of even European public service television is becoming swamped with versions of infotainment programmes, varieties of 'reality reconstructions' (such the crime-watch genre) and, not least, talk shows which blend talk about international political crises and the love lives of movie stars into a chatty concoction in which it becomes difficult to separate the basic ingredients. This development is by no means new – in Sweden it can be traced back at least to the early 1970s – but it is accelerating. If the public knowledge project cannot be anchored to a limited number of programmes or genres on television, but instead becomes dispersed or dissipated within many, it begins to lose its focus as a 'project', at least as far as television is concerned.

At another level, there are epistemological assumptions at work, which we need to examine further. Thus, the public knowledge project – both in its programme and audience studies – largely builds on either the 'transfer of information' model, with a focus on messages, or on some discursive model which emphasizes a sociology of knowledge or critique of ideology. There is nothing wrong with this, but the epistemological premises and methodological procedures tend to underscore the rational, cognitive side of televisual representation and the audiences' reception/knowledge. This latter tendency has been modified somewhat in recent years, particularly via some studies of reception of TV news (for example, Jensen, 1990), but if we look at television research as a whole, the predilection remains strong. The affective 'alter ego' emerges largely in the popular culture project, where questions of pleasure, emotion, and aesthetics are seen to have their place.

This aspect of the distinction is interesting not least because there is obviously a lot of gendering going on here. Joyrich (1991–92) points out that the question of affect, even among TV critics, is an interesting one. For decades, critics and researchers have been concerned that television works either to evacuate affect – deaden feelings – among its viewers (especially children), or, alternatively, to arouse intense emotional states or useless sentimentality (especially in women). Affect is associated with the feminine, and the many studies exploring the pleasures and other feelings experienced by women viewers is in keeping with this gender assumption. Two points are to be made here. First, the public knowledge project would certainly benefit by becoming still more alert to the affective dimensions at work within news and current affairs programming (as well as the newer genres) and within the audiences for these programmes. There is considerable affect behind all public knowledge. This could be further analysed and underscored. Secondly, the correlation between cognitive public knowledge and affective popular culture tends to reproduce the social relations of power which pivot on the public/private distinction, and this can be seen as a gender issue. Concretely: whatever pleasures women derive from 'feminine' forms of popular culture, it does not seem that they are politically served by attempts to ghettoize the affective within popular culture, walled off from the project of public knowledge.

What is in question here are the assumptions *behind* the division between these two worlds of television. One can acknowledge the differing interests of the two perspectives, but we would be advised to not assume any essentialistic distinction in either the nature of the programming or the kinds of audience responses that we may classify under the two categories. Indeed, if we make a small adjustment in the terminology and try to keep in mind that with television we are also dealing with *popular knowledge* and *public culture*, this may help remind us that the semiotic environment to which television contributes is transgressive of the original boundary. Moreover, it may help us to see that popular culture is also public, and public knowledge is, in a sense, popular. The upshot of this is that the public sphere, as it is manifested on television and within the audience, is not so easily demarcated from its 'otherness' – from all the other programming and experiential modes which we associate with popular culture. Sense-making within the public sphere should not be seen as something fundamentally masculine and cognitive. In short, our understanding of what constitutes 'knowledge' in relation to television and citizenship must be broadened, and I will return to this theme in the chapters ahead.

Sociocultural TV: ubiquity, culturology and critique

On the third side of the prism, television is a sociocultural experience. What appears on the screen is encountered and interpreted by viewers, and then enters into their social worlds through social interaction, being reinterpreted and inserted in a vast array of discourses. Moreover, television and elements of its output – modes of discourse, themes, topics, forms of humour, etc. – are intertextually circulated through other media. Television is a part of our daily lived reality, penetrating into the microcosms of our social world. It also serves to organize and structure that world, both in terms of daily schedule and interaction within the household (see Lull, 1990) and in offering frameworks of collective perception: television links the everyday world to the larger symbolic orders of social and political life. Ours is a television culture; George Gerbner once described television as 'the cultural arm of the industrial order'.

Indeed, one of television's definitive features is its central position in our semiotic environment. This centrality can be understood in terms of quantity – the sheer volume of output is staggering – but also in terms of its cultural legitimacy. Television functions as a purveyor of shared frames of reference: it serves as producer/reproducer of implicit sociocultural common sense. This view, however, must confront the modifying fact of the large number of channels available, many of them specialized genre channels: in a situation where television is decentralizing, the collective common sense may be on its way to becoming plural and fragmented, rather than unitary. Operating within technological, economic, cultural, organizational and professional frameworks, television is always actively involved in defining, shaping, and giving perspective to the world, and thus in prestructuring viewers' understanding of it. In this social constructivist argument, television functions in ways which parallel language itself; the Sapir-Whorf hypothesis about language shaping our understanding of reality gains further relevance when applied to the electronic media. Its ubiquity has to do both with its quantity and its accessibility. It is both physically and communicatively available. If one is a native speaker of the language used in the transmissions, one can normally become a culturally accomplished viewer in a short time. Television's ubiquity is, in fact, part of the problem as far as the public sphere is concerned. The public sphere as seen on television is embedded in a semiotic flood which threatens to engulf it. Television consists of incessant talk: there is a huge production of everyday speech. Some argue that this daily avalanche is wearing away at coherent speech within society, that the excessive semiotic deluge has become a cacaphony: 'The saturation of signs and messages is now the fact of television's dominance culturally, and that fact is the neutralization of signs and messages, their erasures into television' (Heath, 1990:291).

While Heath overstates the case here in my view, he appropriately calls attention to a drift in television studies and Cultural Studies in which the ubiquity of television implicitly leads to its uncritical legitimation: television is so pervasive, it virtually merges with everyday life. Everybody watches, so it must be OK. Everybody lives an everyday life, so that must be OK, too. Television and everyday life thereby become 'safe' zones – neutral categories, immune to critique, unproblematic because of their popularity. But both are not only problematic, they are also structured, contingent, and mediated by power, though in ways that are highly complex and contradictory. Power is multidimensional, and so must emancipatory strategies be (a theme to which I will return to in later chapters). To ignore power relations, not to mention the political economy of both television and everyday life, is profoundly to cripple one's capacity for critical analysis. C. Wright Mills would no doubt see this as a failure of the sociological imagination.

Perhaps the core dimension of television as a sociocultural experience is precisely that it provides pleasure. On one level this has been obvious – not least to broadcasters – since the dawn of the medium, but it is only in rather recent years that pleasure has come to take an explicit place with cultural theory, and still more recently that it has entered television studies with a degree of theoretical sophistication. Fiske's (1987) exposition was an important step in placing pleasure on the theoretical agenda in television analysis. While he has received criticism over the years for overplaying the interpretive freedom of audiences, his synthesizing of a number of strands of analysis provided a significant step. I will not repeat his whole discussion on pleasure, which by now is well known, but will merely highlight the point that, seen from this angle, much of the pleasure of television derives from viewers' active involvement with the texts; that is, pleasure is to a large degree a 'producerly' experience. The activity of making sense, of playing with the text, even of penetrating its artifice, are all part of this pleasure. While pleasure can emerge from the particular meanings generated, just the fact of making some kind of sense – of appropriating the text for oneself – offers a mild sense of pleasurable empowerment. Feminists have pursued gender aspects of pleasure (see Brown, 1990); even television news can provide pleasure, as Jensen (1990) found among his respondents.

In passing I would just note that we should be open to a complementary angle on pleasure and meaning, namely that there may be a certain type of pleasure derived even in the absense of meaning. Hermes (1993) discusses the disappointment she experienced at first when her respondents seemed to have very little profound to say about the popular magazines that she was interviewing them about. She came to the conclusion that a good deal of our media involvement must fundamentally be devoid of meaning, at least in the sense of providing a significant experience which lodges in our memory and invites cognitive or moral interpretation. And I strongly suspect that what she found regarding popular magazines may well also hold true for television. In other words, as researchers, our own hermeneutic obsessions may blind us to the fact that involvement with the media may not always be producerly and involve 'work'; it can well consist of a 'time-out' from all thought and reflection – from active interpretation.

It is questionable if such no-frills media experiences should be lauded with the label pleasure – one can easily claim that it is closer to the antithesis of pleasure, a sedative, or an instance of the commodified consciousness of consumer society, as Jameson (1983) would argue. In any case, such media involvement must still be seen as providing some form of gratification, some positive subjective experience. We may wish to call even such experiences 'meaningful', but we should still distinguish them from those experiences where active meaning production takes place. Whatever label we choose to define such experience, the point here is that we should be aware that producerly sense-making is not necessarily a universal trait of all television viewing.

Within the evolution of Cultural Studies, one can see how recognition of the polymorphous nature of power, growing epistemological pluralism and relativism, and the imperative to avoid élitist positions and to defend the notions of pleasure and of the popular, have contributed to more nuanced analyses of television and its audiences. Yet at the same time this has also opened the doors to uncritical populist positions which avoid making critical connections between the micro-levels of quotidian culture and macro-level issues of structure and power. (See McGuigan, 1992; Harris, 1992 for detailed discussions of this evolution; for a less sympathetic rendering, see Berman, 1991.)

Aside from Cultural Studies itself, there is a line of research which addresses the sociocultural experience of television in terms which are explicitly culturological, utilizing concepts from anthropology, ethnography and Durkheimian sociology. The boundary between Cultural Studies and culturological approaches, of course, cannot but be permeable and some authors, such as Saenz (1992), seem neatly to straddle the distinction. He argues for the idea that television provides audiences 'with a continuously problematized store of implicit social knowledge' (1992:39), a 'dynamic doxa' which individuals use in the production of their social practices. Derived from the anthropologist Michael Taussig, the concept of implicit social knowledge according to Saenz is 'an essentially inarticulable and imagistic, nondiscursive knowing of social relationality' (1992:39) which viewers interpret and make use of for their own purposes. This knowledge also relates to collective memories and associations, further strengthening television's position as an integrating cultural agent.

Television watching itself is a blend of ritual, aesthetic, literary, poetic and rhetorical practices, according to Saenz. The ideological dimension is ever present, but is often partial and ambiguous. It operates chiefly by refiguring viewers' implicit social knowledge at the common sense level, rather than by transferring a coherent and formalized system of belief. In a similar vein, Newcomb and Hirsch (1984) advocate the model of television as a 'cultural forum'. They link the ritual model of communication made famous by James Carey – 'Communication is a symbolic process whereby reality is produced, maintained, repaired and transformed' (Newcomb and Hirsch, 1984:60) – with anthropologist Victor Turner's notion of the 'liminal' as an in-between stage which is neither wholly within or outside of society, and provides a safe space for rule-bending and experimentation. With the addition of an emphasis on the interpretive variance within the audiences, Newcomb and Hirsch develop a view of television as a site for society's symbolic acting out of its self-understanding – and in a manner which cannot be closed or determinate, since the interpretive free play is considerable.

While Newcomb and Hirsch tip the scales too far in favour of an all-powerful interpretive audience and thus downplay the mediation of power, both their perspective and that of Saenz capture something of the fundamental and important integrative character of mainstream television. The medium unites us not only in that we have shared experiences in viewing, but also in that television contributes to the common implicit knowledge – the dynamic doxa – which is in circulation within society. This culturological line has been given its richest and most probing expression in the work of Silverstone (see Silverstone, 1981, 1988, 1994). In describing the central cultural position which television has, Silverstone says:

In its centrality it articulates the primary concerns of human existence and in ways which are themselves primary. These concerns, questions of life and death, of the familiar and strange, of male and female, of nature and culture, are incorporated even into our own advanced culture through the messages that television communicates. The forms of that communication are themselves basic. They are simple and one supposes that they are effective; they consist in the mythic narratives, part myth, part folktale, and in magic and ritual . . . Television's effectiveness consists in its ability to translate the unfamiliar and to provide frameworks for making sense of the unintelligible. It articulates difference but preserves that difference. And while it transcends the boundary of the acceptable and the known and seeks continuously to extend it, it nevertheless marks the boundary clearly and unambiguously. Within that boundary we are secure and through television we are always within it. (Silverstone, 1981:181)

This compact quote captures not only television's overarching position as an integrative symbolic universe, it also points to television's 'translation service', its capacity to recast the unfamiliar or the unintelligible in ways which make it safe and accessible. No doubt things get lost in translation, but that is partly the point: television offers its own ways of seeing, pulling an almost infinite array of things into itself – rather like a gravitational force field – and putting its stamp on them. Moreover, the modes of sense-making via television lean towards the extra-rational; the mythic dimension – which expresses the eternal need for cosmic security, to generate order and suppress chaos – hovers between the known and the unknown (or unknowable), between common and extra-common sense. Thus, from the standpoint of sociocultural experience, television becomes a resource, the mythic discourses of which we use to help process and organize our own experiences, and to mediate between the horizons of our everyday world and those which lie beyond our immediate reality. This mediation helps to situate and validate the everyday in larger symbolic terms, providing a sense of cosmic coherence. That this mythic dimension may be largely expressed in mimetic terms only serves to heighten its cultural resonance.

Silverstone wrote this text in the early 1980s and one may wish to test this line of reasoning with more postmodern lenses. Thus, the unified, all-embracing portrait of a rather cozy television here seems at odds with the image of the discordant television of today, with its multiplicity of discourses and rapidly shifting segments. If I allow myself considerable room to speculate here, I would posit that people use television today in pretty much the same way as Silverstone describes, still deriving an important sense of cultural anchoring and orientation. However, the amount of output available today and the enhanced tempo of some newer programming, together with genre-mingling and other more recent trends, may mean that the television-based symbolic universes which reverberate among audiences are both more plural than previously (at least in post-public service monopoly societies) and perhaps more kaleidoscopic in character. The destabilized microworlds of modernity are complemented by less-, not more-, stable semiotic environments, as I will discuss in Chapter 4.

Among those using a culturological approach to television, Silverstone is the one who not only seems to take the cultural saturation of television as an important analytical factor – probing its many articulations with other features in our lives – but has also been the most sensitive to the relationship between ideology and culture. The relationship is complex, and difficult, and in my view Silverstone steers an exemplary course. As I suggested above, the ideological dimension is ever a potentiality and often an actuality, yet all culture, including the output and experience of television, cannot simply be reduced to ideology. The level of integrative codes do not only serve to reproduce social relations of domination; all meaning does not a priori simply serve the interests of power. Moreover, ideology is not singular and unified; it too, like televisual texts and the sense-making of audiences, is polyvocal and fractured. If power and emancipatory impulses are plural, so is ideology. The critical task, according to Heath, is to counter the 'normalization' which television fosters, to retain 'the critical distance that television carefully erodes in its extension, its availability, its proximity' (Heath, 1990:297). Ricoeur (1981) calls it 'distanciation', and there are probably few phenomena which are so difficult to distance ourselves from as television, precisely because of its unrelenting ubiquity.

Critical understanding of television must go beyond the levels of both televisual text and the empirical data of audience experiences, and see the larger societal configurations in which television is embedded, particularly those of power, precisely as Lodziak (1986) argues. Television tends to invite certain subject positions via its modes of address, and exclude others. If television tends to privilege the subject position of 'consumer' over that of 'citizen', this pattern is not merely the creation of the televisual discourse alone, but is also fostered via other major constellations of power within society. Media institutions, media output, and media reception all meet up with social structure and power relations. If our role as citizen is by implication dimunitive in the face of television, it is also the case that this pattern is generally pervasive; television's contribution is largely one of homologous coherence, not one of exception. I am not arguing that we are confronted by an hermetically sealed, media-driven social system – on the contrary, I see many stresses and tensions in a complex social formation which is in transition. The point is that we understand the phenomenon of television – like the public sphere with which it overlaps – as intricately interwoven into mutual reciprocity with an array of other political, economic and sociocultural fields. It is via such interplay that television in its present forms is made possible by, and makes possible, these other fields.

Perhaps the most obvious example of this interrelationship is the character of the political system itself and, more specifically, the public sphere. In the space of several decades, television has moved to a position of prominence – for example, many people, in response to questionnaires about their news habits, place television as their primary source of information as well as the news medium in which they have the most confidence. Television journalism is in many ways shaped by the political traditions of our societies, while at the same time politics as we know it today is very much an expression of its adaptation to television. Political campaigns are simply the dramatic high-lights of this, for even the day-to-day processes of politics are adapted to the logic of the media, not least television. As countless studies have shown, the interaction between journalists and power holders, the ensemble of news val-ues, the framing of events, the accepted modes of discourse, the style of interviews, and so on, all express an integration of television and political cul-ture. One could say that, to a significant extent, the official political system exists as a televisual phenomenon; on the other hand, it is crucial that politics in the larger sense does not become reduced to a media phenomenon. That many viewers may be ambivalent about what they actually derive from tele-vision journalism, as Hagen (1994) found among Norwegian audience members, may have as much to do with the character of the political system as with the modes of television's representations.

Concern for the democratic quality of the prevailing social order and its public sphere requires that television must remain an object of critical con-cern. Treating this object prismatically – as an industry, as mediated discourses and as sociocultural experience – will help us to maintain the hori-zons adequate for such critical concern.

3

Popular television journalism

Mainstream, mimetic television would seem to lend itself eminently to journalism. Via its natural, technical and integrative codes it should be able to enhance public knowledge, its output serving as a positive contribution to the representational dimension of the public sphere. Moreover, television journalism would also constructively stimulate the dimension of sociocultural interaction of the public sphere: television as a sociocultural experience would strengthen public culture and democratic participation. Within the political system, direct participatory democracy is possible to a limited extent only; the remainder is carried out by representation. This political representation has its counterpart in the media: we cannot all be present at all events and developments, but fortunately television can represent them for us.

Many argue that, for all its shortcomings, this is precisely what television journalism does. These defenders posit that since the emergence of television journalism, more people have become more informed about national and international questions. They claim also that in societies which are at least somewhat democratic, governments cannot fully control what is transmitted; critical discourse, albeit at times in very watered down forms, circulates. Public knowledge, though patchy and uneven, is augmented. Not least, television journalism can force some minimal accountability from the powerful, at least among public officials (private economic power admittedly remains more aloof).

This view of television journalism of course has its counterpart. Beyond the liberal-reformist position, which acknowledges deficiencies and calls for improvements, is a more fundamental critical view. This position, which has a number of 'strong' and 'moderate' versions, argues that given television's institutional embeddedness, the nature of its representations – not least its journalistic output – and its qualities as a sociocultural experience, it functions basically to subvert democracy. Its discourses are pervasively ideological, not least on account of its realist aesthetic. It constricts the spread of necessary knowledge, it provides an illusion of informedness while at the same time trivializing important issues by juxtaposing them with frivolous items. The social world appears to a large extent as a scene on which random and unexpected events take place, the overall picture seemingly incoherent and fragmented. Television defines for us what is political and provides the terms for political discussion in ways which, at bottom, support the prevailing constellations of power and wealth. Viewers are positioned as spectators of the political system and socialized to a sense of powerlessness. This familiar list can be expanded, but these are some of the more common charges.

While there may be a tendency for the more severe critics to be academics and the more staunch defenders to be operating within television journalism itself, the lines cannot simply be reduced to critical outsiders versus supportive insiders. In his review of the various arguments, Corner (1995) concludes that there is ample evidence to support both positions, and it is important to underscore the need for evidence, in the face of both easy theorizing and defensive professionalism. We would do well to avoid the extreme arguments on either side of the debate. Corner argues for a 'wary ambivalence', which I take to be a sound starting point, but that is not to say that the respective arguments are necessarily equally compelling in all circumstances.

My own wary ambivalence is situated a few notches off dead centre in the direction of the critics. However, I too feel that the arguments and evidence from the defence cannot be wholly dismissed. Television journalism does – with many qualifications – foster forms of awareness and public knowledge conducive to the democratic character of society. Its contributions to the public sphere can by no means be deemed entirely negative. Yet, whatever their conclusions, all such overarching evaluations are of limited utility.

What I wish to do in this chapter is to look at some of the current trends within a number of genres of television journalism. In keeping with the prismatic nature of the television medium, I first take up an aspect of television journalism's industrial character, specifically, the deeply rooted professional tension between its 'televisual' and 'journalistic' dimensions. Turning to the sociocultural side, given that the most pervasive developments within television journalism can be captured within the term 'popularization', I explore some notions of what the 'popular' may mean here. This is admittedly an elastic, yet useful concept. From there I look at aspects of television journalism as an audio-visual text, including some of its current formats and modes of representation. I conclude with a short discussion which takes us back to the sociocultural side, namely questions about possible dialogic character and its mobilization of a moral point of view. From these angles of vision I will try to grasp television journalism's promises and pitfalls as part of the public sphere.

Television journalism: an essential tension

Communication theorists are fond of saying that there is no 'pure' information, no language which does not embody presuppositions and value orientations, as well as implying certain social relations among its users. There is a rhetorical slant to every representation of knowledge about the world. Television journalism is no exception: it can never merely present an unproblematic 'mirror of events'. Yet communication theorists comprise only a very small fraction of the population, and it is questionable whether the majority share this understanding. The concept of objectivity and the related distinction between 'information' and 'entertainment' have also been part of the practical, professional self-understanding of journalism since its inception (see Schudson, 1978, and Hartley, 1992a, for two quite different discussions on this theme within the history of journalism). While information and enter-tainment are concepts which readily circulate in popular and professional discourses, they are by no means unproblematic from a theoretical perspec-tive. In part they echo the distinction between pleasure and effort, and the division between the popular culture and the public knowledge projects referred to in the previous chapter. Let us briefly look at the institutional unfolding of this force field between the ideal of objective information and popular entertainment in television.

Television journalism's position within journalism as a whole has never been completely unproblematic. If one goes back to the origins of broadcast journalism, one can see that in historical terms it took considerable institu-tional and professional adjustment to solidify the position of journalism, first on radio, then on television. The print bias was culturally well-entrenched. Yet the electronic media and not least TV journalism had become a fact of life; accommodation was required. Gradually, broadcast journalism became accepted, not only professionally but also popularly. Its history varies somewhat within different countries, but generally one can say that forms of journalistic practice were developed which soon gave broadcast journalism a respected position as a complement to the printed press. As politics in west-ern society became more television-oriented and as television's position in the public life of society became dominant, TV journalism's standing became unquestionable, though there always remained lingering discomfiture in some circles over its 'television-ness'.

In the USA, TV journalism has been defined since its beginnings, on the one hand, by the abstract goals of journalism and, on the other, by commer-cial imperatives and the cultural understanding of TV as an entertainment medium. For many years, one accepted that television journalism had an obligation to the public interest, yet was not a major source of income. That gradually began to change in the 1970s, with new modes of presentation in local TV news. There emerged a style of TV news production which came to be known as 'Happy Talk' (Powers, 1977, traces this development, with a con-siderable dose of irony). With such strategies as a more sensationalist tone, an emphasis on the charisma and image of newscasters (a journalism back-ground was not necessary: screen 'presence' was more important), the launching of co-hosts who engaged in informal and humorous banter among themselves (at times bordering on slapstick), an elaboration of the weather report and the growth of human interest stories, local news programmes soon become an economic asset.

Questions about the concept of journalistic professionalism, which I men-tioned in the previous chapter, intensified. The move towards 'Happy Talk' met with much internal professional criticism, but the economics were beyond dispute. Critics began to console themselves with the fact that at least the prestigious national network news programmes maintained the best tradi-tions of TV journalism. But by the late 1980s, as the national networks in the USA began to lose up to a third of their viewers to the newer cable TV net-works, even this began to change. First the budgets of the news divisions were drastically cut, and then the flashier styles, faster tempo and even somewhat more sensationalist news values began to manifest themselves – even on the network news programmes.

While in Western Europe the commercial imperatives were less pronounced, even here competition for audiences began to appear as soon as second channels were introduced. Moreover, in Sweden, and presumably in other countries with public broadcasting, television journalists and producers were hardly following the research recommendations for such didactic measures as slower tempo. Slower tempo and more instructional modes of expression in TV journalism were no doubt perceived as being risky. Such measures would break the cardinal rule of TV: they would be boring. The viewer might then switch the channel or turn off the set. The Geneva-based media analyst Baldi (1994) finds in his analyses of European programming trends that infotainment, incorporating both talk shows and reality-based programmes, has been the most forceful growth trend in the five major markets in recent years.

The 1980s witnessed the dramatic transformation of television globally. I will not recount all these changes here, but for purposes of this discussion I can just mention that the old regime in the USA – dominated by the three networks – as well as the public service model in Europe, have both been altered by, among other things, the loosening of government regulation, the increasing absorption of the television industry into international conglomerates, and the rise of satellite links and cable stations. The internationalization of television journalism, both in the sense of institutional and technological factors, as well as shared sets of conventions, codes and genres, has been proceeding accordingly. One should not ignore differences in reporting which do still exist: there are still national variations in organizational, political, economic and cultural factors, as Wallis and Baran (1990) demonstrate in their comparative study of television journalism. Moreover, as the work of Cohen et al. (1995) on the 'global newsroom' shows, we can find cultural differences at work in the ways the same 'raw material' of footage and facts are 'packaged' and given different narrative angles by different national broadcasters, to attain congruence with various 'meta-stories' circulating in the respective cultures. Overall, though, the drift towards an international standardization of basic journalistic discourses in television is evident.

Though the essential tension between information and entertainment persists today, one cannot help but sense that the stridency of the voices defending traditional notions of informational journalism have been muted as the imperatives of television as an industry tighten. Television journalism finds itself in a different media environment. Viewers have more options. The spread of such technologies as remote control and video make audiences more fluid and transitory. The struggle to capture and maintain viewer attention escalates. From an economic perspective, the growing prominence of the popular in TV journalism seems, in retrospect, inevitable. From a professional perspective, many have come to argue that there is little point in following some traditional recipe for journalism if it does not attract viewers. Early in the game it was apparent that journalistic programmes on television could not deviate too far from the prevailing notions of what 'popular TV' was all about. (For an excellent recent study on how market forces shape the outcome of American local television news, see McManus, 1994.)

Probing 'the popular'

From Chapter 1 we can recall the notion of what constitutes a 'public'. Habermas is insistent about the idea of discursive interaction among citizens. A 'public' is not an inert mass of people, nor is it a product derived from opinion polling. Publics exist only in so far as there are active exchanges of views and information among citizens: this is the interactional dimension of the public sphere. While it may be Utopian to expect this to become the pattern among a majority of citizens, this vision should at least guard against accepting certain 'cut price' versions of citizenship as indicative of healthy democracy. To burlesque the point somewhat: atomized TV news viewers responding to questionnaires is not a portrait of a viable democracy.

Thus I discussed the dimension of social interaction in the public sphere and television as a sociocultural experience. For television journalism this means we need to consider how it functions *as communication*: at some level the criteria for 'good journalism' must in part depend on its capacity to attract and engage the audience, to stimulate the processes of meaning-making and critical reflection (Rosen, 1986, develops this point). In Fiske's (1989:185) terminology, this is journalism's 'producerly' quality. Embedded in this notion of the producerly is the capacity to evoke and provoke, to stimulate response and interchange with other people. As Fiske points out, this can only take place within specific cultural contexts; there are a variety of such contexts and thus it seems reasonable to suggest that there should be a variety of modes of journalism which aim at different sectors of the population.

Fiske's notion of producerly I call the communicative or *pragmatic* dimension of journalism, as distinguished from the *thematic* dimension. If the thematic dimension has to do with journalism's referential functions, that is, its representations of social reality, the pragmatic has to do with not only the relationship between journalism and its audience, but also journalism's role in fostering interaction among the audience – in helping audience members to interact as citizens, transcending their status as 'audience'. Journalism can be treated as a factor which potentially promotes or hinders the communication among citizens that is necessary for a viable public sphere, and can in principle be evaluated even on these grounds. Obviously it cannot do this in the absence of other social and cultural factors, but it is not unreasonable to assume that television journalism's particular contribution can make a difference here.

Two qualifying comments are appropriate here. First of all, I am not advocating that the pragmatic dimension be operationalized to serve as the basis for empirical testing with viewers, whatever the research approach. This would be a rather futile task. Rather, I am merely suggesting that we incorporate this pragmatic dimension into our horizons when we analyse and evaluate journalistic output. This is by no means a new thought – in Sweden, for example, the work of Findahl and Höijer (for example, 1981, 1985) have long advocated analysis 'from the standpoint of the viewer' – but its link to the perspective of the public sphere should be made explicit. Secondly, I am fully aware that the distinction between pragmatic and thematic dimensions hovers perilously close to a replay of 'form-and-content' discussions. However, in today's intellectual climate, armed with semiotics, hermeneutics, discourse analysis, and so on, actual analysis need not resort to such ontological reductionism. Clearly the two dimensions are interwoven in the overall structural coherence of any particular text, via the discursive configurations, codes and intertextuality of journalism. (I note in passing that 'structural coherence' does not in any way preclude multiple interpretations of the text.) Meaning, whether of the more analytic or experiential variety, and pleasure, are not found exclusively in either the thematic or the pragmatic, but in the relationships between them.

Analytically then, what is 'the popular' and how does it relate to the thematic and pragmatic dimensions? The popular foregrounds the pragmatic. Fiske, following Stuart Hall, situates the popular with 'the people', that is, the heterogeneous majority who stand in contrast to the various sectors of the élite 'power bloc'. In this line of reasoning, the popular is that which enhances the pragmatic dimension for the majority. Applying this perspective to journalism, Fiske distinguishes between official, alternative and popular news. Official news is 'serious' and essentially speaks with the voice of the power bloc. Alternative news is the small minority of outlets offering left radical perspectives. Popular news is the staple of the majority, the people. Fiske argues that to 'encourage a wide diversity of people to want to watch it, and to remember and think about its events, TV news must meet the key criteria of popular taste, those of relevance and pleasurable productivity' (Fiske 1989:185). Relevance here involves making connections between one's own everyday experiences and that which appears on television news. Television news must be made to matter to a wide variety of subcultures in modern society, inviting divergent readings and social interaction.

To elicit talk about the events it portrays, television journalism must fit easily into contemporary oral culture; television news needs to address its audiences with affective intensity and should 'discard its role of privileged information-giver' (Fiske 1989:193). Objectivity should not be its central criterion; rather Fiske envisions a broad repertoire of journalism where the serious sectors stand for such traditional concerns, while the popular modes concentrate on providing multiple perspectives, preferably devoid of hierarchy, which can evoke discussion and disagreement.

This helps to provide some contour to journalism's pragmatic dimension. Yet there are some elements here which can be misleading. First of all, Fiske's three-part typology of news is too categorical and misses precisely the current dynamics of popularization; for example, even what he terms official TV news is becoming more 'popular' in its modes of representation. The drastic increase in visual cuts and sound bites (see Gitlin, 1991a, and Hallin, 1994, for American perspectives) and the rise of political adversity (see Diamond and Bates, 1988) are but two examples of this. The proposed division of labour between the official and the popular in TV journalism becomes tenuous in the face of television journalism's development. Secondly, what of the thematic dimension? He does not by any means dismiss it, but it remains comparatively undertheorized in his writing. He states that broadcast news 'needs . . . to balance popular tastes and pleasures with educational, socially responsible criteria' (Fiske 1989:193). He also mentions 'criteria of social importance and social responsibility', admitting to the difficulty of defining them (Fiske 1989:191). Yet there seems to be an imbalance: he appears too willing to give the former priority, his 'escape clause' being that objective information and educational criteria are matters that can be left to serious journalism or to schools. However, if the trend towards the popular is so pervasive, are we wise to put our faith in some shrinking last bastion of serious journalism? (And most people stop going to school at an early point in their lives.)

A difficulty in Fiske's line of argument is that his notion of relevance is too anchored in people's already-established experiential horizons. This unnecessarily predefines certain topics or themes as falling within the domain of the serious and beyond the possible range of the popular. What is suppressed in this view is the legacy from the traditional canons of journalism, namely that there are indeed 'objective' developments in society which can impact on people's lives, regardless of whether or not these developments fit in with people's already existing horizons.

Looking in my thesaurus, I find that among the words suggested as possible synonyms for popular are 'public', 'civic' and 'civil'. It is this sense which Fiske captures so well in his discussion of popular TV journalism – the popular as democratic and vernacular forms of discourse, accessible to the vast majority. Yet, given that popular journalism on television is not a static category but a process touching virtually all journalistic activity, his category of serious information is left in a precarious position. As television journalism becomes more popular, at the same time as the serious press continues to decline internationally (for example, in Britain the circulation of the *Sun* is ten times that of *The Times*), it will not do for popular television journalism to pass the buck and say, 'Let serious TV journalism take care of social responsibility'. Popular television journalism must be obliged take up serious matters, and in a manner which *both* takes the thematic (and its criteria) seriously and which is popularly pragmatic enough to make them matter. Popular journalism needs to be 'educational' in the sense of broadening people's horizons, of making new connections between the accessible, experienced world and the world beyond those boundaries. Popular pragmatics must be weighed with serious thematics – a truly tall order.

Another check in my thesaurus revealed many words listed under 'entertain', among them 'divert' and 'beguile', as well as 'engross' and 'absorb'.

Here we seem to come again to the essential tension: the entertaining element of the popular side of today's TV journalism can indeed cut both ways. If there is to be a balance between the popular and the socially responsible, or between thematic and pragmatic aspects, then the underlying criteria for such balancing must be carefully considered. I see no compelling alternative to the long-established ideal that journalism must somehow aim to provide people with informative material to help them make sense of the world and to fulfil their roles as citizens. How this is to be done, and the balance between thematic and pragmatic can be discussed, but if the thematic is simply jettisoned – if we just give up on criteria for the referential status of television journalism's representations – it becomes difficult to visualize a democratic future. This does not discount a constructivist understanding of both social reality and of journalism, but argues that all coverage have as reliable factual foundations as possible.

In considering how to balance the thematic and the pragmatic within journalism as a whole, I concur with Fiske's idea that there must be a wide variety in the modes of expression – many genres – speaking to different sociocultural groups within the citizenry. In that case, television journalism would have a strong leaning toward popular formats. It is a question of optimizing the journalistic use to which the medium is put, allowing for the conditions and circumstances which shape its possibilities. We can of course never prove that television journalism could have been anything other than what it was at any particular moment; we can only fall back on an understanding of its potential. This potential is coloured by the prismatic conditions of the medium as an industry, representation and sociocultural experience. It is from this understanding that we must derive our ideals for television journalism and develop our critique of its current practices.

Old and new formats

That television journalism is changing is something we can confirm by looking at tapes of transmissions from 10 or 15 years ago. My guess is that in most western societies an examination of these older programmes would make many viewers acutely – and ironically – aware of the artifice used to generate impressions of reality. (We may well not have to wait 10 years to perceive today's artifice as constructedness seems to be becoming more visible in the present media environment.) It would be difficult to argue against the claim that over the past decade or so, the dominant trend in journalism generally, and TV journalism in particular, is towards it becoming more 'popular' in its modes of representation.

There have been a variety of responses to what is perceived as the increasing popularization of television journalism, and the reactions from commentators within the journalistic profession have been no less divided than those from outside it. Traditionally torn by a professional ideology which privileges, on the one hand, hard political news/information and, on the other hand, the economic/commercial requisites of media institutions,

journalists themselves seem to have mixed opinions about these developments. One of the upshots of the popularization trend is the further
destabilization of the signifier 'good journalism': there seems to be an increasing uncertainty as to what this means in today's context. Even the criteria
which separate journalism from non-journalism – that is, popular culture –
seem to have become less firm (see Dahlgren and Sparks, 1992).

Television journalism is now involved in a phase of intensive experimentation with a variety of new strategies and genres, or what Altheide and Snow
(1991) call formats. Format is the manner in which material is defined,
shaped, structured and presented, constituting a mediating link joining technology, subject matter, economics and audiences. What characterizes the
growth of the popular, or 'entertainment values' in television journalism?
While a number of general patterns are familiar enough – such as sensationalism, personalization, heightened dramatic conflict, quicker tempo, and
fewer abstractions – specific formats manifest the trend in specific ways, with
varying implications. If we begin with the contemporary formats of television
journalism, a partial list of the most prevalent ones would include the following, divided schematically for simplicity's sake, into 'older' and 'newer'
formats:

1 Older formats
(a) Traditional news broadcasts. These have been progressively revising some
    of their strategies, while essentially retaining their traditional format.
(b) Traditional current affairs magazines. Many of these, such as the classic *60
    Minutes* in the USA and programmes in similar moulds, consist of inves-
    tigative journalism. They combine filmed narrative representation with
    interviews of power holders, as well as other citizens who may figure in the
    news. The topics can range from political and social issues to particular
    criminal cases.
(c) Journalistic talk shows. This established format proceeds largely via dis-
    cussions between journalists and élites. This format is evolving; the
    discussions are becoming increasingly less question-and-answer and more
    'chummy chat'. Journalists are often becoming celebrities through such
    programmes.
(d) Documentaries. Some news programmes will, on occasion, include a
    longer 'feature' of a documentary nature, but the full half-hour or one-
    hour television documentary is an increasingly rare journalistic format.

2 Newer formats
(a) Tabloid-style news broadcasts. The prototypes can be found in USA local
    TV news shows; there is a variety of idioms within this format, but the
    basic style approximates that of evening tabloid newspapers, with consid-
    erable sensationalism, human interest stories, personification, crime and
    disasters.
(b) Vox-pop talk shows. Often with a media personality heading the pro-
    gramme, these shows centre on audiences in the studio and even at home
    expressing their views. They may take up current political affairs, but

more often focus on themes having to do with controversial social topics and emotional issues from personal life. The juxtaposition of lay and professional perspectives is a common ingredient.

(c) Infotainment magazines. Morning 'breakfast shows' are included here, but this format can be found in the early and late evening as well. Explicit entertainment segments are mixed with more serious material, even including short traditional news segments..

(d) Transnational satellite TV news. CNN, of course, is the prototype here. This format consists of 24-hour news transmission, organized chiefly around continual news segments. These include continual updates on ongoing important stories. There are also specialized news areas covered by special segments, especially business and entertainment, as well as interview programmes. One tendency in the news coverage here is to do much less editing than traditional news programmes and transmit much more 'raw footage', providing a strong sense of immediacy.

There are of course other formats, such as the so-called 'reality-based' programmes, of which the lurid 'crime reconstructions' are internationally the most infamous (Kilborn, 1994), analyses some of the varieties of 'reality television'). The overall categorization is negotiable, yet the version here does at least suggest that television journalism consists of an array of formats – some old, some new, some transmutational and some hybrid.

By far the most common format of television journalism remains the traditional news programme. While its conventions are still thoroughly recognizable, this format has been evolving steadily, especially over the past decade. The programme *Aktuellt*, for example, which is the main evening newscast of Channel One in Sweden, has undergone a number of decisive changes. The use of sophisticated logos and graphics has become the norm for *Aktuellt*. There is greater attention to the decor of the studio and a new personal style on the part of the anchorpeople in the newscasts. More significantly, the 1980s marked a dramatic increase in the tempo of the programme. The number of visual cuts and sound bites has increased dramatically, meaning that the average time for each such unit has been correspondingly reduced. While each transmission now also includes a longer, in-depth reportage, it is this increased tempo which most manifests a turn to the popular. This in turn has necessitated changes in the way stories are constructed and interviews are presented, with some alteration in news values. Hvitfelt (1994) found that in recent years the news programmes on Swedish Television and on the commercial channel have manifested a decline in the amount of information offered and an increase in sensationalism, thereby following international trends. Thus, popularization here would seemingly have had a largely negative pedagogic impact: the faster tempo, together with sensational elements, while more in keeping with other television programming, must serve to reduce rather than enhance comprehension and reflection. This said, all the other familiar critical issues about traditional news programmes remain.

The rise of CNN can be seen as an offshoot of the traditional news programme genre and undeniably constitutes a major development within television journalism. (There is already a large literature on CNN, much of it devoted to the Gulf War. But there are other issues as well, such as the relationship between CNN and national, public service news. See for example, Larsen, 1992.) CNN's cameras often take us close to the action, and much material is pumped out to global audiences in an only semi-edited state – as so-called 'real time' coverage. These production values of rawness and immediacy – almost a hyper-realism at times – do not necessarily enhance our understanding: the close-ups on trees may obscure the forest. Moreover, CNN's sense of 'liveness' is not without its own ideological baggage, as this form of mimetic television relies heavily on the traditional notions of journalistic immediacy blurring its own constructedness.

Yet such production values are understandable in a setting which is hysterically competitive and in which the technology now permits almost instantaneous coverage. To spend a few hours editing a story, filling in the background, weighing different interpretations, checking the sources – in other words, following the procedures of traditional broadcast journalism – would mean risking 'losing' the story to a competitor who might break it earlier. CNN's approach, given its 24-hour transmissions, is rather that of the continuous update. As CNN built up its following, viewers (and other media dependent on CNN) expected 'fast-breaking developments' as soon as they happened. CNN did not dare to risk undermining this position.

At the other end of the scale, we find versions of infotainment programmes which not only operate with very different sets of news values, but also undermine most traditional conceptions of what journalism is about. Some of these are structured as celebrity-oriented talk shows or as magazine-style shows with entertainment segments mixed with journalistic segments; in both versions political élites are interviewed with varying degrees of 'seriousness'. In other infotainment programmes, political élites appear in their capacity as 'media celebrities' and become part of the entertainment. Some recent examples from Sweden: the foreign minister and an androgynous rock star changed clothes to emphasize the point that 'clothes make the man'; the prime minister appeared and was tested to see how many seconds it took him to knot his tie; politicians have had their horoscopes read, played blind-man's-bluff, and have sat in cages and answered silly questions in a parody of game shows. One line of response to this treats it as harmless fun, giving the politicians an opportunity to present a 'human face', while another laments the degradation of dignity.

More to the point is that in the context of Sweden, for example, this trend can be associated with a number of other changes. The phenomenon of politicians appearing as entertainment can be understood in part as a response to the shrinking sound bites they are allotted on the news programmes. Infotainment programmes permit politicians not only lots of public exposure, but also a setting in which they are hardly ever challenged with any difficult questions. Moreover, this trend on television signals something more fundamental in the evolution of Swedish politics. Traditionally, within the formal political system, power can be seen to have rested on three legs: the power of decision making, the power of setting the political agenda, and the political power to mobilize opinion – in that order. The order is now being reversed, with the power to mobilize opinion playing a much more prominent role. But, at the same time, the shift is away from the political party to giving more weight to the persona of the politician. This trend has long been characteristic of politics in, say, the USA, but is now becoming more common in Western Europe as well.

The logic and functioning of the media is central in this transformation. If opinion is coming to play a more prominent role, this could be lauded. However, eight-second sound bites, cosy chat shows and silly entertainment do not enhance democracy. In fact, 'opinion' in this context becomes less a manifestation of a reasoning public and more the pay-off of instrumental strategies of publicity, which Habermas and others have so thoroughly critiqued. Personification constructs an impression of affective proximity, but tends to deflect critical reflection on political issues as such. The impression of the 'apolitical' here is precisely political in its implication.

Elusive information, accessible stories

Returning briefly to the question of comprehension on the traditional news programmes, information processing has constituted one trajectory in journalism research for many years (see, for example, Robinson and Levy, 1986; Gunter, 1987; Graber 1987). With a strong anchoring in cognitive psychology, such research has sought to chart the understanding and processing of new information, particularly in relation to existing cognitive frameworks, or schema, as they are sometimes called. On the whole, the results of such studies of television news viewing make for unhappy reading: the levels of comprehension are generally appalling.

A corollary to the issue of comprehension is the more fundamental question of recall, of memory. Most people can recall few news items from a news broadcast they have just seen, even when prompted. Interestingly, it has also been found that 'interpersonal communication' can make an important difference in this regard: people are better able to recall, comprehend and relate news stories to their own lives via talk with other people – a finding entirely in keeping with the notion of a 'public' discussed above. In his review of this research literature, Davis (1990:175) concludes that to enhance information processing, 'The ideal news program would have a slower pace'. He also suggests that, to take into account varying educational backgrounds and interests, more news programmes, tailored to different audiences, should be offered. Both suggestions, of course, run counter to the logic of television as an industry.

One can bemoan the strict boundary between such research and investigations into the media which derive from the various critical and ethnographic schools. There are clearly difficult epistemological issues at stake. The concept of information or knowledge operative in this research invites questioning: it tends to use a cybernetic analogy which downplays the contextual and inter-subjective dimensions of knowledge. Still, the critical schools have been too cavalier in their avoidance of the questions around how people handle factual information; they have ignored the thematic dimension. To be concerned about what facts and information people comprehend from television jour-nalism does not require the relinquishing either of a critical stance towards journalistic representations or an interest in the interpretive sense-making of viewers.

While there is much that could be done to improve the processing of infor-mation, pedagogic enhancements of television journalism have their limits. It is somewhat contentious to question what indeed are the limits to television's pedagogic potential. Postman (1985), in his broadside against television, asserts that everything the medium touches turns into show business, includ-ing news and politics: entertainment automatically overwhelms serious information. There is of course much truth in his argument. However, Postman refers back to a somewhat mythical golden age of public discourse, which we would do well to question, and, more importantly, seems to ignore the possible positive roles that the pragmatic dimension can play, even in the learning process. The question of the medium's 'innate' or 'essential' qualities is begged: in other words, does television's performance as we know it have to do with some essential quality or with the way it has been used culturally?

Findahl (1988), in summarizing research in this area, suggests that it is not the case that television cannot convey knowledge. It does this on an unprece-dentedly wide scale. Rather, the difficulty lies in successfully transmitting in-depth, analytic knowledge – at least to a majority of the population. This is because more complexity puts more demands on both television (its pro-duction must be more carefully handled) and the viewer (who must exert more effort). But Findahl goes further and contends that the cultural context of television use – its commonly understood function and role, which derives not least from the nature of its overall programming – is significant. What he is alluding to is the traditional distinction between television as a public ser-vice medium, catering to a variety of tastes and addressing itself in a sustained manner to informational and cultural uplift, and commercial television, as an entertainment/advertising machine. Whether or not the implied image of public service evokes a romanticized past, a strong version of this model of television is not on the political agenda in most parts of the world today. In short, whatever expectations we can reasonably place on television's role in the public sphere, they should not be predicated on its delivering in-depth knowledge or detailed, abstract information to a majority of viewers.

I lean towards a 'soft essentialist' view of the medium's potential: even with the best of intentions, the technology of television and its modes of rep-resentation make it unsuitable for conveying abstract, or analytical information. Pedagogical measures could enhance the informational efficacy of the medium, as could other, more edifying cultural contexts of television. Yet there is a ceiling; beyond that, for more analytic forms of knowledge, we simply must rely on printed (albeit digitalized) media. The power élite does this, which I think is very significant.

On the other hand, television is exceptional in its ability to mobilize affective involvement and convey the amorphous entity called implicit social knowledge, as I discussed in the previous chapter. And I would emphatically underscore that this quality is by no means entirely detrimental to its role in the public sphere. Affect is of course tied up with TV representations' pragmatic dimension, with its popularity, with its pleasures. Indeed, the meanings and even the 'knowledge' – in the broadest sense – derived from television news programmes is by no means solely dependent on the transfer of information. In the previous chapter, all the points made about television as a sociocultural experience are no less relevant to television journalism than to other genres. The ritual model is decidedly at work in journalism.

Those features which constitute the familiar, repetitive aspects within journalism normally remain as assumptions which are taken as read – a part of the cultural air we breathe. Narratological and rhetorical analyses of journalism reveal structural features, deeply ingrained in the culture – inarticulate and imagistic – which organize the perceptions of events and actions in the world and their representations in journalism (see, for example, Bennett, 1988; Bennett and Edelman, 1985; Hall, 1984; Mander, 1987; R.R. Smith, 1979; Knight and Dean, 1982). These recurring features, which of course extend to the visual dimension (see, for example, Griffin, 1992), contribute to our understanding of what is 'normal' and routine in various fields of the social world – for example, the familiar inventories and categories of news, actors, actions, events, types of conflict, measures taken, and so on – with which we as viewers of television journalism are readily familiar as part of the 'schema' we carry with us. Further, these recognizable structural elements are in themselves carriers of meaning – they prefigure our understanding and help channel our sense-making along common paths (even though there is a spectrum of interpretive tendencies at work among audiences). These narratological elements contribute to what Bennett (1988) calls 'normalized news', which hovers on the border between culture and ideology. As Bennett and Edelman (1985) posit, it can never be a question of going beyond narrative frameworks (since there is no 'pure' information) but rather being cognizant of which ones are operative, what their ideological implications might be, and what possible alternative ones might be mobilized.

These familiar narrative frameworks are central to making the world of news so recognizable. We can miss most of the factual information and not even realize it, because the narrative elements in themselves are so overwhelmingly recognizable. Such structures communicate to viewers culturally resonant notions of social order and disorder, implied definitions of normalcy and deviance (see Ericson, et al., 1987), and – not least – help construct coherent images of the public, which are inserted in various ways within journalism's discourses of actuality (Chaney, 1993).

Tele-tabloids

Tabloid news programmes constitute one of the most visible manifestations of the popularization of television journalism. These can be seen as deriving from the Happy News local news programmes in the USA in the 1970s. In Sweden, a version of Happy News was never attempted in the 1970s, no doubt because it was simply too culturally remote, both for producers/journalists and for the public. Yet by the end of the 1980s, the times were ripe for the launching of a 'lighter', tabloid evening news programme. TV4 began as a satellite-cable production some years ago, but has more recently become a ground station, operating on a commercial basis formally within the framework of public service. Its programming aims to maximize the number of viewers, with heavy doses of Swedish game shows and imported American series. Its evening news programme at 10 p.m., *Nyheter*, was launched as a clear alternative to the evening news on the two public service TV stations. The language is a bit more vernacular, the visuals more audacious, and the dramaturgy somewhat less predictable. The technique of 'reconstructions' is not uncommon (and modest use of this has even begun creeping into the news on the non-commercial channels as well). The style is relaxed and personal, with the role of the reporter being somewhat enhanced.

Amid stories of suffering, mayhem and victimization there are also a good number of encouraging items. The upbeat human interest stories are also matched by the positive personal style of the reporters. In this regard, TV4's *Nyheter* has a more friendly tone than many of the more sensationalist and lurid tabloid news programmes found in other countries. Indeed, its approach is more heartening than even the traditional news programmes on the public service channels. There is an atmosphere of supportiveness, as if to say to viewers, 'We understand that things can be difficult at times . . .'. There is a heavy focus on personalization in its news stories, to give political issues concrete human faces. TV4's *Nyheter* uses less official sources for its news items and devotes less time to official politics; human interest stories are more common there than on the non-commercial channels. It wants to offer 'news you can use'.

The news programme *Nyheter* reproduces the major strengths and weaknesses of the evening papers: certain aspects of the world are made more accessible to its audiences, while the rather systematic avoidance of abstractions sets limits on what can be explained and understood about the world. The editorial director accepts the comparison with the evening tabloids, saying 'Like TV, the evening press bypasses the brain and goes directly to the stomach' (quoted in Lindell, 1992).

From the critical left there is a compelling view which sees tabloid news in terms of commodity aesthetics (see Knight, 1989 and Sholle, 1993, for two detailed examples of such analysis). With an anchoring in the logic of television as an industry, coupled with a semiotic approach to texts, such analyses link the process of signification to the imperatives of political economy. As Sholle concludes: 'The tabloid's characteristics: textual fragmentation, spectacle and reality effects, floating of meaning, passive populism, and normalizing exclusion, all function to position the audience within the general stance of consumerism' (1993:70–1). This is no doubt true, but it may be worthwhile to pursue further some of the communicative dynamics at work. Tabloid TV news is undoubtedly strong on the pragmatic dimension: its format can be termed popular precisely because it communicates in ways which are 'producerly'; it is accessible, evocative and provocative. Compared with the more traditional 'serious' news programmes which privilege stories about élites, national and world politics and similar themes, tabloid television news offers a world which is much more anchored within the horizons of everyday life and its universe of experience. There is an immediacy and sense of proximity in tabloid news which distinguishes it from traditional news. This more readily facilitates identification and involvement. Even foreign news items are often given this slant: we see the war in Bosnia and the untold suffering it causes as a profound and cruel disruption of the lives of ordinary people, with the fates of actual individuals providing the 'hook' for many news items. This concreteness would seemingly promote response more readily than stories using more abstract representation, at least initially – we cannot in the long run discount the phenomenon of what can be termed 'empathy weariness'.

Internationally, victimage stories are a staple on tabloid news (though less so in the case of Sweden's TV4's *Nyheter*). Langer (1992), in his discussion of tabloid news, suggests that while serious news tends to situate viewers in a position of detachment, victimage stories involve the subjectivity of viewers more directly. They are emotionally charged mini-episodes which portray the ordinary routines of daily life being disrupted and shattered by unforeseen events and circumstances. The victims are usually typified by their ordinariness – the great 'we' of the politically subordinate. That these news discourses position themselves with the lived experiences of the subordinate rather than with the dominant groups would suggest that they are not reproducing ideology in the classical sense. Yet, while endorsing the experiences of the victims and indeed of all 'ordinary people', victimage stories tend not to locate such experiences in concrete social and historical circumstances which are amenable to political intervention. Instead, folklore and fatalism appear as the implicit motifs. In Langer's words:

> In victim stories, the world we know is played with, tossed around, stretched and pulled out of shape, and in the end gleefully destroyed; but only momentarily because it always seems to spring back into shape (like the characters in an animated cartoon), in time for the next day when further misfortunes unfold. (1992:126–7)

This ping-ponging between threat and reassurance is significant. Langer goes on to say that it is not just an ideology of fatalism at work, but also a form of 'anarchic existentialism', where the world is governed by the capricious and the unpredictable. In his view, we can specify a number of sources of pleasure in tabloid news: watching destruction, the experience of uncertainty, and the more traditional pleasure of narrative. These may of course vary and we might wish to specify other sources (for example, the reassurance that, despite all, this world remains basically unchanged and has as yet not made *me* a victim), but what we have here is a rather prototypical case of popular journalism (indeed, one could well use the epithet 'populist') which is successful in its pragmatics but deficient in its thematics. The programmes are engaging and do invite involvement, but the issues and topics taken up and the subject positions fostered tend to deflect attention from issues of power, where fundamental political decisions are at stake. Like the tabloid press, the emphasis on the social here leans often towards moral order and disorder, for example, corruption and other scandals. One can only speculate what the results would be of going beyond the equation of 'the more appalling, the more appealing' – of merging popular pragmatics with 'serious' thematics.

Defenders of traditional news values have been engaged in what Langer calls a 'lament' over tabloid news, attacking its triviality, its deflection of attention from more serious matters, its pandering to baser instincts, and so on. Yet we should be clear that, ultimately, there is not a difference in *kind*, only one of degree, between tabloid news and the more traditional news formats. All television news contains tabloid elements. Langer writes:

> What may distinguish unworthy news, however, is its excesses, its flamboyant gestures: it takes some of the codes and conventions of news in general and inflates, exaggerates and displays them more directly. The unworthy news may get its bad name, not because of its popularity or its shameless persistence in bulletins, but because it is unruly, more openly acknowledging and flaunting devices and constructions which the serious news suppresses and hides. Perhaps, in the end, this is why the lament is so harsh on this kind of news, because it is what news is, only more so. (1992:128)

Thus, tabloid news more openly reveals itself to be artifice; it flaunts its constructedness.

Talk shows: élite and vox-pop

The television talk show can hardly be called a genre or grasped as a unitary format. Over the years, this overarching category has proliferated, cloned and evolved to generate a wide range of programme types. Here I will take up just two kinds of programme that, with some difficulty, can be contained within the confines of two identifiable formats. The first – what I call élite talk shows – has always resided well within the boundaries of what constitutes television journalism. It has, however, been clearly evolving in a popular direction. The other – what I term vox-pop talk shows, where the voice of the people can be heard – has had a more problematic identity as journalism, at least as far as the spokespeople for traditional canons are concerned. That such programmes should be understood as a part of the public sphere is, however, beyond doubt.

The basic format of having journalists from the major media interview public officials on the air goes back to the pre-television days of radio. The format of such programmes as *Meet the Press* (in the USA) helped solidify this form of journalism in the early days of television. On such programmes, influential journalists would pose questions to important power holders. The tone was normally not only serious, but deferential, even if the journalists might 'get tough' in the questions they posed. The journalists were there to draw out the views of the officials, who were firmly the focus of the programmes. In the USA, a change began to occur in the 1980s, first in the Washington area and then spreading to other cities (and to some extent, to other countries). The format of round-table, élite talk shows began evolving into what have variously been termed 'assertion journalism' and 'talk-show journalism' (see Rosenstiel, 1992). In this evolution, it was journalists, not least from the print media, who were now becoming the 'stars', using skills that win talk-show audiences: 'a knack for asserting opinions, thinking in sound bites and having an attention-getting public persona' (Rosenstiel 1992:74). In this development, these journalists' interpretation of events were almost becoming more significant than the news coverage of the events. By the late 1980s, there were over 20 such programmes in the Washington area which regularly used print reporters as their guests.

From the standpoint of television, this development is not hard to understand. The executive producer of an established élite talk show says, 'I need someone who is glib, colorful, whose thoughts can be condensed into a conversational style' (quoted in Rosenstiel, 1992:78). It is more important to be able to stake out positions and provoke conflict than it is to present a reasoned analysis. From the standpoint of the newspapers, it cannot be all bad to have one's journalists on television, with the name of the newspaper clearly subtexted on the screen. And for those élite print journalists who take the step to become what we might call 'opinion celebrities', it's a clear career boost. In this format, there is a blurring of the lines between officials and journalists; they are in a sense all 'media stars', sitting and discussing together. The popularization going on here is that once again we see the primacy of the pragmatic over the thematic, form over substance. Yet, compared to the vox-pop talk shows, the popular involvement with these programmes is limited.

In terms of the topics covered and modes of discourse employed, the vox-pop talk shows run the gamut from confessional, therapeutic discussions around issues of sexual intimacy to traditional opinion formation around concrete political issues. The latter, however, is clearly in the minority. The almost explicitly therapeutic character of some talk shows, where participants air such topics as identity crises and marital conflicts, merges into what may be seen as an implicit therapeutic dimension in much of television programming (see M. White, 1992). It is not possible to grasp all the variations within the large outpouring of such programmes, but one can make a general distinction between 'panel programmes', which consist largely of experts or other prominent people having group discussions, and those programmes which more accurately fall into the vox-pop category.

In vox-pop programmes, 'ordinary people' participate, sometimes only as a part of a panel but more often as members of a studio audience. Some of the key features of these programmes can be summarized as follows (I base this in part on Livingstone and Lunt, 1994:39):

(a) both experts and lay people are often present; much of the programmes' focus has to do with the interchange between them;

(b) the host of the programme, usually a media personality, stimulates, guides and facilitates discussion, and allows people to speak – from their seats, by coming to a podium, or by giving them his or her microphone. However, the host does not and cannot entirely steer the course of the discussion;

(c) the discussions themselves use debate, diatribe, testimonial, story-telling, and other discursive modes, mostly within a conversational style. Discussions are often lively, not least because conflicting opinions have been guaranteed in the selection of participants;

(d) Personal experience and common sense have considerable status and often appear as forms of knowing which are superior to expertise;

(e) Each programme transmission tends to be organized around an explicit theme of public or personal import;

(f) These shows are relatively inexpensive to produce and are mostly not a part of prime time programming;

(g) Most programmes are transmitted either live or recorded in real time with little editing.

In Sweden, the first major programme of this sort to make a significant public impression was called *Ikväll med Robert Aschberg* (Tonight with Robert Aschberg); Camauër (1993) has done a detailed analysis. It began, in prototype form, in the late 1980s on the satellite channel TV3, and continued until 1993; Aschberg has gone on to do similar kinds of programme series. Aschberg is Swedish, but TV3 transmits from London to Sweden, Norway and Denmark. In Sweden, almost two-thirds of all households now have cable and can thus receive TV3 and the other satellite channels. The programme became so popular that Aschberg's face was used for a while as an emblem for TV3 in its advertising. He also was awarded the Swedish prize of 'Journalist of the Year' in 1990 – throwing further confusion on the legitimating discourses of what constitutes good journalism and perplexing many within the profession.

Aschberg's blend of talk-show journalism and tabloid TV is an interesting phenomenon, mixing American and Swedish sensibilities (in the early years of his programme, Aschberg evoked some of the style of the late American TV host Morton Downey, Jr). Aschberg has a characteristic sceptical laugh, which he uses frequently. He seems to invoke in his audience something which might (following John Fiske) be called the pleasure of suspicion: guests, especially élites and experts, are invariably treated as if they should not be taken fully at face value. Aschberg generates an aura of doubt around most people and topics. He breaks a number of cultural rules (in the Swedish context) regarding polite conversation, such as interrupting and emphasizing conflict rather than consensus. He questions the official versions of events; all authority is brought down to earth; he tilts towards sensationalism and personalization; his tone is conversational. He uses irony as one of his chief strategies, which in my view is one of his more innovative moves, as irony has not had a prominant place in public culture in Sweden. There are lots of opinions, but few facts; lively discussions and interactions, but not much analysis. He says of himself that he is cynical, and invites the audience to be so as well. The cynical position, however, undercuts the possibility of a political standpoint or a moral position; even moral indignation seems out of place in this setting. The result, from the standpoint of public knowledge, seems to be that after the fireworks, not much light remains, as Camauër (1993) notes. On the other hand, Aschberg no doubt captures a mood; the obvious carnival quality and his cynical style not only resonate with a deep seated political disaffection, but are also indicative of an atmosphere where the traditional frameworks of trust in authority and optimism in the future have waned. Also, the format itself, while American-inspired, signals a development within Swedish culture. The core of the programmes' viewers are younger, more shaped by media culture than their parents. A generation ago there would not have been such an audience, nor would there have been a population from which programmes such as this could draw the televisually competent guests to participate in such a format.

There have been a number of studies and debates on talk shows and talk on television more generally (Livingstone and Lunt, 1994, is clearly the most ambitious and systematic analysis thus far: see also Carpignano, et al., 1990; McLaughlin, 1993b; Tolson, 1991; Morse, 1985; Deming, 1985; Tolson, 1985). One line of study (Tolson, 1991) focuses on the talk of the hosts and guests on public service television, normally not 'ordinary people' but rather media personalities. Tolson suggests that talk on television can be categorized according to genres which cut across the various programme formats on which talk is prevalent. These modes of talk, not surprisingly, are found to dissipate any singular 'communicative ethos' on television; they are pluralistic and aimed at various sectors of the audience which operate with varying sets of cultural knowledge. Television chat gives rise to 'synthetic personalities', who are ambiguous as regards their sincerity; moreover, such talk creates a growing ambivalence as to the functions of entertainment and information.

Carpignano et al. (1990) privilege the talk show as a new site within the public sphere which embodies strong democratic potentials. Among other things, they point to the fact that these programmes are geared to public debate, using conversational discursive modes – they establish bonds of familiarity with the television audience; the studio audience, via its talk, participates in the scripting of the programmes; common sense prevails over expertise. Their argument can be seen as a counter-effort to retrieve television from the condemnation of traditional left critique. In her response to this analysis, McLaughlin (1993b) criticizes the authors for valorizing the working class in their analysis, assuming that this segment of the population has privileged access to politically viable common sense. She also levels a feminist critique towards what she sees as a gender blindness. In sum, her argument is that while Carpignano et al. are right in emphasizing the alternative discourses which emerge from such programmes, they ignore the dominant discourses (of power, gender, and so on) which the talk shows also generate. Their analysis, in her view, rests too strongly on a faith in the audience's interpretive freedom and it further ignores how the discourses of the programmes are largely still implicated in the prevailing structures of power and dominance. Peck (1995) is very explicit about this. In her analysis of talk shows the recurring ideological dimension lies precisely in that the interpretive frames always privilege the personal and individualistic over the social and the structural.

Livingstone and Lunt's (1994) major contribution, which includes audience research as well as analysis of a large set of programme materials, arrives at a more complex set of conclusions. In their view, all efforts to 'explicate unambiguously the political and social functions of the genre of audience discussion programmes must be doomed' (Livingstone and Lunt 1994:174). They point out that these programmes, for example, provide a platform and give a voice to groups in society which previously have been largely excluded from public communication. At the same time, they acknowledge that this fact in itself can be countered by the argument that such access need not necessarily lead to any changes in power relations, but can instead simply provide an *illusion* of participation. While the emancipatory potential of vox-pop programmes cannot be easily evaluated, the authors point out that they should be seen as representing a 'postmodern' condition:

> The very form of audience discussion programmes is anti-genre and a host of oppositions traditionally used to analyse the mass media are deconstructed by these programmes, including text/audience, production/reception, sender/receiver, interpersonal/mass communication, information/entertainment, hot/cold, critical/involved. Audience discussion programmes, like most television . . . represent the moving away from reporting of an external reality to a self-referencing and self-constituting system. The audience discussion contributes to this trend by bringing what used to occur in private conversation into the public realm of the media. (Livingstone and Lunt, 1994:175)

While the programmes can serve a variety of purposes for viewers, Livingstone and Lunt see the audience discussion programmes as a particular kind of social space, one which in some ways has a marginal status – being mostly 'low-brow culture' and providing a carnivalesque opposition both to everyday life and to established forms of authority. In this space a public sphere is generated which mediates between the experiences of everyday life and established power. This mediation is accomplished not least by the mixing and shifting of multiple discursive conventions, using elements from debate, storytelling and therapy, among others. There are many contradictory elements which enter into both confrontation and negotiation, chief among them perhaps being the tensions in the sets of assumptions, knowledge, ordinary experience and expertise. These programmes are a far cry from the Habermasian ideal of rational debate and opinion formation. Livingstone and Lunt (1994:179) see in these programmes the merger of the game show and current affairs programming. The generic *mélange* of entertainment, information and opinion can be seen as a process whereby popular culture is undermining and overwhelming reasoned political dialogue and criticism. Also, the conversationalization of public discourse itself is by no means immune to manipulation by the power establishment. Yet, claim Livingstone and Lunt, these programmes also seem to offer important possibilities for popular involvement and participation.

Though one may experience Livingstone and Lunt's hedging on firm conclusions as mildly frustrating, it is nonetheless compelling. In a sense, we are returned to the wary ambivalence with which we began – but not entirely. In the course of their analysis of vox-pop shows, Livingstone and Lunt felt the need to question some of the traditional terms and assumptions operative within media research and critical theory, and, in so doing, point to some postmodern strands of thought which do not lead us to give up on the ideal of democracy and a viable public sphere, but rather critically to reflect on what these and related notions may mean in the modern world of the media.

Morality and dialogue

If we consider the Kantian distinction between cognitive, moral and aesthetic, it is significant to note that media research has for the most part skipped over the middle category. Cognitive issues of information and ideology, aesthetic concerns of representation and pleasure, and other permutations are quite familiar, but we see little attention to dimensions pertaining to the moral. I am not referring here to questions of the morality which is portrayed or advocated in television fiction, nor to 'moral panics' over specific programming; such concerns take us into issues such as the effects of sex, violence and lifestyle role modelling on various categories of viewers, and this does have a long research tradition. What I am interested in here is what can be termed 'the moral response' on the part of viewers, as part of the pragmatic dimension of televisual communication.

This has to do with viewers' sense-making at the normative level, particularly in a reflexive manner which includes their own moral subjectivity and potential practice. How can we begin to specify the televisual conditions for moral sensibility? How are media representations angled to promote or deflect a sense of moral obligation on the part of audiences? Occasionally, there are commentaries on this theme. Enzensberger (1993), writing on the growth of irrational violence in the world, notes that the nature of media representations of such occurrences, coupled with the (valid) sense of powerlessness most people feel about contemporary social development, leads inexorably to a moral blight. In other words, we must not neglect to look beyond the screen and examine the larger societal contexts of moral sensibility. And moral sensibility no doubt varies with people's perceptions of their possible social and political efficacy.

Yet we do know that television can mobilize sympathy and empathy, and that this can have important political reverberations (television coverage of the latter phase of the Vietnam War is often cited as a major case in point). At the same time we cannot discount the effect of empathy weariness: the constant flood of horror images must at some point contribute to the routinization and normalization of our view of human suffering (after seeing images of the first major famine, the others become somewhat less shocking). And there are other factors which may hinder a moral response such as the modes of representation. The Swedish Red Cross has been puzzled as to why some limited news coverage of the truly dreadful circumstances in some Romanian orphanages elicited such a generous financial response from the population, while the tragedy of the wars in former Yugoslavia, which has received so much coverage and constitutes suffering on such an immensely larger scale, initially prompted a proportionally far less generous response. Could it be the dramaturgy – clear victimage in the case of the Romanian children and, initially at least, ambiguity in the case of former Yugoslavia (at first framed as 'ethnic conflict')? We can only speculate.

In recent years, it has been particularly the experience of television coverage of the Gulf War which has elicited reflection on moral response. In an illuminating discussion in the course of a review of some the literature about this coverage, Robins (1993) summarizes the arguments about the distancing of viewers to the suffering via the Nintendo-style mode of representation. This evokes the simulation of video- and computer games; the real war is turned into a 'virtual' war, conducive to 'screen voyeurism' but not to moral reason. But Robins goes still further, into the terrain of psychoanalysis and collective subjectivity. He invites us to consider the limits of 'an exclusively rationalist approach to reason', an approach which has informed the prevailing notions of how the public sphere is ideally to operate. He maintains that if we cling to that paradigm, we cannot really begin to understand what happened to the moral sensibilities of viewers during the course of the coverage. In particular, he holds that the desire for security, cosmic order, clear boundaries, and so on – what we may see as the pull towards the mythic – is often stronger than the desire for rational knowledge of the real. In short, we have for too long tended to disregard the strong role which fear plays in the psyche. 'The collective expulsion of fear becomes the basis for affirming group solidarity' (Robins 1993:323). In the case of the Gulf War, Saddam became, via media representations, the embodiment of not only evil, but also of threat. Fear is then first projected outward against this 'Other', then mobilized to unite 'the civilized world'. Whatever the merits of the case for or against the actual intervention, this is indeed a snapshot of the media-based psychic mechanisms at work. Their significance is that they are potentially operative in all situations which involve us/them divisions, and few sociopolitical contexts are devoid of such divisions. Robins concludes that it is not a case of choosing between rational reason and unconscious sensations, but rather of acknowledging their co-presence:

> If reason is to be civilized, then it must accommodate our primitive and basic fears. It cannot be based on the repression, the evasion or the expulsion of these unconscious materials . . . We all have the potential for compassionate behaviour. What the Gulf War showed us is how effectively that potential can be neutralized. (1993: 326–7)

Robins' introduction of the unconscious here is an important move which I will pursue in Chapter 5. I would just make one modification here: while the unconscious is the site of repression, displacement and other mechanisms relevant to fear and conflict, it is also the site of creativity, of imagination, of empathy, of solidarity. In other words, the unconscious may well be at least as significant as – or even more important than – rationality in regard to moral sensibility.

Another one of the few discussions on morality, sensibility and media representation is Tester's (1993) extended essay. His position is to concede that the media can evoke moral response, but often do not: normally, 'Media significance means moral insignificance'. Tester sees two basic conditions which must be filled to achieve moral response: there must be a dialogic response and a seriousness of purpose. These are slippery terms, but he argues that they are essential and are undercut by the anaesthetization of images: following Adorno, he contends that the increase in images results in a decline in their value (an argument similar to that of the critical political economy of the tabloid, discussed above). This argument has been heard over the years, but this does not make it less significant. To the extent that it is valid, we come up against an impasse; the logic of the media, the nature of the media ecology we live in, the social ecology of reception, coupled with the objective limits to efficacy (that is, people's powerlessness) all mitigate against moral sensibility within the public sphere. Moral reason, moreover, as a mode of reason which is situated at least in part within the dynamics of the unconscious, is not fully amenable to cognitive rationality. Again, as we seem to hit a dead end, we must consider our options; it is a question of trying to rethink the basic terms of the analysis.

Thus, for example, the 'dialogic' to which Tester refers can perhaps be understood in ways which can even be located, albeit in a limited fashion, within the essentially monological character of the mass media. There are a variety of modes of address, of interpellation, and different subject positions are possible. Stoehrel (1994), in her study of non-tabloid current affairs magazines on Swedish television during the 1980s, found that a variety of ideal typical narrative strategies were employed. These can be seen as different modes of storytelling, often co-present within a single journalistic story. One she termed 'documentary realist', which is the traditional, objectivist mode which aims to convincingly convey information. Another, less common one, she calls the 'aesthetic strategy'. Here the use of poetic and evocative devices address the viewers' intuitive and emotional sides, inviting them not only to witness events, but to experience them. Instead of just representing an external reality, this strategy also tries to portray – and to speak to – people's inner reality, their subjective states. In her view, this reaching for the intersubjective dimension goes beyond both comprehension and associational interpretation and leads meaning production into the domain of normative reflexion.

Stoehrel makes use of the distinction between explicit knowledge – derived formal propositions about external reality – and implicit knowledge, which is largely tacit and moral-practical. She further suggests that while 'experience' is mostly physical and immediate, it can also occur via texts. We 'understand' (in the hermeneutic sense) the text of a story when we can identify with different situations and persons within the story, using largely implicit knowledge. It is here, in her view, that the dialogic dimension comes to the fore, and it is this which encourages the viewer to reflect on moral distinctions. In terms of practical journalism, she sees a dilemma: while the documentary realist strategy, with its emphasis on explicit knowledge, risks closing off the dialogic dimension, the aesthetic strategy can lose sight of the external, factual aspects which condition inner realities. Her point, however, is to underscore the potential of the dialogic dimension and moral response.

As our societies careen under a tumultuous modernity and as they continue to segment themselves between 'informed élites' and the 'entertained majority', the politics of representation and knowledge have become crucial. The democratic character of the future is by no means guaranteed, nor is the nature of popular television journalism. We can see popular television journalism as the dominant – and a problematic – institution of the public sphere. However, to more fully understand television, the public sphere, and the conditions of democracy more generally, we must try to situate them on a horizon which encompasses some of the key features of the contemporary historical situation. To do this thoroughly is, of course, an enormous undertaking and can never be fully realized. Yet it is important to at least indicate the contours of this horizon, and this is the modest task of the chapter which follows.

PART II
SHIFTING FRAMES

4
Modern contingencies

The impossible task is set by the *foci imaginarii* of absolute truth, pure art, humanity as such, order, certainty, harmony, the end of history. Like all horizons, they can
never be reached. Like all horizons, they make possible walking with a purpose.
Like all horizons, they recede in the course of, and because of, walking. Like all
horizons, the quicker is the walking the faster they recede. Like all horizons, they
never allow the purpose of walking to relent or be compromised. Like all horizons,
they move continuously in time and thus lend the walking the supportive illusion of
destination, pointer and purpose . . . The march must go on because any place of
arrival is but a temporary station . . . The linear time of modernity is stretched
between the past that cannot last and the future that cannot be . . . The present is
always wanting, which makes it abhorrent and unendurable. The present is *obsolete*.
(Bauman, 1991:10–11)

That we are caught up in a major historical transformation is pretty well
accepted in most quarters today. And though there are many 'takes' on our
contemporary situation, with differing vocabularies and at times considerable
controversy, most commentators acknowledge that we live in rather confusing times. Increasingly we come to see that the present historical juncture can
only with difficulty be grasped and rendered with the unrevised blueprints of
what we generally call modernity. Indeed, many writers term the historical
present 'postmodernity' or, more accurately in my view, 'late modernity' (for
example, Fornäs, 1995) to accentuate the distinction. The advent of modernity as such is a contentious issue, but most authors place it in the sixteenth
or seventeenth century. However, it was just over one hundred years ago that
the social agenda began to manifest what we today include as one of the
definitive features of the contemporary world: the growing tendency towards
reflexivity. This collective self-monitoring of where we find ourselves, what we
can do about it, and even what we can know about it seems to have emerged
in earnest at the end of the last century. I am thinking in particular of the
work of Marx, and that of the classic sociologists such as Weber, Simmel,
Durkheim, and Tönnies. Not least, Nietzsche occupies a prominent position

in this regard. In particular, the post-World War Two era testifies to an intensifying problematization of our historical condition. Indeed, this reflexive probing is dramatically accelerating, to judge by the avalanche of such literature produced over the past decade.

I will not try to summarize or synthesize the vast literature on modernity, nor can I offer a full-blown perspective of my own. What I will do is present a number of important themes to provide a useful backdrop, allowing my discussions on the public sphere and television to stand in clearer relief, situating them in some current societal (and epistemological) conditions. The importance of the literature on modernity for my concerns here is that this line of investigation forces us to re-examine some of the common assumptions and conceptualizations about both the media and democracy. Without this re-examination and some of the reconceptualization which it invites, our understanding of the possible conditions and dynamics of the contemporary public sphere will be decidedly hampered.

The first theme I will deal with has to do with the fundamental way in which we view modernity and the conditions for knowledge itself. While I can give only the barest treatment of such an overarching theme here, there is something of fundamental importance and utility to extract specifically from the debates around the status of the Enlightenment. From there I sketch the contours of a view of capitalism which is compatible with an understanding of major patterns of contemporary culture. This leads me to a short presentation of three important features on the sociocultural landscape of modernity: the pluralization of our microsocial worlds and identities; the disembedding of social relations; and the mediazation of the semiotic environment. All three have a bearing on the topic of television and the public sphere. At the end of the chapter I address the evolution of the distinction between public and private, and then conclude with some reflections on contemporary political circumstances.

Falling rates of certitude

Societies are constantly in transition; this perpetual change has been termed modernization, and can conveniently be examined from the standpoints of economics, politics, technology, and culture. In terms of accounting for change, depending on one's theoretic inclinations, one may emphasize one of these factors over the others, or argue for weighting the interplay of some factors over others. How one periodizes the present is also often a feature in such analysis. Thus, in the debates over postmodernism which raged during the 1980s and into the early 1990s, two key themes concerned what is an appropriate theory of history and how to best periodize the present. While there is as yet no consensus on these points, it seems that the controversy has subsided and these points of contention now command less attention.

Where does that leave us today? The term postmodernism continues to carry a conceptual valence, but as a signifier it appears to have a modified accent. It has now less to do with a problematization of history and periodization. Instead, the term points to a trajectory within two related regions: philosophy/social theory and culture. Within philosophy, we see an accelerating self-examination on the grounds of knowledge itself. Within culture, not least within the mass media, patterns of 'postmodernism' are seen as historically specific and pervasive sets of attributes, even if they have not yet reached the ubiquity that some (for example, Jameson, 1991) claim. The present epoch of late modernity manifests both modernist and postmodernist cultural characteristics.

We seem to have stumbled on a wry paradox: information as well as our formalized knowledge about the world is expanding astoundingly, at the same time this growth includes the advancing insight about the situated and contingent character of all knowledge. The net result is that, in some ways, our knowledge may be shrinking in the face of a rapidly changing world. Our desire to understand our contemporary circumstances, to reduce uncertainty, is strong and can lead us enthusiastically to embrace one particular interpretation or vocabulary over another, Yet, with enhanced reflexivity, we see that our view of the historical present is to a great extent shaped by it. We realize, at some level – even if we normally partition off the insight in a remote recess of our mind – that any particular intellectual trend in which we may participate may well have passed within a few short years. Historicism as a perspective is hardly new, but with our increasing collective reflexivity it seems to be assuming an ever stronger position. Yet, as Lawson (1985) and others remind us, for all the attention and indeed, celebration, accorded the notion of reflexivity, we should not lose sight of its limits. From a constructivist point of view, not only are there epistemological breaking points to reflexivity, but also, carried to its extreme, it can implode, leading us into an unproductive vortex.

From this cautionary angle, we can view postmodernism – in simple terms – as a dialogic counterpoint to some of the claims anchored in the Enlightenment tradition and its vision of modernity. In other words, postmodernism, in its better moments, can be seen as the Enlightenment's reflexive encounter with itself. Thus, postmodernism in this regard has come to be associated with a sceptical stance to the Enlightenment's aspirations to generalize and universalize, to its teleological mode of explanation, and to the forms of technocratic rationality which have emerged in its wake. Feminist theorizing has also contributed greatly to these developments, questioning not only pervasive gendered assumptions cloaked as universals, but also probing the nature of the epistemological foundations of western rationalism more generally (see, for example, Benhabib, 1992; Hekman, 1990; Nicholson, 1991; Yeatman, 1994). The growing critique of modernity over the past century challenges the assumptions which link, on the one side, increasing rationality and a faith in science, innovation and progress generally, with, on the other side, enhanced social harmony, moral development, justice and happiness.

What is at issue today is the nature, the status of this dialogic counterpoint, its premises and the alternative vision it offers. Do the voices that speak from the Enlightenment's shadows offer a constructive critique of the

Enlightenment or do they constitute an attack on its very foundations? Can there be an enlightened suspicion of the Enlightenment, a reasoned critique of western rationalism? These questions came to a head in the debates between Habermas (1987) and a number of leading French theorists. Habermas of course is an insistent critic of the historical present, particularly of what he sees as the deformations wrought by capitalist modernization. Yet he wishes to maintain the privileged position of reason, emphasizing his claims for valid universal structures of human existence and norms of action/interaction. He thus rejects the postmodern move to incorporate philosophy into literature more generally. He is also critical of the move to inexorably situate knowledge with power, a point which takes on prominence in his debates with Foucault (see Kelly, 1994).

Habermas' project is to retain the goals of the Enlightenment, to struggle for their fulfilment; the alternative, in his view, is to relinquish modernity itself. Postmodern theorists, he argues, are, at bottom, both nihilistic and reactionary. For a while at least, there was a quality of trench warfare here, with respective positions being established, but neither side winning or acceding much terrain after the initial clashes. (There is a large primary and secondary literature here; see McLennan, 1992, for a very pedagogical port of entry into the issues.) However, there are now also more positive signs, of manoeuvres going on around the flanks, permitting new openings. Many commentators have pointed out that there may be more common ground in these debates than Habermas or his opponents recognize or admit. The 'project of human liberation', for example, remains the prime concern not only of Habermas but also of the postmodern, counter-Enlightenment critics; much of the controversy now centres around how to conceive of emancipation. Moreover, as Smart (1993) points out, there seems to be a third direction emerging, beyond Habermas' and his opponents' either/or positions. This view shares Habermas' anchoring in and respect for the Enlightenment legacy, but by implication gives some credence to his critics, without accepting their positions in any unqualified manner.

This third way comes into focus via the cumulative reflections from a number of analyses. In particular, I would mention the work of Bauman (1991, 1992), Beck (1992), Heller and Fehér (1988) and Giddens (1990, 1991); see also Wagner (1994). Despite the differences among them, these authors suggest that to understand and come to terms with modernity need not require an all-or-nothing view of the Enlightenment. In keeping with Foucault's (1984) notions of the interrogation of the present, expressed in his encounter with Kant and with his more overarching history of rationality, they call into question the idea of a unitary modern reason. These authors note that, while concepts such as progress and development may have lost their unequivocal rhetorical power to evoke, it is less a question of jettisoning them and more of seeing them in a new light. Our efforts for order and innovation inevitably carry with them threats of chaos; measures to achieve happiness can generate new dissatisfactions; moves towards universality can be confronted by heterogeneity and result in exclusions. It is this awareness – and acceptance – of contingency and indeterminacy that I see as the core of a constructive postmodern mode of social theory. In Bauman's words:

> Postmodernity does not necessarily mean the end, the discreditation . . . the rejection of modernity. Postmodernity is no more (but no less either) than the modern mind taking a long attentive and sober look at itself, at its conditions and its past works, not fully liking what it sees and sensing the urge to change. Postmodernity is modernity coming of age: modernity looking at itself at a distance rather than from the inside, making a full inventory of its gains and losses, psychoanalysing itself, discovering the intentions it never before spelled out, finding them mutually cancelling and incongruous. Postmodernity is modernity coming to terms with its own impossibility; a self-monitoring modernity, one that consciously discards what it was once consciously doing. (1991:272)

Postmodernity thus becomes the name we give to a critical interrogation of certain features of the Enlightenment, in particular its foundationalist attempts to anchor reason and to legitimize systematic, cognitively-based knowledge at the expense of other forms. In this usage, the term does not a priori embody a reactionary politics, nor does it simply point to insignificant epiphenomena. Like the older Frankfurt School critical theory, it does not posit an alternative system, but rather constitutes a set of probes and interventions, seeking out and challenging problematic assumptions. Naturally, this can be (and has been) in ways which are constructive and productive, as well as in ways which are less so.

We should treat the postmodern mode as a particular kind of awareness, one at the brink between the (relative) theoretical certainties of the past and the contemporary strands of thought which question them. The postmodern mode suggests to us a falling rate of certitude, that from now on we will have to learn to feel more comfortable with pluralities of perspective, where none has a privileged legitimacy. It underscores the contingent quality of knowledge, of society, of the self. We have to live with a lot of ambiguity (a key notion in Bauman's (1991) rendering of postmodernism) and the anxiety and sense of disorder it produces – and do our best to muddle through. The events in Eastern and Central Europe of 1989–90 taught us several things, not least that – for good or ill – we should allow for the historically unexpected.

Thus, this interface between postmodern thought and the traditions of the Enlightenment should not be seen as an either/or proposition. We must try to position ourselves in the force field between them, as for example Hebdige (1988) illustrates in his own analyses, and Best and Kellner (1991) explicitly argue for in their survey of postmodern theory. Dews' (1987) exploration of the intricate relationships between the tradition of critical theory and postmodern thought remains one of the most ambitious. Looking beyond critical theory as such, there is no discipline in the humanities and social sciences which has not begun to rethink the very grounds for its activity, and for the possibilities of knowledge more generally, as any check through publishers' catalogues over the past years will verify.

Postmodern perspectives on the historical present are by no means all of a piece. While some such lenses can focus on the grimness and precariousness of our contemporary situation, others have manifested an excessively festive nihilism and implicit social optimism – blithe positions which have, in a short time, shown themselves untenable. Bauman (1991) is right in pointing to the antinomies of certain strands of postmodern thought; there is a regressive dimension which easily colludes with commodification, the privatization of societal concerns, and selfishness. It can be mobilized to legitimate the growing split between rich and poor; in Bauman's (1991:259) acerbic words, 'There is no shortage of postmodern formulae meant to make the conscience of the seduced spotless'. The inventories of traditional social ills are still glaringly and painfully visible: class-based economic deprivation and pauperization in many sectors of the population, growing unemployment, violent crimes both inside and outside the home, environmental pollution, discrimination and oppression based on gender and ethnicity, decline in social services, deteriorating infrastructures, and so on. Both the post-communist societies in Eastern Europe and the more established democracies in Western Europe are demonstrating a number of unsettling – and in some cases, quite horrifying – tendencies.

Yet Marxism and the leftist legacy have by no means been immune to this growing awareness of contingency and ambiguity: they too are children of the Enlightenment. With the decline of the paradigmatic class-model of historical change, it is not always so clear today what should count as 'progressive' or what the criteria are for 'emancipation'. The political upheavals of the 1960s challenged the classical Marxist conception of class struggle by pointing to the multiplicity of sites and mechanisms of power and domination irreducible to class and (economic) exploitation. And today's so-called new social movements emerge within a heterogeneous political context, trying to oppose different forms of oppression towards specific groups. They address current needs for multiple forms of struggle – feminist, ecological, ethnic, cultural politics, the politics of everyday life. Whatever one's theoretical affinities might be, it is important to avoid tendencies to monothematic renderings of the historical present.

Flowing capitalism

Our understanding of modernization must incorporate the dynamic interplay of economic, political, technological and cultural processes, as Fornäs (1995) and others suggest. Each one of these aspects is a necessary dimension but by itself insufficient. That said, we should not conclude that these four sets of forces are always equal in their import.

Further, it is my view that the economic dimension must be rendered as political economy, and that any meaningful grasp of our contemporary situation must still incorporate at its core an understanding of the dynamics of modern, global capitalism. This is because capitalism sets the conditions for – without fully determining – many parameters of social reality. In the context of media studies, this argument is given clear expression in, for example, Golding and Murdock (1991), as I discussed in Chapter 2. There is a whole minefield of issues and controversy here – both within and external to Marxisim – about 'economic determinism' and 'economic reductionism', to which we must be alert. I cannot delve into all those debates here, but will offer a few brief remarks.

First, to underscore the importance of contemporary capitalism is not to advocate any kind of economic reductionism in social analysis; the base-superstructure reasoning can be left on the shelf. Rather, in keeping with modern political economy, I would emphasize the interplay of the economic and the sociocultural (though detailed theorizing of their relationship is beyond the scope of the present discussion). Even if political economic analysis itself is not the focus, it must not be eradicated from the field of vision. The sociocultural must be understood within a framework which encompasses political economic contingencies; processes of collective meaning-making can only be fathomed in tandem with their material conditions. Within media studies and sociocultural analysis more generally (including much of Cultural Studies), this orientation has been best represented by various strands within what is loosely termed neogramscianism (see Harris, 1992; McGuigan, 1992; Milner, 1993, for helpful overviews).

Secondly, for the political economy (and sociology) of culture perspective, it is not insignificant just how capitalism is perceived – that is, which contemporary features one chooses to emphasize. Particularly as we move to theories of modernization, where in terms of explaining historical change capitalism usually has to share the stage with other forces, interpretations can vary. Capitalism, since its origins and with increasing rapidity, has been revolutionizing production, consumption, social relations, knowledge, information and the patterns of communication. Yet it does not do this in a monolithic, unilateral way, but via interplay with other factors. One theoretical approach to modernity which I find particularly stimulating not only argues for an appreciation of the complexity of capitalism but also, importantly, makes explicit the links between the political economic and the sociocultural realms. This is Lash and Urry's (1987, 1994) thesis about what they (borrowing a term from Claus Offe) term 'disorganized capitalism'. Their attempts to rethink some of the traditional categories and dynamics of capitalism, while retaining a strong critical perspective, could be said to exemplify a postmodern mode of inquiry within political economy.

In their first book Lash and Urry (1987) argue that notions of a post-industrial capitalism are quite premature; it is rather a case of understanding how capitalism, without relinquishing its fundamental logics, has been dramatically modifying its operational modes, which also means that the sociocultural interplay has been transformed. They present a list of by now familiar interconnected features such as: the globalization of markets; the decreasing capacity of nation-states to regulate transnational conglomerates; the decline in western industrialism and the industrial working class; the waning of class politics; and the growth of service industries. Like other commentators, notably Jameson (1991), they also claim that we are witnessing an increased pluralism and fragmentation in the cultural sphere, arguing that disorganized capitalism itself is engendering a postmodern culture; the circulation of capital as well as of culture is accelerating. Like Harvey (1989), they also emphasize the changes in our sense of space and time which follow in the wake of modern capitalist development; further, this new cultural mode involves, among other things, a shift in the semiotics of everyday life – where signs have themselves become referents – as well as a decentring of identity. Lash (1990) further explores the parameters of the new postmodern culture.

In their second book with this orientation, Lash and Urry (1994) introduce the concept of 'flow' to capture better the dynamic dimensions of modern capitalism. There is a consequent move away from an emphasis on structures and organizations to one on the flows of people, ideas, images, technologies and capital, resulting in analyses of 'economies of signs and space'. In their words:

> Our analyses of these economies of signs and space has been focused upon the overlapping, non-isomorphic patterns of such flows, their organization through time and space, their overlapping effects within particular sites, and the relative causal influence of different flows in different historical epochs. We have considered the ways in which such flows both subvert endogenously determined social structures . . . *and* provide the preconditions for heightened reflexivity. (Lash and Urry, 1994:321)

There are several things at work here. One dimension is their accentuation of the limits of the perspective of the nation-state in attempting to elucidate current developments. In their first book they argued for the specificity, the differences between various nation-states of the North Atlantic rim, even though these societies may all be categorized as advanced capitalist, and post-Fordist (which has to do with capitalism's modern flexibility to relocate quickly investments, to restructure labour markets, to use computerized information technology, and so on). Here the analytic strategy moves to go beyond what they see as 'society-centric' formulations:

> Rather we have shown that such differences are the complex product of the interplay between each society's history and the current flows of capital, technologies, peoples, ideas and images, where those flows are also seen as having a history and a geography and where there are certain local nodes in particular societies involved in the propagation or reproduction of particular flows. (Lash and Urry, 1994:321)

One important upshot of this view is that they force a transnational perspective into any understanding of the national; the global configurational dimension comes to the fore. Likewise, the local takes on a new importance, as both the global and the local together compete with the national, as the necessity of a multiperspectivism becomes increasingly compelling. More original, perhaps, is their underscoring of the flow concept. Even while they may overstate their case regarding structures and institutions, the interjection of flows opens up not only a more dynamic view generally, but also one which more readily lends itself to emphasizing precisely the interplay between the political economic and the sociocultural. This is done without reducing one or the other and without having to assign any determinist priority 'in the last instance' of one over the other.

All this is poised at a rather high level of abstraction, and we must take their theorizing as an attempt to break new ground, rather than as a final, problem-free solution to many big questions within historical materialism. If we descend a bit from the theoretical heights and pinpoint some of the more concrete implications which Lash and Urry draw from their analysis and which may have bearing on the public sphere, I would point to a number of suggestive aspects. One is that social classes are seen as the 'victims of such disorganization' (Lash and Urry, 1994:323). They suggest that classes traditionally congeal around specific geographical places, national space, and organized hierachies. One could add that the disorganization of capitalism even hinders the traditional efforts towards the international organization of class. The flows of disorganized capitalism contribute to an erosion of classes in that classes become displaced – in the sense that they are simultaneously rendered both local and global by the flows of people, images and information. By implication, this semiotic fracturing and its consequences for both individual and collective identity work is deemed more compelling than any attributed class consciousness based on the traditional objective laws of capitalism. Class boundaries, one could add, even lose a good deal of their self-evident, objective qualities with the flows of capital and technologies in post-Fordist contexts. This is taking place, Lash and Urry are quick to point out, while at the same time social inequalities are manifestly growing.

Lash and Urry also point to other implications of disorganized capitalism. Their analysis is poised on the slender fence between what Seidman (1990) terms the millenium versus the apocalyptic view of modernity. If Berman's (1982) account of modernity tried to balance the worst and the best, Lash and Urry's spectrum seems slightly more skewed to the latter – ranging, so to speak, from the worst to the less worse. They can envision a positive disorganized decentralization, which may open up some spaces for a benign redistribution of knowledge and power. Alternatively, dreadful dystopias cannot be excluded from the possible future. Indeed, the signs are quite visible in the present, where:

> these flows create nightmarish scenarios, of increasing 'wild zones' consisting of collapsing empires (USSR), imploding nation-states (Yugoslavia), ungovernable First World cities (Los Angeles), tracts of desertification (southeast Africa) and countries dominated by narco-capitalism (Columbia . . .). Such wild zones are characterized by a collapsing (or collapsed) civil society, a weakly developed 'civilizing process' and flight to 'tame zones' for those that are able to escape. Such tame zones are areas of economic, political and cultural security, often with strong boundaries separating them off from the wild zones . . . Such divisions can of course be seen within local areas where electronic surveillance techniques keep the one-thirds and the two-thirds societies apart. (Lash and Urry, 1994:324).

The communication revolution, likewise, they see as potentially liberating or repressive. They see possibilities for 'small communitarian public spheres' (1994:324) making use of decentralized data banks and interactive computer networks; these may even develop a new logic of place, new skills, and new constellations of power relationships beyond the traditional institutions. On the other hand, they can also foresee power/knowledge dystopia where 'even moral and practical knowledge is transformed into cognitive and technical systems which normalize and regulate what was previously private (including the private and critical activity of book reading . . .' (1994:324). They add ominously that, 'A visual culture is publicly controllable in a way in which literary culture is not'.

What we have here is a critical reading of modernity, an attempt to take into account the dramatic transformations of capitalism's *modus operandi* and link them with processes of modernization in the sociocultural sphere. There is a recognition of postmodern culture's distinctiveness and theoretic importance in shaping the modern world, and an attempt to articulate the realms of political economy, culture and subjectivity. While Lash and Urry highlight dynamic flows they do not jettison structures; class does not simply vanish but becomes relativized with other factors, resulting in a more prismatic view. The overall perspective is agnostic and it neither expects nor offers any guarantees. The perspective is, in itself, an expression of the theoretic force field between the critical tradition's Enlightenment origins and its more sceptical postmodern mode.

Such an orientation is not unique to Lash and Urry; from various (and partly incompatible) positions parallel strategies are at work in, for instance, Hebdige (1988) who works within the field of Cultural Studies; Eder (1993), who focuses on the sociology of social movements; and Laclau and Mouffe (1985), whose interpretation of the Marxian philosophical legacy lead them to a (much debated) post-Marxist standpoint. In none of this literature is there a denial of the significance of economics generally, nor capitalism in particular. Rather, within loosely neogramscian frameworks, the interplay between the sociocultural and the political economic is articulated in such a way that a multiplicity of subject positions and emancipatory projects can take on theoretic relevance for understanding the dynamics of social change.

Destabilized microworlds

These larger dynamics of capitalism can be seen to constitute strong homogenizing forces, via commodification, consumer culture, and pervasive instrumental rationality. Yet such integrative tendencies also have their centrifugal counterpoints. Indeed, a salient feature of modernity's sociocultural realm, which has been discussed by countless commentators, has to do with the differentiation within the whole fabric of what I loosely call our microworlds – the immediate, everyday settings and experiences which constitute our lived reality. In this section I will focus on two basic and by now quite familiar themes, namely the pluralization of social microworlds and of identities, and the disembedding of social relations, highlighting their relevance for the perspective I am developing. Following this, I will pick up on another, related feature of the sociocultural landscape, namely the nature of the semiotic environment.

The notion of the pluralization of social microworlds has a strong anchoring in phenomenological sociology, particularly in the work of Schutz (1970) and Berger and Luckmann (1967). The argument is threefold: first, for the majority of us, most of the focus of our daily attention is on that segment of the social world which is immediately available to us and is anchored in our own lived space and time. Secondly, this everyday world is actually composed of a plurality of relatively distinct contexts, 'multiple realities' in Schutz's term, each of which involves different aspects of identity, different stocks of knowledge, frames of relevance and reference, and so forth. Experientially, these plural 'worlds' are held together and given whatever overarching coherence they may have largely by the individual's biographical factors. Thirdly, a common diagnosis of the predicament of modernity is that overarching, *collective* normative and cognitive integration is weak, at least in secular terms. Coherent integration of the various experiential worlds is lacking, which many see – at least in part – as a consequence of the fading power of traditional religion in the modern world.

With the growing reflexivity of modernity, identity itself – who we are both to ourselves and to others – has become increasingly problematic. If identity is contingent on social context, the pluralization of social microworlds fosters a counterpart on terms of multidimensional and even contradictory identities, with no one identity being necessarily fundamental. The sociocultural milieux of modernity do not often provide unequivocal experience of the self; subjectivity comes to lack a unified core. For most people, the social settings and discursive configurations in which they are enmeshed yield multiplicities of subject positions, at times with no one position necessarily experienced as more fundamental than others. This need not always be seen as something exclusively negative, yet it is clear that the experience of an ambiguous self can be painful and produce anxiety. Indeed, in late modernity the psychic prerequisites for a coherent sense of self are often absent, starting from the earlier stages of life. Consequently, identity becomes a project, subject to crisis and innovation, forged out of existential uncertainty on a shifting social terrain. Giddens (1991), among other theorists of modernity, has made the question of identity a central focus of social theory, while psychologists and psychoanalysts (for example, Frosh, 1991) increasingly thematize identity within social and historical frameworks.

The upshot of all this is that it brings the sense of ambiguity and contingency of modernity down to the level of daily personal experience. A good deal of what we see in the sociocultural realm can be related to these conditions of our microworlds: the discomfort of low certitude fosters searches for secure answers, hence, for example, the position and cult of expertise even in everyday matters. Bauman discusses how experts, as self-proclaimed servants, turn into managers:

> Once the relationship of the individual to both nature and society has been effectively mediated by expert skills and their attendant technology, it is those who possess the skills and administer the technology that command the life-activities. The life world itself is saturated by expertise – structured, articulated, monitored and reproduced. (1991:214)

And expertise, of course, is a marketable commodity.

The disembedding – and re-embedding – of social relations can be understood to a great extent as a consequence of the modern media of communication and the impact they have on our traditional coordinates of time and space. These coordinates, or implicit cultural maps, are evolving quickly, with ramifications for the patterning of social relations and the structuring of subjectivity. Harvey (1989, 1993) coins the term 'time/space compression' to capture these developments, which he links to the post-Fordist tendencies of transnational capitalism. The change in tempo is felt in daily life, as events, decisions, information and experience speed up. This can be both stimulating and debilitating; our environments change faster and we have to respond accordingly.

The spatial dimension is perhaps even more significant. On the one hand, with modern communication and transportation, we experience the world as shrinking. On a deeper level, there is more at work here. According to Harvey, spatial aspects of modern capitalism – for example, the high mobility of finance, the location of investments and jobs, the geographically uneven development – impinge on community, identity, and conditions of social life generally. Space is not merely an objective specification of locale, but a key dimension of the social construction of reality: spatial practices construct our senses of place, provide anchoring to our lives, and are not least intimately tied up with questions of power.

Harvey's arguments obviously parallel those of Lash and Urry though Harvey, more anchored in the traditional historical materialist paradigm, tends to give the economic realm a determinist position, while Lash and Urry emphasize the interplay between the flows of capital, technology, people, ideas and images. Both versions, however, underscore the links between cultural experiences of time/space and the vicissitudes of capital, as well as the tensions of flux and fixity at work in both arenas.

From a more Weberian angle, Giddens (1990) writes about a growing separation between space and place:

> 'Place' is best conceptualized by means of the idea of locale, which refers to the physical settings of social activity as situated geographically . . . The advent of modernity increasingly tears space away from place by fostering relations between 'absent' others, locationally distant from any given situation of face-to-face interaction. In conditions of modernity, place becomes increasingly phantasmogoric: that is to say, locales are thoroughly penetrated by and shaped in terms of social influences quite distant from them. What structures the locale is not simply that which is present on the scene; the 'visible form' of the locale conceals the distanciated relations which determine its nature. (Giddens, 1990:18–19)

This line of reasoning paves the way for his notion of the disembedding of social relations, by which he means '"the lifting out" of social relations from local contexts of interaction and their restructuring across infinite spans of time-space' (Giddens, 1990:21). Conceptually, this further scrambles our coordinates: the 'social' is now free to manifest itself in many ways beyond immediate, co-present face-to-face interaction. One very large segment of modern life in which this is operative is bureaucratic organizations; another is the administrative state. But no doubt the most salient arena is within the media, which allows social relations to be extended across space and time and thus become re-embedded in new configurations. I will turn to the media in a moment; Giddens' general point here is that the disembedding – and re-embedding – of social relations, the separation and recombination of time and space, are central to the dynamics and experience of modernity.

While the themes of the pluralization of social life worlds and identities, and the disembedding of social relations via the transformation of time/space orientation, are salient under late modernity, I must hasten to add that – in the name of prosaic sociological accuracy – it is important that we do not exaggerate their actual pervasiveness in everyday experience. That these developments have received much attention and generated a considerable academic literature can blind us to the fact that, experientially, for example, many people may often feel that their identities are a problem only to the extent that they are bored with what they feel to be a very static and circumscribed self; that most of the population seems to cope competently most of the time with the separation of space and place; and that they can normally negotiate their plural social worlds and identities without too much difficulty. Alternatively, we should not forget that people's sense of time and space, as well as their identities, is also very much tied to family relationships. And family structure has certainly been experiencing profound disruption in modern times, which may well be as much a cause of people's experience of dislocation and fragmentation as the themes addressed by more recent theory.

The semiotic environment

These are important, discernible dimensions of late modernity, seen from a macrosociological vantage point, and, as I hope to show later, are of considerable relevance in any attempt to theorize the possibilities of a public sphere. These themes within modernity – and others one could itemize – are of course entwined with the media, which I have deliberately left lurking in the background of this discussion for a while. I have done this in order to present an orientation which explicitly inserts the media into a framework as a part of a larger configuration of factors engendering our present historical juncture – this to avoid a view which is too mediacentric or mediadeterminist. Nonetheless, the media of communication reside at the core of modernity. Thompson (1990:3–4) writes about the 'mediazation of modern culture', whereby 'the transmission of symbolic forms becomes increasingly mediated by the technical and institutional apparatuses of the media industries'. Mediazation is admittedly a somewhat clumsy word, but it points explicitly to that historical process in modernity where more and more of our social relations are dependent on various forms of media, and where a large portion of our lived time within everyday life is filled by the use of both mass media and more selective and even personalized 'minimedia'.

So far we are on familiar ground: there is little dispute regarding the quantitative dimensions of mediazation. But how can we theorize the qualitative side of mediazation? Is the sociocultural world left pretty much as it was, only that we now have the media as intermediaries? Or can we chart changes in the processes of signification and in prevailing sensibilities which have deeper ramifications? Murdock (1993) posits that modern communication systems are fundamental to the constitution of modernity; moreover, he sees a reciprocal interplay at work:

> I want to make the case for the proposition that the organization of communications is not only constituted *by* the general dynamics of modernity but is constitutive *of* them, and as we move towards the present it comes to play an increasingly central role in shaping both institutional and cultural formations and the textures of everyday life. As a consequence, we cannot theorize modernity without taking formations of communication centrally into account. (Murdock, 1993:522–3, italics in original)

The dynamics of this interplay proceed in many ways; let me mention three useful approaches, which refract these dynamics in slightly different ways from different points of departure. One line of analysis addresses how media institutions and the cultural environment reciprocally play off each other, and builds on the notions of media logic and formats (Altheide, 1985; Altheide and Snow, 1991). The media constitute communicative forms and processes through which phenomena are presented/represented and via which sociocultural experience is interpreted; the media serve as matrices which give specific discursive shape to communication. Media logic refers, on the one hand, to the structural conditions and attributes – the vast array of procedural considerations behind various medias' and media genres' representational modes. On the other hand, it also depicts the cultural competence and horizons of expectations of the audiences, which in turn impacts on how journalism, politics, sports, religion, and so on are represented and experienced. Media formats are the specific ways a particular medium's or genre's materials are defined, selected, structured and given final expression. The argument is that an ever-growing portion of social life and institutional activity adapt themselves to the requirements of media formats: today, 'more experiences are reflections of previous encounters shaped by formats that in turn direct future experience' (Altheide and Snow, 1991:1). There is an element of the Sapir-Worf hypothesis here, as Altheide and Snow suggest: sense-making is consistent with and bounded by the grammatical structure or internal logic of a language. Under modernity, the mass media have become the 'language' of our public culture.

Another version is found in Meyrowitz's (1985) theses about how the electronic media in particular refigure our sense of time and place, by defining new 'electronic situations' in which people can insert themselves, offering new options for individual and collective sense-making and identities. Building on Goffman's distinction between the communicative (deliberate, literal messages) and the expressive (unintentional non-verbal and verbal communication), the qualitative distinction between the experiential presence of, say, books and television, is readily highlighted. Using Suzanne Langer's concepts of discursive and presentative symbols, the abstract and arbitrary nature of language is contrasted with the more iconic nature of visual images.

Thus, the distinctions between traditional and electronic media point, on the one hand, to the familiar comparisons with regard to their respective capacities to communicate analytical, conceptual thought versus affective, intuitive experience, as well as to the nature of the demands placed on the audience. On the other hand, Meyrowitz's framework leads him to conclude that with the dominance of the electronic media we now have a more democratic and accessible public culture, the traditional boundaries between public and private spheres and social roles have been greatly blurred (though this is not socially unproblematic), and that physical and social space have now become disconnected from one another. The parallels with Giddens are apparent, but we should note that in Meyrowitz's scheme the dimension of power is virtually absent.

A third line of inquiry, in many ways compatible with the above two but theoretically more complex and ambitious, is Lash's (1990) notion of 'regimes of signification'. With a point of departure in the premise that it is sociologically warranted to speak of identifiable differences between modernist and postmodernist tendencies within contemporary culture, he introduces the categories discursive and figural. (These derive from the early work of Lyotard, which admittedly does not make for easy reading. A collection of English translations is available in Benjamin, 1989; helpful secondary discussions are found in Bennington, 1988, and Readings, 1991.) These categories can be seen as ideal types. According to Lash, the cultural forms of modernism and postmodernism can be understood to signify differently, that is, they follow different semiotic logics in their representation and thus contribute to different sensibilities. The modernist mode is associated with discursive processes of signification, which, in Lash's words:

> 1) gives priority to words over images; 2) valuates the formal qualities of cultural objects; 3) promulgates a rationalist view of culture; 4) attributes crucial importance to the *meanings* of cultural texts; 5) is a sensibility of the ego rather than the id; 6) operates through a distancing of the spectator from the cultural object. The 'figural' in contradistinction: 1) is a visual rather than a literary sensibility; 2) devalues formalisms and juxtaposes signifiers taken from the banalities of everyday life; 3) contests rationalist and/or 'didactic' views of culture; 4) asks not what a culture 'means', but what it 'does'; 5) in Freudian terms, advocates the extension of the primary process into the cultural realm; 6) operates through the spectator's immersion, the relatively unmediated investment of his/her desire in the cultural object. (1990:174)

At first glance, this may look like just a more elaborate version of Altheide's media formats thesis and Meyrowitz's discursive/symbolic distinction. And on one level it is; all three frameworks could be used to highlight the essential tension within television journalism to which I referred in the previous chapter, for example, the dissimilarities between, for instance, a sensationalist, tabloid TV talk show and a serious newspaper of political and economic affairs. All three frameworks in different ways evoke issues of epistemology, how we make sense, and the tensions between cognitive and aesthetic ways of knowing. Lash's version, however, is somewhat better situated theoretically, in that it more forcefully connects with theorizing about modernity, capitalism and postmodern culture, as we have seen (Lash and Urry, 1994). At the same time, it is also better articulated, with developed conceptualizations touching on subjectivity and the unconscious, and how these operate within the context of communication. Indeed, in my view it is this analytic connection, even more than the periodization of signifying regimes, which is most fruitful. I will pursue these topics in the next chapter.

The distinction between discursive and figural modes of signification is compelling; it captures something of what we experience daily around us in our media-based semiotic environment. In the public sphere, it is emblematic of the whole discussion about the popularization of television journalism as television, and thus reverberates with similar ambiguities. Within television journalism, within communication more generally, the two sides are often positioned in opposition to each other – normally with affect getting the lesser support. We are not only asked to choose between them, but to choose correctly – and to not choose affect. The problem is that any model of communication which tries to eliminate the arational, in the end risks becoming irrational in denying this dimension of human subjectivity. In the figure/discourse distinction we see the classic tension between reason and affect, between information and experience. Indeed, the discourse/figure couplet can be seen as a specific instance of the encounter between Enlightenment and postmodern thought.

But to return to discourse and figure in the framework of modernity and the media: as Lee (1993) suggests, the distinction needs to be sociologically more specified. It is not simply the case that postmodern trends are replacing modernist ones across the board, although they are beyond doubt on the ascent. For instance, if we take classic realism and narrative forms as one index of modernist culture, Abercrombie et al. (1992) remind us how pervasive these still are in the popular media. And despite what television looks like today, and even despite the well-grounded alarm over reading levels within various western societies, I would be cautious about simply depicting the majority of people today as being 'post literate' and unable to think beyond the analytic levels which characterize TV game shows. A lot of people are still reading an awful lot. Rather than displacement, it is more of a question of a growing tension between discursive and figural modes within the media, within the public sphere. Many commentators have raised the theme of 'the informed élite versus the entertained majority', which captures something of the trend within the public sphere, though not necessarily (or at least not yet) characterizing the actual literacy levels of the majority. Popular mainstream television, for example, even if it retains much of the classic realist strategies, at the same time leans heavily towards the figural mode of representation. The discursive, on the other hand – as a manifestation of modernist, analytic, text-based culture – is alive and well in such sectors as the serious press, specialist journals, data banks, and research and development, which are associated with not just with the upper strata of societal hierarchies, but with centres of power and decision making. In other words, the discursive seems to be withdrawing to smaller, specialized enclaves. The figurative modes of postmodern culture tend to cluster in those media which are most accessible to most people.

We should not be overly hasty and simply relegate the figural to 'entertainment' or see it as totally incompatible with progressive politics; but there are, undeniably, dilemmas here. As public culture becomes increasingly a figural media culture, so does social order itself become in part an instance of mediazation. As Chaney (1993:33) asserts, '. . . contemporary culture has become overwhelmingly a representation through spectacle . . . that is as things to see, and to see through, so that the image has become the paradigmatic means of conceptualization'. Further, he notes that 'Leisure exemplifies the form of participation in society of spectacle which is essentially individualized . . . Public drama is privatized as personal experience' (Chaney 1993:35). In a similar vein, Lee (1993) comments on the contrast between the rational public subjectivity and reasoned public opinion – which was the normative ideal of the public sphere in the bourgeois epoch – and the forms of mass mediated public subjectivity generated by consumer capitalism. The latter, writes Lee:

> creates an imaginary space of viewership and participation in which individual choice and freedom exist at the level of consumption. The specificity of interest and embodiment bracketed by the liberal public sphere returns in undisguised form as the basis for a mass subjectivity characterized by a potentially infinite differentiation of desire . . . The multimediation of mass publicity creates a different dynamic than the print mediation of the early public sphere . . . Instead of an ideal reader/citizen, one form mass-mediated subjectivity takes is that of viewer/consumer. (1993:171)

The figural mode and the frames of leisure and consumption, then, are integral components of an overwhelmingly obvious characteristic of modern culture, namely its consumerist character. Featherstone (1991), Jameson (1991), and others have theorized this dimension explicitly. Citing Haug, Featherstone writes:

> The centrality of the commercial manipulation of images though advertising, the media and the displays, performances, and spectacles of the urbanized fabric of daily life therefore entails a constant re-working of desires through images. Hence the consumer society must not be regarded as only releasing a dominant materialism, for it also confronts people with dream-images which speak to desires, and aesthetize and de-realize reality. (Featherstone 1992:270)

There are some excellent efforts to confront the consumer media culture within the mediated public sphere itself: the Vancouver-based magazine *Adbusters Quarterly: Journal of the Mental Environment* (1992–) is an energetic example; occasional films, television programmes, art exhibits, and – of course – many books invite critical reflection on the mediated consumer culture. Colleges and universities have had media studies programmes for many years and, more recently, in some schools in a number of countries, 'critical media pedagogy' has emerged. On the whole, however, there is little critical confrontation of the semiotic environment within the public sphere.

The quantitative attributes of mediazation and the qualitative aspects of figural, image-based modes of signification foster a specular form of social order which is largely attended to via the frames of leisure and consumption. This is obviously a sweeping claim; we would do well to remind ourselves that the situation is by no means one-dimensional, but constituted via tensions, and is variable in sociological context. Even micro-level qualitative audience research lends credence to this view: see, for example, Jensen (1990), who found that in discussing TV news viewing, his respondents revealed a palpable diversionary dimension in their experience of viewing – a contradictory dimension which they experienced as not fitting in very well with their more formal views of news and citizenship.

Going global?

A perspective on the mediated semiotic environment which partly merges with the consumerist angle is that of globalization. Globalization is, of course, not merely a question of the media. McGrew (1992) contrasts those views which are at bottom mono-causal with those which argue for multiple logics of globalization as an historical process. Recalling Lash and Urry's perspective, the transnational flows of capital, technology and peoples, as well as ideas and images, are blurring national boundaries. Other commentators add political, military and legal factors, and most underscore the often highly uneven and inegalitarian nature of globalization processes. On the other hand, there is also a growing 'discourse of globalization', a 'global babble' which sells rather spurious notions about 'global ecumene'. As Ferguson (1992) argues, there is a considerable amount of fuzzy, mythic and ideological thinking at work here. Within the European context, Schlesinger's (1993, 1994) sober appraisals about the limits to what the media can accomplish in terms of pan-European identity, and his reminders about the powerful grip that nationalism can still exert, are instructive antidotes. With more realistic horizons, a number of authors have been probing globalization specifically from the standpoint of culture (see Featherstone, 1990, 1993; Hannerz, 1992; Robertson, 1992; Tomlinson, 1991), in particular pointing to the multiple interplay between global and local cultures. Here the media may figure prominently, though in a more carefully contextualized manner (see also Moores, 1993b).

While it is impossible for me to take up the many pertinent issues which arise in these discussions, I do wish to raise one point from the globalization theme which has direct bearing on the discussion of media culture and the semiotic environment. Recalling Giddens' and (Meyrowitz's) claims about the dis/re-embedding of social relations, and the disconnection of social place from physical space, one may ask: Can social relations, or communities, which are essentially constituted via media consumption be equated with those which are anchored in face-to-face interaction? Is there any significant distinction to be made between mediated and non-mediated communication, and, if so, what are they and on what grounds do they rest? In his critical reflections on Giddens' global modernity, Tomlinson (1994) offers a number of suggestive points.

Giddens suggests, as we have seen, that globalization 'stretches' the relationships between local settings and distant events and processes. The disembedding of social relations means that they can be established at a distance, separate from physical co-presence. The 'world opens to us'; physically remote people and activities enter into our everyday consciousness. Giddens states explicitly, 'Although everyone lives a local life, phenomenological worlds for the most part are truly global' (Giddens, 1991:187). Tomlinson raises the question of the nature of these relations – how we are to compare them with our face-to-face relations. He acknowledges that in a sense all relations are mediated since they proceed via language, but he asserts there are still important distinctions we should not ignore. Thus, the degree of mediazation, the modes of experience involved, the intensity of involvement, the depth of familiarity with the other, and so on, all involve subtle but important distinctions. Speaking face to face with a friend, speaking with that person on the telephone, and watching a national leader on television are qualitatively different encounters.

Tomlinson is cautious about privileging 'immediate lived experience', yet argues that it would be foolish to discount a fundamental difference between mass-mediated and non-mass-mediated experience. This becomes especially relevant when we consider community. Giddens suggests that we understand community as 'an embedded affinity to place', and in that regard implies that community is being eclipsed by the conditions of modernity. However, he holds out global community via the media as an historically new situation, keeping in mind that 'global' may not necessarily have to encompass the entire planet, but only mean 'physically remote'. Tomlinson, on the other hand, posits the distinction between an experience of local community versus that of mediated global community. First of all there is the issue of scale: the global can trail off into a virtual infinity of numbers. The global/remote is also dispersed, and tends to have few effective political, economic, institutional or linguistic factors holding it together. And, finally, mediated global community is basically monological, with all the limitations which this implies.

It might be argued that nationalism is a sort of mediated global (or, more accurately, extensive geographical) community, but Tomlinson counters those arguments by emphasizing precisely all the institutional, political, economic and ideological work which lies behind such 'imagined communities'. By themselves, the media cannot provide us with 'a robust sense of global belonging', and so, for example, we must be cognizant of the conditions and limits of the 'communities of affect' via popular culture and the media discourses which Hebdige (1988) writes about. Yet, even given the distinctions between mass-mediated and non-mass-mediated communication, and the consequent characteristics of media-based communities, it is apparent that tempo-spatial co-presence no longer has an automatic monopoly on orientational significance for individuals. Even if the immediate here and now still commands most of our attention, the geographically and temporally remote is no longer, by definition, irrelevant. The processes of mediation are altering people's cognitive maps, loyalties and frames of reference.

The problematics of public and private

The flows of capitalism, especially in the sociocultural realm of ideas and images, the processes of transnationalization, the pluralization of social life-worlds and identities, the disembedding of social relations, and the figural side of the semiotic environment and relations of consumption which it fosters, all contribute to problematizing a conception of the public sphere. Indeed, Habermas himself, from the vantage point of the late 1950s and early 1960s, and with a somewhat different vocabulary, pointed to some of these themes in his interpretation of the decay of the bourgeois public sphere. In his analysis, the public sphere was an historically specific category emerging from within bourgeois society. Yet, at the end of his *The Theory of Communicative Action*, he explicitly distances himself from the older Frankfurt-style critique of mass culture which informed his *Structural Transformation of the Public Sphere*. His newer theoretical orientation, he says, 'makes us sceptical to the thesis that the essence of the public sphere has been liquidated in postliberal societies' (Habermas, 1987:389). While history has bypassed the earlier bourgeois society and its form of public sphere, we can still treat the category of the public sphere in a 'generic' sense and see how it can be most productively understood today. To that end, it is necessary to explore a little more fully the notions of public and private, and to see what trajectories have contributed to shaping the relationship between them in the present situation.

The public/private distinction, pointing to different sorts of social activities, settings and modes of discourse, is a complicated one and has a long history within several theoretical contexts. Any attempt to develop a perspective on the mass media and the public sphere must come to terms with the larger ramifications of the categories of public and private. We must remember that the distinction is an historically evolving one. It must be understood as a product both of discursive practices within everyday life, and of larger, macro-institutional arrangements. It derives both from political, economic and legal conditions as well as sociocultural practices. Moreover, the distinction is never fully clear-cut; it is always untidy and at times contested.

Thompson (1990) charts two fundamental contexts in which the public/private distinction has been operative in the history of modern Europe. The first, with its anchorings in liberal political philosophy, derives from the fundamental distinction between the state, on the one hand, and the private economy and domestic realm on the other. The second context, derived from legal and political thought and today actualized by the modern media, has to do with public in the sense of 'publicness', that is, visible or accessible to the citizenry (which of course is the tradition on which Habermas builds his analysis). Thompson's discussion, however, does not pursue the context which we might, in simplified terms, describe as having emerged from these two, in particular from the former: namely the patriarchal gender system. For feminism, the boundaries between public and private can be seen as a cornerstone of the entire patriarchal edifice.

With the emergence of the nation-state, formal political power became institutionalized within the state, while the economic sphere and the realm of familial relations was, in theory, situated outside the control of the state. Of course this principle became greatly modified in practice, not least as the state had to respond to the circumstances generated by the capitalist economy, resulting, by the end of the last century, in the incipient interventionist state whose contours became firmly established in the present century. This development contributed to a rather large grey area between the public and the private sectors, as the regulatory activities of the state expanded, and especially as its corporatist character deepened. Also, this grey area grew as other, intermediate organizations continued to grow; Thompson mentions political parties, charities, pressure groups and co-ops. Likewise, the intimate realm of family and household was theoretically distinct from the state, but came under increasing regulation, especially due to expanding social welfare policy initiatives.

One can draw different conclusions from this historical narrative. Conservatives may bemoan the 'decay' of the 'pure' categories, but progressive interpretations would emphasize, for example, that state involvement in the social and economic realms, despite its problematic class biases, has nevertheless manifested positive steps to counteract some of the social devastation of capitalism. To various degrees in different countries, the working class was able to negotiate benefits (especially via social democratic parties) within the centres of state power – while at the same time the capitalist sectors came to understand that a modicum of stability in the social realm and regulation in the economic realm lay in their interests as well. And even in the domestic arena, social policy has contributed in a variety of ways to the welfare of citizens, though here we must be particularly alert to the gender bias of even the more progressive welfare states. What emerges from this narrative of the boundaries between state and non-state as the foundation for the public/private distinction is a sense of its political nature, and how it resides in a tripartite force field between philosophical and normative ideals, structural power relations, and discursive practices.

The historical evolution of 'publicness' constitutes the core of Habermas' analysis of the public sphere. This sense of public is distinct from the first one, but, as Thompson states, 'overlaps with it in complex and historically varying ways' (1990:240). Thus, the state's decision making became more 'public' in the course of modern history, 'although this broad trend was neither uniform nor complete: new forms of invisibility and privacy have emerged, and the exercise of state power in modern societies remains in many ways shrouded in secrecy and hidden from public gaze' (1990:241). However, along with the uneven unfolding of visibility of the state arose the fora that we have come to see, via Habermas, as the original bourgeois public sphere, as well as the idea of 'the public' as the citizens engaged in discussion over current affairs. Publicness ultimately becomes a theme which comprises political, economic, and legal, as well sociocultural elements.

If we leave Habermas' account and instead follow Thompson, the development of mass communication can be seen as having a dramatic impact on publicness. The media make the publicness (that is, visibility) of events – in both the private/personal domain as well the state/public domain – relatively independent of spatial constraints. Thus, both mediated public events and mediated private events are endowed with a new publicness, which in turn is for the most part experienced in private, domestic settings. These become the main sites of reception for mediated publicness. Thus, despite all the shortcomings of the media, Thompson underscores that:

> Since access to publicness is no longer dependent on physical co-presence, a wider range of individuals, and especially individuals in so far as they inhabit private domestic settings, are able to experience a greater spectrum of events in the public and private domains . . . *Hence, any individual situated in a private domestic setting equipped with a TV set has potential access to the sphere of publicness created and mediated by television.* (1990:244, italics in original).

But the transitions in the public sphere engendered by the modern media of communication have to do with more than the spatial aspect. The media despatialize the public sphere, enhancing its accessibility. Media discourses themselves contribute to drawing our cultural maps of public and private (see Meyrowitz, 1985, in regard to television; Kress, 1986, from a different angle, discusses the press' role).

Moreover, the trend towards informal modes of discourse in the media – the paradigmatic example is the television talk show – can be seen both to further enhance accessibility and to modify the public/private boundary (see Tolson, 1991; Livingstone and Lunt, 1994). However, mediazation also renders the public sphere less of a dialogical encounter between citizens, and shifts its character in the direction of monological representation, dominant in the semiotic environment. Power holders can readily manage and manipulate their visibility – impression management on television has become a refined speciality – but they cannot fully control it, as Thompson points out. The 'stretching' of social relations across time and space, the disembedding of senses of place, can be seen to come with a price, namely that the nature of mediated social relations cannot be simply equated with the nature of social relations experienced face to face: there *are* differences. However, this is a price well worth paying, for the net gain is large, namely enhanced visibility and accessibility. It just means that the complementary dimension of interaction – 'discursive elaboration' is Thompson's phrase – becomes paramount. Reception and social interaction – that is, sense-making through social constructive talk – remain modifying factors to the definitional power of the media, even if the processes of decoding are more socially patterned than some reception studies and notions of the popular have suggested in recent years.

Turning to the gender system, feminist theory speaks through multiple voices, but virtually all strands emphasize the centrality of the public/private dichotomy. This is the key to understanding the historical structuring of gender relations and the subordination of women (see, for example, Pateman, 1987; Hansen, 1987. B.L. Marshall (1994) explicitly situates the problematic within the social theories of modernity). Both the historical evolution of state and civil society, as well as the liberal tradition in political philosophy, are charged with manifesting a false universality, whereby the general category of the individual turn out to be male gendered. The 'social contract' which lies at the heart of the liberal political tradition is a fraternal one (Brown, 1988; Elshtain, 1993; Pateman, 1988) from which women have, to a great extent, been excluded. What has emerged is a gender system (Hirdman, 1991) composed of the dynamic interaction of an array of mechanisms within the political, economic, legal and sociocultural realms.

In this gender system the demarcation between public and private becomes pivotal. Pateman (1992) points out that in the liberal vision, it is not so much a question of the worlds of private and public life being fully separated. On the contrary, they are quite interrelated, but profoundly articulated by patriarchal mechanisms. Thus, for instance, the family in its modern form is not so much a 'natural' phenomenon as it is a social pattern shaped by policies of welfare, employment, education, and so on (see Pateman, 1992; for a discussion of the Swedish welfare model from a feminist perspective, see Eduards, 1991). These policies, in turn, are systematically predicated on unspoken and largely unconscious assumptions which associate women with nature, the personal, the emotional, love, the private, intuition and morality, and men with culture, the political, reason, justice, public, philosophy and power. The gender system operates not least via the deep layers of tacit cultural assumptions.

One of the key upshots of the gender system has been its contribution to shaping two distinct and overarching sets of morality in the modern world, one deemed suitable for public life, the other for the private sphere (Poole, 1991). Poole uses a looser conceptualization of public and private, treating public life as composed – at bottom – of the rationalized institutions of capitalist production, market exchange, and bureaucratic administration. He remarks that: 'Both the market and the bureaucracy operate "without regard for persons" and on "calculable rules" . . . It is the exclusion of the personal, the emotional and the domestic which is essential for modern rationality' (Poole, 1991:47). He then argues that this distinction 'maps on' to another, namely that of male and female, where the latter traditionally has stood for, among other things, an ethics of caring. He sees the relationship between public and private as being marked by 'exclusion, subordination and opposition, and the distinction between masculine and feminine forms of identity is in large part constructed in terms of this structure' (Poole, 1991:156). Poole's distinction of public and private varies somewhat from the framework I am currently using, but what is suggestive here is that the notion of distinct systems of moralities within public and private spheres articulates with Habermas' notion of communicative rationality and ethics in the lifeworld confronting the instrumental rationality of the system. Moreover, it also suggests the possible correlation between key elements in feminist thought and the idea of communicative rationality. Indeed, we find this theme within the sympathetic feminist critiques of Habermas (see in particular the collection by Benhabib and Cornell, 1987; also, Soper, 1990, has a helpful review of this collection).

Of course it is not just the system of moralities which derives from sexist distinctions of public and private. Even the divisions of labour within domestic life and other questions of gendered practices take on significance for the public sphere. If women, for example, are disproportionately burdened with domestic labour, then they are not in a position to participate equally in the public sphere. The critical feminist perspective assumes a central role in the struggle to realize a democratic public sphere and, more generally, to counteract the encroachment of instrumental rationality in the institutional lifeworld. Feminism, in short, is a critical contribution to the democratization of civil society. As I have indicated, feminism embodies many different voices, and, in regard to philosophical orientation and the formulation of politics, there are a variety of positions with a mixture of inflections, especially from liberalism, Marxism and postmodernism. (Among the vast literature here, useful orientations can be found in Benhabib, 1992; Hekman, 1990; Phillips, 1993; Bock and James, 1992; Butler and Scott, 1992.) While feminism has thoroughly dealt with the public/private distinction, it has thus far had little to say about the public sphere and the media as such. We still need what McLaughlin (1993a:614) advocates, namely 'both a feminist theory of the public sphere accounting for the media and a feminist media studies accounting for the public sphere'.

Political permutations

The three different, yet intersecting contexts of public/private which I have taken up – political and economic macrostructures, the theme of publicness and visibility, especially as it pertains to the media, and the gender system – are all operative in shaping contemporary boundaries between public and private. Or, more accurately, I would say that all three contribute to keeping the boundary fluid and negotiable. For what has been eroded by the reciprocal interplay of these contexts is the idea that there is a unique, delimited, and specific social space which constitutes the realm of the political. The site of the political, as Laclau and Mouffe (1985) posit, is diffused across the terrain of the social, rendering the boundary between the public and private very permeable, though not dissolved. Indeed, as Fraser (1990) indicates, the maintenance and/or dissolution of such boundaries becomes a central and contested topic in the politics of advanced capitalist society.

In contrast to the bourgeois epoch, in today's world that which we would term the private sphere is hardly a stable and secure space. Microworlds swathed in the current semiotic environment tend not to promulgate universal sets of values. Self-identity is increasingly a reflexive struggle, and accomplishments in this regard seem increasingly temporary. The public world of politics enters the private domain; issues previously deemed private are projected into the political realm. Whether or not one sees as adequate Habermas' reconstruction of historical materialism in the framework of life-worlds resisting colonization by systems logic, it is apparent that within post-war politics, both the structural conditions and the ideational climate are problematizing the traditional coordinates of orientation (for example, Heller and Fehér, 1988).

The institution of politics under late modernity is not what it once was. If we conceive of modern democratic politics as emerging in the last two centuries parallel with such phenomena as capitalist production, urbanization, and the industrialization of information and opinion, it could be argued that political modernization has lagged behind. There is a stagnant, moribund quality to much of the official political realm, which stands in stark contrast to the dynamic post-Fordism of the contemporary global capitalist flows discussed above. The political realm, as Mulgan (1994:9) writes, 'has the feel of something archaic: a set of rituals, a container of tensions, a symbolic link with the past rather than a dynamic force of the present'. This is not to say that the major political questions have been answered, only that the solutions provided seem to inspire less and less. Issues about the nation, state power, group and class interests, and the promise of a better future are still very much with us, as is the political machinery itself. However, the ideational climate which has enveloped and expressed such issues does not galvanize attention nor resonate in people's imaginations to the same extent as before.

Involvement is being syphoned off in two directions: the microcosmic and the macrocosmic. The microcosmic has to do with the personal and everyday life, with meaning, identity, values; with issues of sexuality, culture, lifestyle; with relationships in the home, at work, in the neighborhood. The macrocosmic points to the global, to the transnational arena, as well as to the planet as such; to the species and its survival. The end-point of this transition is by no means in sight, and it is difficult to extrapolate what the contours of politics will look like even in a decade hence. Yet, at present, it is apparent that many of these kinds of micro- and macroscopic issues do not readily lend themselves to administrative measures such as legislation, since they have more to do with cultural patterns of behaviour. Thus, as Mulgan points out:

> Politics becomes a sensibility more than a set of institutions . . . less part of the definition of the collective, the nation, the class or republic, and more part of the armoury of the self-defining, self-creating individual, continually required to make decisions on everything, including what to eat, where to work, and what relationships to maintain . . . It vanishes from the committees and parliaments because it has gone everywhere, into the bedroom and the kitchen, the workplace and the bar. (1994)

In a similar vein, Giddens (1991) makes a distinction between what he calls emancipatory politics and life politics. The former, with liberal and conservative as well as radical manifestations, aims at liberating people from the chains of tradition – reducing exploitation and domination. It usually makes appeals based on criteria of justice and equality. Life politics, on the other hand, which emerged only in late modernity, 'is a politics of life decisions' (Giddens, 1991:215). Emancipatory politics have to do with life chances; life politics dwell on life choices. According to Giddens, at the centre of the questions raised by life politics are issues about self-identity and its relationship to various domains of social life. These include the private sphere as well as local, national and global contexts. It is not the case that life politics simply replace emancipatory politics. Instead they are intricately interwoven. For instance, freedom of life choices presupposes a modicum of well being that the emancipatory politics of life chances strive for. This evokes not least the traditional questions of class, distribution and equality.

Yet life politics do not mesh well with the existing structures of political life, and 'may well stimulate the emergence of political forms which differ from those hitherto prominent, both within states and on a global level' (Giddens, 1991:228). Contemporary social movements are the most obvious expression of this logic, where increasingly 'cultural texture', as Eder (1993) calls it, in the form of values, identities, knowledge, discourses, and so on, mediate between social structural features and collective action. And cultural texture derives not least from the mass-mediated semiotic environment: Luke (1989) argues for the importance of the media as mobilizing agents in these movements. Giddens' labels of 'emancipatory' and 'life' politics are not wholly satisfying – could one not speak of the emanicpatory aspects of 'life politics'? – yet the distinction captures something of the complex permutations under way within political life in late modernity. These developments have implications not only for the conception and the arena of politics, but also for the identity of political actors. The evolution of politics of course has ramifications for the public sphere; these can be explored via the notions of civil society and citizenship, themes I address in Chapter 6.

This chapter has emphasized that modernity or, more specifically late modernity, as the historical present, can most constructively be approached through postmodern modes of thinking. This includes a general epistemological modesty and sensitivity to multiperspectival possibilities. Furthermore, recent literature on modernity emphasizes a number of important substantive strands which can help to specify the historical and sociocultural contingencies of the public sphere itself. I have mentioned: the basic features of disorganized, transnational capitalism, with its various flows and the interplay between the political, economic and the sociocultural; in everyday life the plural social lifeworlds and identities , as well as the shifting coordinates of social time and space, and the consequent disembedding and re-embedding of social relations; the mediazation of the semiotic environment and the current tension between the discursive and the figurative regimes of signification; the multidimensional distinction between public and private, and the political 'openings' which derive from the permeability of the boundary.

With this overall sketch of some of the key contingencies of modernity, let us now focus attention in more detail on some themes which are central to any theoretical perspective on the public sphere – themes which I have only referred to in passing in the course of the past chapters: the question of the 'rationality' of communication and processes of subjectivity.

5

Communication and subjectivity

In this chapter I turn my attention to some theoretical aspects of the process of communication. This follows up the more general reflections on the mediated semiotic environment in the previous chapter, as well as tying in with previous discussions on social interaction and subjectivity in the public sphere.

As an initial frame for the discussion, and with the aim of clarifying a few points relevant to my overall perspective, I will use some aspects of Habermas' (1984, 1987) *The Theory of Communicative Action*. There are innumerable expositions and analyses of Habermas' overall approach (see for example, Ingram, 1987, and S. White, 1988, for two extensive treatments). I take Habermas as my point of departure, however, not only because his is an ambitious attempt to relate communication theory to social theory, but also because in this work he retains thematic links with his earlier text on the public sphere. For my purposes, the controversy around his theory of communicative action can be seen as a condensation of the more general debates about Enlightenment and postmodern thought, as well as the status and purpose of critical theory, to which I referred in the previous chapter. My position will be one of critical solidarity with Habermas, while suggesting that his version of a rational communication unnecessarily constrains the utility of his theoretic model.

More specifically, the themes I will be addressing have to do with the universalist claims in Habermas' model, and his view of language, culture, the unconscious and subjectivity. I end with some reflections on imagination and emancipation. While each of these topics is in itself immense, I will be highlighting only a few key points which have bearing on my own arguments. There are innumerable issues which spring from these considerations, and it would be easy to allow the discussion to meander over an enormous terrain of contemporary thought. I will try to hold a tight course, which inevitably means that a good number of issues, though fascinating in themselves, will have to wait for another occasion.

A universal model?

While rationality is a word with a variety of meanings, Habermas grounds his usage in the traditional view that it refers to an attribute of action, namely that action which is guided by knowledge and can be coherently defended through argumentation. The process of reasoning thus figures centrally in communicatively convincing others not only of the validity of one's knowledge, but also of the rightness of one's norms and beliefs, and, hence, the rationality of one's actions. I would not dispute the classic criteria of rationality as such, but it is Habermas' model of the communicative reasoning process where I see difficulties. Habermas' use of the classic view of rationality is incorporated into his elaborate theories of communication and the evolution of modern society. Since the late 1970s, Habermas has been developing a critical theory which has made use of a number of empirical traditions of social theory, including Parson's sociology, Piaget's research on cognitive and moral development, and especially speech act theory. All of these, in different ways, emphasize the presence and unfolding of rationality in the social world. In Habermas we have a very different view of the processes of reason from that in the earlier critical theory of Horkheimer and Adorno, who ultimately see in the Enlightenment the seeds for domination, that is, its own negation, in the forms of capitalism and instrumental rationality. Habermas, in contrast, sees the Enlightenment as an 'unfulfilled project' and one of his key goals is to redeem the notion of reason. He wants to demonstrate that the reasoning process need not automatically lead us into domination and destruction, that it still retains a liberatory dimension.

A cornerstone of his contemporary thinking is the distinction he makes between strategic or instrumental rationality, guided by criteria of technical effectivity, and communicative rationality, which is grounded in negotiated intersubjectivity and normative thinking. Though striving to realize the potential of the Enlightenment's rationalist legacy, Habermas is also critically sensitive to its shortcomings and failures. It is particularly his adherence to this legacy which places him at odds with some postmodern strands of thought, as I noted in Chapter 4. Habermas finds in speech act theory, and the analytic philosophical movement from which it derives, an orientation for coming to grips with the dimension of rationality within everyday language use. For Habermas, speakers are always making claims, at least implicitly, about the validity of their statements. Even in ordinary speech situations, people will attempt to justify their claims and positions via argument. Thus, for Habermas, rationality is pre-structured, built into all speech situations. The implicit appeal to reason, though not always in fact realized, lurks beneath the surface of all social interaction. This constitutes a thematic intersubjectivity which we can view as an immanent resource holding out the promise of realized rationality. Indeed, Habermas defines rationality in his communication theory as precisely the quality that makes speech (or action) justifiable against criticism, that is, that beliefs and claims can be defended through the use of validity claims – claims which in turn can be criticized. He sees the process of reasoning as providing arguments to underwrite beliefs and actions; the supposition here is that ends/means distinctions are always possible with regard to speech and action, and that even habitual, or tacit knowledge, is accessible and susceptible to explicit, propositional formulation. While the 'ideal speech situation' of course does not exist (and we should not hold our breath in anticipation), Habermas' point is that it functions as an implicit model – a horizon – within ordinary speech settings and thereby plays an important role in structuring inter-subjectivity.

In argumentation, rational speakers will appeal to potentially consensual grounds to justify their claims. The claims, implicit or explicit, can invoke cognitive, moral and expressive dimensions. Cognitive appeals refer to factual reality and a shared understanding of the factuality in question. Moral claims invoke rightness; they make use of normative discourse. Expressive dimensions include both emotional and aesthetic modes of reasoning. Here the claim is not to the truth, but to 'truthfulness', that is, it is a subjective mode, which alludes to the speaker's own authenticity and sincerity. Historically, in Habermas' view, such strategies of communicative action have not always been operative; they are a product of modernity. Further, he underscores the point that understanding among speakers – intersubjectivity – cannot be assumed or ascribed, but must be achieved.

This is in many respects an attractive model; and while we may find it compelling as a vision, we should also be aware that a good deal of communication in everyday settings, and even in the public sphere, *does* embody this pull towards the rational. This tendency is enhanced under some circumstances; in this volume, for example, an academic text, I am closely wedded to the procedure of rationally justifying my claims in an effort to attain intersubjectivity with the reader. As an operating principle of the public sphere, the notion of contestability – of claims, of decisions, even of the 'rules of the game' themselves – is immeasurably valuable. As Benhabib (1986) suggests, from the standpoint of critical theory, this entails a major paradigm shift. The older critical theory was, at bottom, aligned with a traditional philosophical concept of truth; this has now given way to a model of discursive argumentation and legitimation. Meaning is constituted via communication; it is an achievement, not a given. In Benhabib's (1992:5) words, Habermas' communicative rationality represents a shift 'from a substantialistic to a discursive, communicative concept of rationality'. What we have here, fundamentally, is a move away from the epistemology of the subject towards a view of the irreducibility of intersubjectivity.

At the same time, even in my very compressed rendering, a number of problematic issues can be detected. A basic one has to do with the position of the mass media: to what extent can the model address the processes of mass communication? There is an uncomfortable tension here, as Peters (1993) observes. Habermas' model strongly privileges face-to-face encounters and one could almost conclude that his position, therefore, would be that the media inevitably foster systematically distorted communication and thereby contribute to domination. Indeed, this implication hovers over his *Structural Transformation of the Public Sphere*, where strong traces of Adorno's critique of mass culture can be detected. However, in the final chapter of his *The Theory of Communicative Action* (1987), as well as in his (1992a) update on the public sphere, Habermas is quite explicit in his ambivalence, saying that the media can function both in oppressive and liberatory ways. Yet it is difficult to see the liberatory potential of the media if one is wedded to such a rationalistic understanding of communication and intersubjectivity. If the relevance of Habermas' communication theory lies chiefly with face-to-face speech, this would at least underscore its utility for the public sphere's dimension of social interaction. However, his implicit sense of social encounters seems modelled on something akin to the academic seminar. It is my understanding that Habermas' model of communicative action, with its emphasis on achieved intersubjectivity and the contestability of truth claims, is a very helpful one – even in the case of television. Yet it needs to shed some – but not all – of its rationalist attire and allow for what I call the arational.

Arational modes of meaning-making and paths to intersubjectivity sidestep the either/or of the rational versus the irrational. They appear in the more metaphoric and poetic forms of speech and text, as well as in non-verbal forms of communication such as images and music. In the Kantian distinction between cognitive, aesthetic and moral forms of knowledge, the arational clearly has a home in the aesthetic. However, I would also make room for arational dimensions to cognitive and moral forms – tacit, intuitive and unconscious processes of reasoning may figure here as well. They need not by definition lead us into darkness – though they can. However, they can also open the doors of imagination and emancipation; the point is, there can be no guarantees, regardless of which mode is operative. The appropriateness of the arational is contextual; it will not 'work', nor should it, in all circumstances. But by giving the arational an entry ticket and allowing it to play a role, we will have a more serviceable theoretic framework.

I can note briefly that McCarthy (1991) indicates that Habermas in his more recent writings has begun to take into account the '"illuminating power" of aesthetic experience' and acknowledges how this may affect 'our cognitive interpretations and normative expectations, and transform the totality in which these moments are related' (McCarthy, 1991:186). I take this to mean that Habermas is allowing more space for the aesthetic in his communication theory. I would push still further, however, and argue for the broader notion of the arational. I will be returning to the theme of the arational, in the context of a discussion on the unconscious, below.

Another issue has to do with the question of universalism. Habermas' position is explicitly anti-foundationalist. That is, he is rejecting a view which asserts that philosophy can demonstrate some absolute grounding or validity to our knowledge or morality. On the other hand, he does make universalistic claims for his views on action, communication and the establishment of intersubjectivity: he sees his framework as offering a general 'proceduralist' model. There is a tension here, in that his universalism can be construed as covert foundationalism, which has elicited considerable debate. White (1988) says that this tension is hardly surprising, in that it mirrors one of the most central questions of contemporary philosophy, namely 'what it means to create some legitimate commonality among different forms of life, with "legitimate" here carrying the sense of reciprocity and mutual respect' (White, 1988:154). From White's point of view, both 'contextualists' and 'universalists' have different, but complementary, contributions to make.

We are living in an increasingly pluralistic world, where difference is multiplying along innumerable axes. Yet we are forced to live with each other – to interact. Somehow we must coexist and make it work, not only to maximize cooperation, but also, more modestly, to avoid killing each other; we have to find ways of dealing with our conflicts. In White's view, the contextualist contribution is to emphasize difference and then (at best) to seek 'communicative links' between them, promoting mutual understanding. The universalist perspective can be seen as building upon this approach, highlighting the implications of that intersubjectivity which is accomplished: the motivations, mutual recognition, good reasons, and common communicative features which are not the monopoly of any one form of life. Thus, on this point, while Habermas is emphatically universalistic, I would modify this with a recognition of context and contingency, though allowing that these must always remain relative, never absolute.

Language and lacunae

A central difficulty in Habermas' model is its selective view of language, a view which emphasizes its transparency. This rendering of language allows for speakers to represent reality, negotiate norms, and express their subjectivities. Here language is largely a rule-bounded institution, where speech acts are the basic unit of communication, but language is accorded little or no productive dimensions of its own. In principle there need be few discrepancies between meaning and utterance; there is at bottom an intentionalist logic at work. In other words, Habermas is saying that people use language to convey what they want to say about themselves or the world, and there is no tension between what they say and the meaning of what is said. Moreover, the role of language in shaping the reality which it describes is largely ignored.

This view of language can be deemed pre-semiotic, in the sense that it ignores much of the insight which followed with de Saussure and the rise of linguistics and semiotics regarding the social nature of language. Semiotics sees language as a sociocultural system, though in its poststructuralist guise the emphasis tends to shift away from the systemic aspects in favour of the unstable side of meaning. In our sense-making, we strives for closure and stability, but always confront difference, instability and polysemy. Like an amoeba flowing along the social terrain, meaning often refuses strict boundaries and spills over, exceeding – as well as falling short – of our intentions. In a collection of essays which follow up on many of the points of his debates with the postmodernists, Habermas (1992b) reaffirms and nuances his position, especially his notion of 'a weak but not defeatistic concept of linguistically embodied reason' (Habermas, 1992b:142).

In his rejection of postmodern thought, Habermas sees a line from Nietzsche to Derrida which threatens rationality, or more generally, reason itself, with some pre-linguistic, primordial 'Other' – a regressive force which would lead us down the path of irrationality and chaos. The critics, however, reply that what Habermas misses here is precisely the semiotic (or perhaps we should say post-semiotic) view of language which disrupts rationality simply by virtue of its mobile and polyvalent quality. Derrida's 'differences' and 'deferrals' in the processes of signification, and the heterogeneity they point to, do not subvert rationality in the name of the irrational. What such operations do is call into question reason's illusion of mastery, to challenge the alleged transparency, omniscience and self-presence of rational language. As Coole puts it:

> The Other then emerges only as a sort of mobile negativity, a disruptive force but not one that might be installed as an ontological alternative to reason, a counter-symbolic. Its irruptions are but strategies for opening spaces through which the unnameable and hence uncolonizeable, might be glimpsed/created as a subversion of reason's closures. The other is not then a new foundation, but a demonstration of the untenability of all foundations . . . Postmodernism is not then on the side of truth(untruth) or goodness, but openness, an openness which springs from the structures of meaning itself. Indeed, its subversions are the sort of permanent guarantee against closure that Habermas' communicative participants might themselves rely on if their consensus, too, would not harden into a new closure and in this sense postmodernism is continuous with an earlier critical theory. (1992:85–6)

Moreover, as Rajchman (1988:166) indicates in his review of Habermas' attack on postmodernist thought, he himself never takes up questions of sexuality, of the body, of language and gender themes which have made postmodern theory useful for many feminists. From a different angle, Keane (1984), in an early response, noted that non-verbal communication ('body language') vanishes in Habermas' approach; we might say that people become reduced to 'talking heads' in this view of communication. All non-propositional speech and the inherent rhetorical dimension of all discourse are seriously devalued in their communicative significance:

> With varying degrees of intensity, to be sure, all communication is marked by rhetorical characteristics that are generated by the play or tension within the chains of signs and utterances employed by speaking actors . . . . The rhetorical quality of speech acts flow precisely from this play of equivalence and difference, synonymity and antonymity. (Keane, 1984:178)

This is important because rhetoric here points to the generation of new meanings by speakers – that people produce new meanings, new linguistic formulations, and new subjectivities – via speech. The unpredictable, the new, the imaginary – qualities I have touched upon in earlier chapters – find no real home in Habermas' communication theory. There is little room for what Ricoeur (1994) calls the 'semantic innovation' which follows from the irreducible metaphorical dimension of all language use.

It seems that Habermas has joined ranks with the Anglo-Saxon schools of linguistic philosophy which have tended to take the norm of representational accuracy and logical coherence – a perfectly valid norm in innumerable situations – and turned it into a theory of how language and subjects function. This, as Taylor (1985) indicates, has disastrous consequences, not least that the expressive and constitutive dimensions of language get short-changed. Taylor shares Habermas' strong emphasis on intersubjectivity, on not reducing our analytic horizon to the monological subject as a bearer of language and knowledge. Yet for Taylor, intersubjectivity is established via language without necessarily having to invoke notions of ideal speech situations and implicit validity claims.

In his more modest view, language use *per se* between people serves to create a 'public space', where speakers are united by the commonality of their mutual address. Even through the expressive use of language – without reference to validity claims – we constitute a common vantage point, which can 'bring us together qua participants in a common act of focusing' (Taylor, 1985:260). The 'usness' or togetherness thus generated is as diverse as the world of human relationships, and Taylor goes on to affirm that even though purely expressive speech can serve to establish an intersubjective public space, the nature and degree of intersubjectivity is ultimately dependent upon cultural contexts. Language use is inexorably tied up with social relations and practices, and contributes to their constitution.

Within his complex model, Habermas distinguishes between communicative action which is propositional and that which is non-propositional, that is to say, between that communication which makes claim to say something, to represent something about the state or nature of things, and that which does not. Non-propositional communication action includes not only expressive dimensions, but also, in its non-verbal forms, such aesthetic modes as music and visual abstraction. Habermas develops and emphasizes propositional communicative action, but by enhancing the status and significance of the non-propositional it may be possible to achieve a better theoretic balance even within the framework of his own model.

Cultural contexts

Alexander (1991) pursues this theme in calling attention to what he terms the cultural weakness of Habermas' theory. In his view, Habermas has a strong rationalist bias towards *conscious* activity. This means the bringing up to full awareness of the assumptions and motivations which underlie one's arguments and behaviour. Alexander rightly questions the cultural contingencies of such self-transparency. While Habermas makes strong points about the distinction between mythical and modern modes of thought, Alexander suggests that the mythical is still very much with us – and always will be. The relation between rationality and tradition remain a lingering question within modernity. Alexander posits that while much evidence about modernity confirms the differentiation of culture, society and personality, much remains within modern individuals which is unconscious, fused and irrational. Our views of the social world are coloured by language and preconscious motifs. Even our own 'world views' are not fully transparent to us; they too are shaped by extra-rational factors:

> Modern, rational people continue to infuse values, institutions, and even mundane physical locations with the mystery and awe of the sacred. It is for this reason that physical, social and moral reality is organized into centres and peripheries. Even for

modern people, moreover, . . . 'concretize' abstract relationships by evoking metaphors and other tropes. Finally, there seems to be abundant evidence that moderns still seek to understand the contingency of everyday life in terms of narrative traditions whose simplicity and resistance to change makes them hard to distinguish from myths . . . . None of this implies the elimination of rationality in Habermas' sense. What it does mean is that there is much, much more besides. (Alexander, 1991:71–2)

Another culturalist response to Habermas' model has to do with its emphasis on consensus, the striving to reach agreement by speaking parties. Keane (1988a) calls attention to the fact that this idea of consensus, which we must see as a precondition for rational communication, fails to come to terms with the problem of cognitive and ethical relativism. In other words, Habermas tends to downplay the very real possibilities – seemingly increasingly likely in the contemporary world – that people can be incapable or unwilling to enter into communicative action oriented to reaching understanding and agreement. Habermas' model privileges language games in which speakers are:

(a) already in explicit agreement about the need to reach mutual understanding; (b) already capable of distinguishing between the performative and propositional aspects of their utterances; and (c) already share a tradition and, thus, a common perception of their social and political situation. (Keane, 1988a:231)

Feminists in particular (see for example, Young, 1987; Porter 1991; Hekman, 1990) have argued against simplistic dichotomies of rationality and affectivity, contending, among other things, that moral reason in particular suffers when all needs and feelings are banished from the halls of rational discourse. These writers claim that the rationality/affectivity polarity feeds into the public/private distinction in ways which are detrimental to women. Young (1987) posits that the opposition between reason and desire in Habermas problematizes his lingering notions of the unified subject (albeit now predicated on intersubjectivity) upon which his work is premised. Young finds much which is promising within Habermas' communication theory, but in his denial of desire he misses something crucial both to communication theory and to the human subject.

Young evokes Kristeva's (1984) distinction between the 'symbolic' and the 'semiotic', two somewhat confusing labels which in fact point, respectively, to the rational, referential functions of utterances and to their unconscious, bodily, sensuous aspects. All speech has at least some trace of each dimension, and meaning is generated to a great extent via the tension between the two. From this perspective, the unity of the subject as sender and receiver of meaning begins to unravel. 'The subject is in process, positioned by the slipping and moving levels of signification, which is always in excess of what is grasped or understood discursively' (Young, 1987:72). The implications are apparent: communication is not just motivated by the goal of consensus, but also by pleasure, by the expression of desire, by the negotiation of identity, and so on, often in ways not accessible to the subject. This trajectory can be pursued in a postmodern direction, but for the moment it is more productive here to see

it as a port of entry into the arational and problematic status of the unconscious within Habermas' theory.

Repressing the unconscious

Normally we assume that consciousness is, if not self-evident, at least conceptually unproblematic, while the unconscious is the great mystery. Yet, as
Ricoeur (1974:99) says 'The question of consciousness is just as obscure as
that of the unconscious'. Without pursuing Ricoeur's own line of reasoning
in much detail, we can simply say that once we admit to the reality of the
unconscious, this inevitably changes our understanding of consciousness. It
is no longer just what is immediately apparent to us, but becomes instead
something which is integrated within a larger portrait of the psyche. Without
some kind of access to the unconscious, our understanding of consciousness
remains rudimentary, if not wholly inaccurate. To embark on any discussion
of the unconscious plummets us directly into the various interpretations
and schools of psychoanalysis and analytic psychology. I will maintain a
rather ecumenical position in this regard, though some contention is
unavoidable.

Elliott (1992) has analysed the notion of the unconscious at work within
Habermas' communication theory. What emerges is a very negative view
operative in Habermas' scheme. At base, Habermas seemingly treats the
unconscious as a defective feature of our subjectivity. Distorted communication (not least in the public sphere) contributes to repression, accompanied by
a privatization of language which further undermines the capacity to self-
reflect and establish genuine intersubjectivity with others. The ensuing
distortions within the unconscious are thus linked to the pathological aspects
of social structure (that is, in Habermas' terms, most notably, the colonization
of the lifeworld by the instrumental rationality of systems logic). From this
position, Habermas then can conclude that emancipation lies in removing
unconscious determinants to human action and speech, to promote self-
reflection and autonomy.

It is not the case that this is by any means all untrue, but it does seem we
again have a situation where Habermas is only acknowledging part of the
story. What is missing basically are those features of the unconscious which
distinguish Freud's thought as a major revolution in the western history of
ideas. Elliott's own position goes still further, arguing for a particular version
of psychoanalytic theory, which I will come to presently.

Habermas undertakes what can be called a 'communications reading' of
Freud, a 'linguisticalization' of the unconscious. He is basically working
within the framework of traditional ego psychology and cognitive development theory. The unconscious, seen as arising from the systematic distortions
of communication and social relationships, reproduces and stores the
pathologies from the social environment. But, according to Elliott, in
Habermas' theory there is no sense of pre-linguistic subjectivity, nothing
equivalent to the Freudian id, or bodily drives. Further, we find nothing

pointing to creative production within the unconscious, nothing akin to dream-work, with its mechanisms of condensation, displacement, reversals of affect, and so forth. In Habermas' emphasis on public speech he neglects our inner realities and their expressions. The unconscious merely registers and records. The emancipatory project, then, is predicated upon mastering the irrational forces, bringing them up to surface awareness and putting them under rational control. In short, the project becomes one of making the unconscious conscious – abolishing the id via rational communication. There is no place for the arational.

While we can travel some way down this path – and it could be argued that this is just what psychoanalysis does, even if it does not attempt to remove the workings of the id – there are limits to the degree of self-transparency which can be attained. Moreover, as a strategy for emancipatory politics, there are indeed severe limits. Habermas ignores the fact that certain deep aspects of our psychic make-up resist discursive intervention. More significantly, the realm of the unconscious incorporates and reproduces in its own ways elements of social domination: drives and desires, fears and conflicts are embodied within public communication, often not manifestly accessible to any of the communicating partners. Without attention to these dimensions, with only a reliance on the power of rational communication, it would seem that the platform for the critical hermeneutic interrogation of ideology is undercut. Television and other manifestations of our mass-mediated semiotic environment largely sidestep communicative rationality and employ other discursive modes, but we would not be in a position to understand how, if our analytic tools were grounded on Habermas' notion of the unconscious.

At a more general level, Elliott (1992) insists on the importance of psychoanalysis for progressive and critical social theory. He traces a number of strands of social theory which have made use of psychoanalysis; he looks not only at Habermas but at the even older Frankfurt school as well as the post-Marxist trajectory of Laclau and Mouffe (1985). Much of his argument is aimed at what he sees to be the limitations of the Lacanian school. This critique does not lead Elliott to simply reject Lacan's efforts and those of the social theorists who make use of him, but Elliott does accentuate the implications of, in his view, the distinct shortcoming in this tradition. This deficiency in turn leads Elliott to propose an alternative path, building on other psychoanalytic theorizing which makes room for a more affirmative role for the unconscious. My interest here is not to enter into the ongoing mêlée between psychoanalytic schools, but rather expressly to spotlight one important aspect of the unconscious which resonates with my discussion on creativity and the imaginary. Elliott brings this dimension to the fore via his encounter with Lacanian theory. I will not retrace all his steps in the encounter with Lacanian theory, but will chiefly summarize his own reconstructive path.

Dealing with desire

A. Elliott's project is to chisel out a psychoanalytic perspective which will aid in the development of critical social theory. While he works his way across Freudian, Lacanian, post-structuralist and feminist strands of psychoanalytic theory, Elliott himself acknowledges that at this stage what he has to offer is primarily suggestive rather than fully developed. Elliott begins with Freud, asserting that in Freud we find the oft-repeated theme that the primary unconscious – which is pre-linguistic – functions as a productive source of drives and affects as well as representations, and thus plays an essential role in the formation and continuity of the self. Unconscious representation is, markedly, the condition for both human agency and autonomy, as well as of repression and deformation. A. Elliott continues:

> For it is within these deep, affective elements of the unconscious imaginary that subjectivity 'opens out' to a self, to others, to reason, and social reality. This 'opening out' of the unconscious occurs within specific symbolic forms of society and politics. The simultaneous empowerment and repression of the self which this signals is not, however, some secondary reordering of psychic processes. Rather, the imaginary dimensions of the unconscious are deeply embedded in, and elaborated through, asymmetrical relations of power which structure modern institutions of social life. As such, the social field figures in this account, not simply as a force which is external, but as a productive basis which constitutes human subjects at the deepest unconscious roots of their lived experience. (1992:257–8)

At the same time Elliott goes on to remind us that the impacts that socio-cultural processes have on the psyche are far from totalizing or unifying. Psyche and social fields 'interlace' in ways which are complex and often contradictory. People are not simply shaped by their sociocultural milieu in a one-way fashion, but they actively engage with and interpret it, generating their own meanings as well – as Cultural Studies has been arguing for many years. In this force field, the unconscious can take self-constitution in directions which are enabling and foster autonomy, or in directions which are alienating and repressive. From the standpoint of critical theory, 'attention to the unconscious dimensions of ideology offers the possibility of disclosing . . . repressive relations between modes of self-identity and forms of social power' (Elliott, 1992:258).

This takes us a considerable distance from the steadfast rationality of Habermas. Of more significance for Elliott is the confrontation with the Lacanian tradition. He finds much which is both innovative and useful in Lacan, such as the fundamental idea that the subject is constructed via language and other cultural discourses of the social field. Also, Elliott shares Lacan's view of the decentring of the subject. However, there are areas he disputes, the most central being Lacan's linguistic notion of the unconscious. By limiting the unconscious to the secondary processes of language, Lacan effectively excludes from the unconscious the crucial work of representation carried out by the primary processes. Thus, for instance, the (unattainable) object of desire is ontologized as 'the lack', but its origins cannot be explained since there is no primary process prior to linguistic representation. In assimilating the unconscious to structural linguistics, Lacanian theory cuts analysis off from the primordial, pre-linguistic production of representation, which is the precondition for the use of language in the first place.

As an alternative route, Elliott, building in part on the work of Castoriadis (1987), offers what he terms the affirmative character of psychical production. Unconscious representation is not seen merely as a cover up or a response to 'the lack'. There may be the psychic experience of absence, but the point is that to be experienced as such an object must first be invested with desire. The importance of this affirmative view is that it posits that the organization of unconscious representation is the fundamental way of deriving satisfaction from our personal and social relations. That is, at the level of the unconscious, the 'work' of representation as such constitutes a source of pleasure. According to Elliott:

> social practices and ideologies are always structured in and through a certain *state of representation*. To raise such considerations is to focus attention toward the social and political dimensions of the imaginary investment in pleasure. . . . The unconscious pleasures attained through states of representation are always organized within the power relations of specific forms of social and institutional life. The reproduction of representational systems of all kinds, from images of sexuality in film and television to the medicalization and technical control of sickness and death in modern social life, touch deeply upon our unconscious investments; gratifications which are mutually imbricated with our existing system of power. Once this is recognized . . . we can begin to look at the *forms* in which social ideologies draw upon the unconscious economies of human subjects. (1992:263)

Thus, desire and the unconscious must be understood within the context of concrete social and political relations. Unconscious desire is profoundly embedded and embodied in social practices and systems of domination. For the public sphere, rational communication is necessary, but if our horizons do not penetrate beyond the conceptual framework of communicative rationality and the ideal speech situation, we will be operating with a crippled critical theory. We will be incapable of grasping the discursive dynamics of ideology and its resonances within the primary processes of the unconscious, within the arational. The strategy is not to erase or transcend the unconscious. Instead, we must strive for critical analysis which can promote self-reflection and transparency, even while being aware of their ultimate unattainability.

In both concrete social settings and in our efforts of social analysis, we cannot become fully transparent to ourselves via communicative rationality. Neither does a critical hermeneutics informed by psychoanalysis offer any such promise. There are, in other words, outer limits to what can be expected of critical theory (see Fay, 1987). But a psychoanalytically-based critical hermeneutics would seem to provide a stronger likelihood of progress in that direction. Struggles for individual and collective autonomy must try to alter the nature of the relationship between conscious intention and unconscious, imaginary representation, bringing to light the dynamics of the latter and its impact on the former. As Elliott (1992:272) writes on the last page of his text: 'While the theory of the unconscious demonstrates the human subject to be non-identical, internally pitted against itself, it equally finds within the recesses of the psyche the seeds of creativity, innovation and self-renewal. In short, the possibility of an alternative future.'

The theoretic importance of the unconscious is not just that it operates as a condition for our subjectivities and identities, but also that it is crucial to all processes of communication. In Chapter 4 I presented Lash's (1990) distinction between discourse and figure, as pointing to different communicative modes, or what he calls regimes of signification. This distinction, which parallels Kristeva's 'symbolic' and 'semiotic' (and can no doubt be found within a number of other conceptualizations), points to a fundamental duality within all communication. It is important not only because we may well be seeing an historical development in which the figurative is expanding within the mass mediated semiotic environment, but even more so because it allows us to make the theoretic connection between arational communication and the unconscious. I mentioned that Lash derives the distinction from Lyotard, who makes the point that within Freudian theory, the 'discursive' corresponds to the secondary processes, where the ego functions within the framework of the reality principle. The figural operates within the primary processes of the unconscious, where the pleasure principle holds sway, where desire is operative.

The significance of this is, among other things, that it suggests to us that we can best grasp the functioning of the unconscious 'by examining precisely how it is *not* structured like a language' (Lash, 1990:177). This is not to suggest that the unconscious does not signify, does not represent; it does so intensely, but the point is that the logic of its activity is fundamentally not linguistic. While it is not simply the case that the discourse/figure distinction corresponds to verbal-textual and visual communication, it does allow for more careful attention to the various *forms* of cultural expression and media output, which Lash argues has been somewhat hampered by the strong Lacanian influence in Cultural Studies.

Lash follows Lyotard's (and Freud's) arguments about the relationship between the two regimes of signification and their position within the psyche. The two regimes, or modes of communication, point to two distinct means for the discharge of psychic energy. Via discourse, energy is discharged in the secondary processes through the transformation of the external world, through our attentional engagement with reality external to our inner selves. By contrast, figural modes, in the primary processes, discharge energy through what is termed cathexis, via the investment in 'perceptual memories' within our psychic selves. The ratio – and the competition – between the two modes will vary immensely in different contexts.

I can illustrate the importance of this view of the unconscious by looking at the theoretic difficulty which arises in its absence. We saw above the rather formalistic approach to language in Habermas' communicative rationality. Ironically enough, a parallel formalism lurks within many of the discourse-based poststructuralist views of the subject. In their efforts to avoid an ontologized, totalized self, such approaches, while suitably undermining notions of self-certainty, at the same time risk an idealist, textual understanding of subjectivity. Here self and meaning reside only in discourse (albeit that the term is given a wide definition), and their relation to social and material circumstances are underdeveloped. And when coupled with psychoanalytic theory of the Lacanian school, the poststructuralist trajectory can foster a view of the self which borders on fiction. One of the most ambitious such discourse-based models is found in Laclau and Mouffe (1985). They develop a theoretical frame whose strengths lie in a strong anti-essentialism, an emphasis on the role of discourse in shaping subject positions, and, not least, a non-deterministic insertion into political issues. In Mouffe's words:

> All social relations can become the focus of antagonism insofar as they are constituted as relations of subordination. Many different forms of subordination can become the origin of conflict and struggle. There exists, therefore, in society a multiplicity of potential antagonisms, and class antagonism is only one among many. . . . There are multiple forms of power in society that cannot be reduced to or deduced from one origin or source. (1988a:91)

The horizon here emerges explicitly as a debate with traditional Marxism and has been termed post-Marxist, but its significance is relevant for broader social theory. Against traditional Marxism, this position, first developed in her previous work with Laclau (Laclau and Mouffe, 1985), suggests that politics is not simply determined by the economic and the ideological; it enters into and helps construct the everyday. Against liberalism, it implies that the subject is not a pre-ordained 'natural' being, nor, alternatively, a product of an ensemble of 'civic' rules and regulations.

That said, however, there is a sense in which this theoretic frame tends to reduce the construction of the subject to the constitution of social and political discourses. This is a problem, since, as P. Smith (1991) indicates, Laclau and Mouffe are not readily able to explain why any subject or collectivity would or should gravitate to any specific discourse. For the project of radical democracy, it becomes difficult to see why its agents should emerge merely via the circulation of appropriate discourses. This weakness derives largely from two features of their view of language: there is, on the one hand, an inadequate historical and material situating of discourses within social structure. On the other hand, there is a deterministic assumption of the relation between discourse and subjectivity. The problem in the latter case, which Elliott explains at length, is that Laclau and Mouffe are wedded to the Lacanian model which sees the unconscious in linguistic, discursive terms. There is no non-discursive intermediary in their model, no place for figural processes of communication.

I will not pursue this conceptualization further, since my purpose is not to elaborate upon psychoanalytic theory. Instead, I can simply affirm that the upshot here is a strong sense of the irreducibility of the unconscious as a dynamic operative within us and through all communication. Its presence can no doubt be captured adequately by other conceptual constructions than this one, but the important point is that we understand that it is something that we cannot eradicate, nor fully reason with. The mythic and rhetorical features present in popular television journalism, the symbolic and evocative dimensions of political talk, the arational features of everyday conversation, and that which lies beyond Habermas' communicative rationality – all these elements can be understood as manifestations of an unconscious which we will always have with us. What a perspective like Elliott's and Lash's helps us to see is that we can live with it, for the unconscious is not just the site of dark forces, fear, conflict and repression, but also of creativity, imagination and renewal.

Reassembling the reflexive subject

Thus far in this chapter I have been discussing a number of themes which stand opposed to the ideal of strictly rational communication: the slippery signification processes of language, its expressive and constitutive aspects, the cultural contingencies of communication, and the psychic region of the unconscious, which is the site the figurative mode of communication. All of these also contribute to what has been termed the decentred character of the subject. We are seemingly never one with ourselves, but always in some ways divided and fragmented within our subjectivities.

Some corners of social theory over the past two decades – especially post-structuralist and feminist varieties – have been offering up a strong version of the dislocated and displaced self. Foucault, for example, is still often credited (or blamed) for promulgating an extreme notion of the discursively generated and decentred subject, yet it tends to be overlooked that in his later work he drew back from the untenability of this severe position (see Dews, 1989, and Poster, 1989). In wryly lampooning the extreme poststructuralist position, Soper writes:

> I am sure that I am a discursively constructed subject. No matter under which aspect I conceive myself . . . I see most clearly that I am the site of intersection of a multiplicity of discourses and practices which have made me who I am. . . . I am aware that I am not an autonomous subject, but relating and deciding, feeling and reacting only through a grid of discourse and practice which I myself have not created. . . . And yet I think to myself, who is it who is certain of this? (1990:146)

While the extreme poststructuralist notion of the dispersed subject has been receiving a suitably sceptical treatment from many writers, few would be willing to swing the pendulum so far as to join with the position of somebody like the German social theorist Luhman, who argues 'there is no dual or even pluralistic self, no "I" distinct from "me", no personal identity distinct from social identity. These conceptions are . . . without sufficient foundations in the facts of consciousness' (quoted in Barrett, 1991:11).

We must end up somewhere between the extreme poles. It is important to avoid the pitfall of essentialist reasoning in trying to make sense of processes of subjectivity or in defining the subject in general. This is by now becoming a commonplace in progressive social theory. But in countering the other extreme, in recuperating some sense of the coherence of the subject against the forces arrayed against it, it is important that we do not slip in an exclusively rationalist argument through the back door. The notion of reflexivity, appropriately modified, is helpful in this regard.

Reflexivity, at the individual and collective level, is of course one of the leit-motifs of the theories of modernity, as we see not least in the works of Giddens (1991), Beck (1992), Lash and Urry (1994) and Beck et al. (1994). In the modern world, as traditional frameworks are eroded, people (and institutions) increasingly come to reflect on their actions, norms and goals; decisions, passive choices, performances, general 'life plan' or 'life style', and much else from all sectors of one's life, come under scrutiny. With the loosening of traditional sociocultural structures and practices, a larger playing field opens up for agency. Less becomes taken for granted, more becomes problematized. Indeed, Lash (1994) suggests that one of the key (albeit extremely complex) trends of modernity has been the weakening of traditional social structures in shaping the individual and their increasing replacement by structures of communication and information. Thus, one can speculate that as historical circumstances increasingly render a unified subjectivity more remote, reflexivity gains in intensity. However, such a grandiose historical perspective is not necessary for my point here. Rather, reflexivity in some degree is a constitutive and operative feature of the psyche. Against external social contingency, symbolic/semiotic instability, and internal divisiveness, we find the ongoing struggle not only to shape an identity but also to scrutinize oneself. But just what does this mean? As Lash (1994) points out, the usual synonym for reflexivity is 'self-monitoring'. He is negative about the strong cognitive, even cybernetic tone to it. This is valid, even if we should not deny that reflexivity can *also* proceed along the lines of logic and propositional knowledge. However, reflexivity also includes (to round out the Kantian distinction) aesthetic and normative dimensions.

Lash opts for the aesthetic dimension, arguing that reflexivity is, at base, hermeneutic. Rather than self-monitoring, reflexivity implies self-interpretation; rather than logic, it involves intuition and imagination. In this sense, reflexivity can be posed against its antonym, namely non-reflection, the 'habits of the heart' – the practical sense embodied in Bourdieu's (1977) 'habitus' – conventional or habitual thought and behaviour in everyday life. While we need to take much for granted if daily life is to function in practical terms, as Berger and Luckmann (1967) argued, we can see the systematic blocking of aesthetic or intuitive reflexivity via communication (not least within the public sphere) as a key dynamic of the processes of ideology. This hinders the play of the imaginary within social interaction, working against dynamic sense-making. Without making new meanings of one's experiences, emancipatory impulses become blocked.

How does intuitive reflexivity proceed? I see two related mechanisms: narrative and tacit knowledge, both of which contribute to the coherence of the subject. Narrative is ubiquitous; we find it in stories, myths, history, journalism, comedy, conversation, and so on. Barthes notes that 'The narratives of the world are . . . present at all times, in all places, in all societies: the history of narrative begins with the history of (hu)mankind' (quoted in Richardson, 1990:117). Narrative is both a form of reasoning and a form of representation; it is the fundamental epistemic means by which people organize and make sense of their experiences. Through narrative we link experience and events to some larger episodic whole, the connections in themselves constituting meaning. We understand the world to a great extent in narrative terms, and talk about it and represent it in narrative terms. Moreover, we grasp, define and constitute ourselves as subjects via narrative. As Ricoeur (1984, 1986) points out, time is the quintessential factor and condition of human existence, and we make sense not only of the world but also of ourselves through 'humanizing' time in our narratives. From the horizon of the present, this helps us to construct awareness of the past and the future both in the social order and within our own biographies. The stories of the social world, as narrated in the public sphere of television journalism for example, interlace with the narratives of self. We strive for a sense of order, of congruity within each, while using each as a horizon to make sense, narratively, of the other. Not least, we engage in collective narratives: stories about the group, the nation, the movement, the political party, thereby affixing individual identity and subjectivity to collective ones.

Just to reiterate the point: narratives of self, of the group and of the social order as a whole do not necessarily follow the logico-scientific mode of reasoning, but constitute a distinct epistemological procedure (see, for example, Bruner, 1986). Narrative is thus a strategy which can (and often does, in my view) operate within the figural mode of signification, resonating with the unconscious. Therefore, we again come up to the limits of self-transparency, to Bauman's (1991) argument about the irreducibility of ambivalence.

As a corollary to this view of narrative as an epistemic category, whose importance is central in the processes of reflexivity, I will just briefly return to the distinction between explicit and implicit (or tacit) knowledge which I introduced in Chapter 3. Any number of versions of this distinction can be found in the philosophical literature (I base this partly on the Swedish philosopher, Molander, 1993), but for my purposes here we can make a schematic differentiation between knowledge as follows:

explicit	versus	**implicit**
propositional	versus	intuitive
instrumental	versus	normative-evaluative
aiming for control	versus	orientational
abstract, universal	versus	contextual, contingent
conceptual	versus	embodied
impersonal	versus	embedded in identity

I will not spell out each pair; the general point is self-evident. Once again, in dichotomizing, the premise is not that one side is somehow better than the other or that we should strive to eliminate one pole. The intent first of all is to argue against conflation: we make use of both forms of knowledge, both are important, and neither one is about to go away or be subsumed by the other. They coexist, often peacefully, at times conflicting. Secondly, with regard to reflexivity, implicit knowledge – characterized by terms such as those found in the above list – is the prevalent epistemic mode we use in the construction of our identities, in generating, modifying, and living with our sense of self. Explicit knowledge certainly comes into play, but it is not this which makes our identity 'come alive'.

Also, I would argue that it is largely through implicit knowledge, with its embodied, normative-evaluative dimension, that *moral* reflexivity takes place, that we cultivate (or not) our moral identities as subjects capable of taking a moral point of view, of generating moral imagination. Indeed, Soper (1990) follows up the ironic comments quoted at the beginning of this chapter with a discussion that it is precisely the universal capacity to make moral judgements, at times even against the grain of established norms and values, which signals the albeit contingent dimension of autonomy and coherence of the subject.

This theme of moral reflexivity takes us back to the discussion in Chapter 3 on television journalism and moral sensibility and empathy. There I referred to the importance of compelling narrative qualities in evoking a moral response. Also, I pointed to the centrality of the dialogic dimension in addressing people's intuitive, emotional side. This emphasis on dialogue resonates with Taylor's point above about the importance of the expressive dimension of language in establishing intersubjectivity in dialogue. In moral reflexivity, in the act of making normative choices in a self-conscious manner, we not only consolidate our identities, our subjectivities, but we do so relationally, with the 'Other'.

Imagination and emancipation

In this final section, I want to return to the theme of imagination and look at it in relation to rationality, or more generally, reason. I situate this relationship against the backdrop of critical, emancipatory social theory.

In the previous chapter I took up postmodernism as a mode of thought which engages the Enlightenment tradition in a constructive dialogue, and mentioned that we now find this dialogue even within critical theory. There are some critics, many of whom share much of Habermas' philosophical and political orientation, who see his work moving away from the critical dimension, indeed, even becoming a form of 'traditional' or 'positive' theory. Such writers make use of elements from Freud, Gadamer, Foucault and other counter-Enlightenment figures in efforts to renew critical theory. Hoy and McCarthy (1994), via an extended debate, present the arguments for the respective sides within critical theory, demonstrating not least the convoluted nature of the issues at stake. Yet the issues cluster around the notion of reason, and they capture this eloquently by referring to a painting by Goya, portraying a man asleep at a desk, with monsters of the night swirling about him. On the desk is engraved the title of the work: 'El sueño de la razón produce monstruos'.

> What interests us here is the title's notorious ambiguity, which expresses a widespread ambivalence about Goya's own era, particularly about eighteenth-century

ideals of enlightenment. The title can be read as either 'The *sleep* of reason produces monsters' or 'The *dream* of reason produces monsters'. The first and primary
reading says that when reason goes to sleep monsters are produced. This slogan of
modern enlightenment is flatly contradicted by the second, counterenlightenment
reading, which says that the monsters are themselves reason's dreams. On this latter reading, reason is not simply a light opposed to the darkness of fantasy, but has
its own dark side. (Hoy and McCarthy, 1994:1)

In this growing dialogue within critical theory, emancipatory projects,
notions of progress, even visions of Utopia itself, all become subjected to
reflexive scrutiny, and become modified – but not necessarily rejected – in the
process. The tenuousness of the modernist project of democracy does not
mean we abandon it, but rather try to rethink it. For the left and for those
who espouse some sort of progressive view (and I am of the opinion that
even though these terms today can be quite problematic, we have not reached
a situation where they are totally meaningless), there is no predefined political programme or automatic agenda which follows from this interrogation.
The postmodern mode, in Smart's words '. . . constitutes a site, a space, or
clearing for political possibilities, rather than a distinctive political
strategy'.

Charting a cautious course between the apocalypse and the millenium also
implies that a rigid distinction between realism and Utopianism is uncalled
for, since neither option is fully identifiable, as both Smart (1993) and
Giddens (1991) assert. Utopian thought becomes not that which is by definition unfeasible, but rather in Ricoeur's (1986:16) words, the product of our
'ability to conceive of an empty place from which to look at ourselves'.
Moreover, 'The decisive trait is . . . not irrealizability but the preservation of
opposition' (Ricoeur, 1986:180). In terms of subjectivity, emancipation and
the public sphere, what is called for is a new lease on imagination. Smart elab-
orates on the idea of grasping the possibilities provided by the present, and
avoiding the all-too-real potential disasters we also are living with:

> The interrogative character of modern reason, the undermining of answers and dis-
> placement of 'solutions' by a radical questioning form of life, simultaneously make
> necessary the constitution of analytic and existential practices that dare think
> and/or imagine the as-yet unthought and as-yet unexperienced, to imagine the
> forms of life that might be reflexively constituted through continuing process of
> (post)modernization. . . . In so far as we find ourselves living with, if not at the lim-
> its of modernity, modern reason needs to be constituted, and to that end perhaps it
> has become necessary to nourish the *post*modern imagination. (1993:106)

This step is really not a radical departure from the Enlightenment, but more
of a reorientation of it; Rundell (1994) argues that we can find in Kant an
acknowledgement of the power of the imagination, that in his efforts to found
a transcendental notion of reason, Kant realizes that imagination too is transcendental, irreducible. Imagination is an essential condition for reason; we
might see it as reason's 'repressed' Romantic *alter ego*. Many observers have
been witnessing and arguing for the recovery of imagination in western
thought, as part of the reflexive encounter with the Enlightenment. Ricoeur
(1994), Castoriadis (1994), Madison (1988) and Kearney (1991) are just some

of the authors who, in various ways, place imagination at the centre of contemporary social thought.

Such thinking of course hovers at a very high philosophical altitude; how does the emphasis on imagination take on a more concrete relevance for us? If imagination refers to a core component in philosophy and social theory, we might find its practical corollary within everyday life in the cognate concept of the imaginary. This term is multivalent and finds use within a number of not always entirely compatible discourses, but let me just point to one rendering which ties in with the discussion here and is not overly abstract. From a social construction of reality perspective, Shotter (1993a) makes the familiar point that, in everyday conversation, the discourses (and words within them) that we use not only refer to objects, but also produce them. To understand better the status of these discursively produced objects, however, Shotter argues for the category of the imaginary, which he sees as 'positioned between the real or the factual, and the nonexistent or the ficticious' (Shotter, 1993a:80). Imaginary objects must be understood as:

incomplete, ongoing, on the way to being other than what they are . . . [T]hey are nonlocatable, either in space and time, but can nonetheless have 'real' attributes in the sense of functioning in people's actions, enabling them to achieve *reproducible results* by the use of socially shared procedures . . . they 'subsist' only in people's practices, in the 'gaps', 'zones' or 'boundaries' between people . . . [T]o this extent . . . we must talk of them as 'negotiated', 'political', 'contestable' or 'prospective' . . . entities, ones which exist 'in' the world only to the extent that they can play a part in people's discourses. (Shotter, 1993a:90)

The imaginary can thus be understood as instances of imagination embodied in the context of social practice. Shotter makes the point that attempts to complete fully the imaginary as factually real objects leads to what he calls 'entrapment'. Processes of meaning production become ossified, freeze dried, as reification rears its head. This perspective emphasizes how the imaginary is essential to keeping everyday life open to new articulations, maintaining a dynamic quality of sense-making. From the horizon of politics, an important orientation becomes how in everyday life this open, discursive quality can be fostered by institutional and cultural formations. If, at the level of theory, it is a question of balancing the security of rational analysis with the openness of innovative imagination, at the level of lived experience the issue is one of the balance between the solidity, the stability, of meaning with its negotiable, contestable antithesis. Critical theory has long warned us of the dangers of identifying reality as the full realization of concepts; the experience of 'already existing socialism' is a grim recent reminder of this. We must allow even such notions as 'democracy' to retain some of their imaginary quality.

Likewise, the concept of emancipation: it must be conceptually meaningful, as well as evocative and compelling. Yet any project labelled as emancipatory can never be defined as fully achieved; the quality of emancipatory, the state of emancipation, must always preserve its anchoring in the discursive, contestable imaginary. Pieterse (1992) has some helpful thoughts on the concept of emancipation in this regard. He notes its Enlightenment origins and its association with an understanding of progress moving towards freedom and equality. He further comments on how there has tended to be a circularity of definitions involving the concepts of emancipation, liberation and empowerment, with each term's definition being rather fluid. Pieterse finds a fruitful step in Foucault's concept of power, which among other things argues that power is not merely something negative and repressive, but also positive, creative and productive. Moreover, we can never get beyond power, never eliminate it; there is no transcendental state to strive for. There are only new configurations of power, new discourses. Overthrowing old constellations of power yield new forms of domination; in terms of the phenomenon of power, there is no future which is fundamentally different from the present. While this perspective on power seemingly constitutes a retreat from common notions of progress, Pieterse still affirms the critical importance of emancipation.

His view is refracted through lenses which bring into focus multidimensionality and constructivism rather than a singular determinist materialism or any other mono-logical mechanism. We see here yet another instance of a critical postmodern mode of thinking. According to Pieterse, we must speak of emancipations, in the plural, and acknowledge a diversity of struggles which aim for an inclusive democratization. The postmodern mode heightens sensibilities towards the unstable, the indeterminate, and this is no less true in the realm of politics; we cannot accept a monopoly on the definition or focus of emancipation. Further, even if we manage to avoid capitulating to the vision of the apocalyptic, we must also remind ourselves there can be no millenium, there is no endpoint in sight beyond (new) antagonisms, beyond politics (see Mouffe, 1993).

The project of emancipation becomes one of a continual striving to level and disperse power. What constitutes the emancipatory is not a final state but rather a direction: 'progressive' is fundamentally that which fosters the distribution of social power. The terrain of such efforts is potentially the entire range of the social, yet in most analyses the salient nodes are far from random. Class may no longer be the only focus, though its relevance has hardly passed into history, as Lash and Urry – as well as many others – have argued. It shares the stage with such struggles as those around gender, race and ethnicity, ecology, and technocratic rationality. In all of these efforts – and here the Enlightenment tradition shows its continuity – emancipation involves a moral vision, a self-conscious ethical horizon. Whether this vision can also encompass a shared commitment to the rules and procedures of a plural democratic order, and thereby form political alliances, becomes a key question for the efficacy of progressive politics on a wider scale.

There are many adjectives one could apply to this orientation to emancipation and to the political, for example, decentred, constructivist, neogramscian. Traditional liberals and Marxists no doubt can add their own, more pejorative adjectives. But I hasten to add that this is merely an orientation, it does not lay claim to being a political programme. What I hoped to show in Chapter 4, however, is that this view of emancipation is coherent with a general rethinking, not only the public sphere, but also of political and social theory.

Commenting on the media from the standpoint of imagination and politics, Kearney writes:

> A postmodern hermeneutics of imagining might thus be in a position to co-join, without confusing, the often opposed claims of poetics and ethics. The poetic commitment to *storytelling* may well prove indispensable to the ethical commitment to *history-making*. Ethics without poetics leads to a censuring of imagination; poetics without ethics leads to dangerous play. But if a poetics of imagining is ever to respond to the ethical crisis of our Civilization of the Image, I suspect it will not be by beating a retreat to the modernist sanctuary of High Art. The votaries of poetical imagination can no longer afford to hold the so-called 'mass media' in contempt. It is not only in novels and paintings that the crisis of imagination is to be addressed but also in television, video and cinema – those media which most drastically epitomize the postmodern paradox of the image. The labyrinth must be confronted from within as well as from without. (1991:228)

The communicating subject, like the project of modernity as a whole, is poised in a position of ambiguity, with no secure foundations to cling to and no guarantees as to the future. However, to say that each moment is pregnant with promise and danger, while perhaps true in a formal sense, is to overdramatize. For the majority of us, for most of the time, our subjectivities, our identities, are not up for grabs. Our unconscious is operative, which may at times lead to repression, other times to creativity. Mostly we just muddle through, occasionally we encounter significant turning points. If we insert this view into the context of television and the public sphere, we find that the theoretic horizon may not be profoundly altered; even in the public sphere, and not least in watching television journalism, we apparently also do a lot of muddling through. But I hope that the reflections in this chapter helped to clarify some of the conditions, indeed, the preconditions, for our communicative and subjective involvement within the public sphere. With this frame of reference, we are less likely either to engage in misplaced critique – such as 'why does television journalism not just present plain facts and cut out the dramatics' – or to indulge in unrealistic expectations, such as anticipating that we can keep objective facts, personal identity and political will separate when we are discussing politics and trying to clarify our opinions.

From these theoretical perspectives on communication and subjectivity, we turn now to the larger contexts of civil society, sociocultural interaction, and citizenship.

6

Civil society and its citizens

A continual difficulty in media studies has been to balance a focus on the media with broader horizons of social theory. Media researchers are understandably inclined to put the media at the centre of their attention, yet our understanding of the media must always be informed by theory and empirical data which highlight their societal contexts. In this chapter, I take a few steps in the direction charted by two concerns within social theory, namely those of civil society and citizenship. The processes of television reception among viewers provide a conceptual link to both of these theoretic terrains.

First, civil society can be seen as offering a way to conceptually gather up the sites of reception and recontextualize them to a larger theoretic horizon which has relevance for both democratic theory and the public sphere. Secondly, if our concerns are with the public sphere, the category of 'audience', although necessary, becomes inadequate. This is because the notion of audience and the discourses in which it operates tend to frame our understanding of reception in terms of people's relationship to television. In this mediacentric perception, the larger horizons remain largely scenic. 'Audiences' certainly exist in the phenomenal world, even if they are far from fixed, and the experience of 'audiencing' is not always a consistent one. But as I have discussed, the public sphere requires 'publics', in the sense of interacting social agents. The category of audience becomes too constricted in this regard. We need to move, in our theoretic vistas, from audience members to citizens.

Reception research still has much to tell us about what takes place in people's sociocultural interaction with television and with each other in front of the screen. My point is that we might derive still more benefit from it by trying analytically to resituate its empirical findings – when and where appropriate – from the sites of reception and the culture of everyday life to civil society, and by recasting viewership as a potential moment of citizenship.

I begin with a brief discussion of some important contributions to reception analysis and try to show that we can see in them the need for a broader contextualization. From there I present the contours of a contemporary perspective on civil society. I follow up this discussion with some reflections on the related theme of talk and the construction of the social world. I then turn my attention to the concept of citizenship, which has been undergoing considerable re-examination in recent years. My hope is that these explorations, though they undeniably complicate our picture of the public sphere, will suggest a richer understanding of its conditions and dynamics.

The contexts of reception

Audience research in the 1980s prompted debates as to the active/passive nature of television viewing, replaying the traditional discussions about the power of the media versus the power of the audience. Reception studies went far in demonstrating that people in front of the screen are indeed active in that they generate meaning from what they see on television. The degree of freedom accorded to the audience in their sense-making was overstated in some corners, as Curran (1990) argues in his critique of the 'new revisionists'; the problems of social structure, the dynamics of ideology and the hierarchical configurations of social power cannot be transcended merely by the interpretive practices of viewers. Yet the new, more robust portrait of the audience is important. It is a conceptual prerequisite for a public sphere.

We must recall that reception should be seen as a phase of the public sphere's dimension of sociocultural interaction; moreover, one of the fundamental features of television is precisely its status as sociocultural experience. Reception can be cast in narrow terms, where it treats just the immediate sense-making of viewers in front of the screen, or it can be given a wider focus, including the entire social ecology of the domestic setting (see Moores, 1993a, for a survey of reception studies). Silverstone (1990) suggestively sketches an anthropology of the audience, emphasizing the embeddedness of television viewing in the larger patterns of everyday life. Though this may be empirically daunting, for a concern with the public sphere, it is conceptually the appropriate stance. Further, the public sphere focus means that reception should chiefly be concerned with television genres with a high degree of referentiality, that is, journalism, and with the 'public knowledge project' (keeping in mind, however, the intertwinement of public knowledge and popular culture, as I discussed in Chapter 2). In these ways, reception research can begin to delineate the articulations between the practices at the site of reception with those within larger sociopolitical circumstances.

Texts by Jensen (1990), Morley (1992) and Ang (1994), each in their own way, are examples of innovative and important developments in reception analysis, and all of them, in different ways, address the question of context. In dealing with television news, Jensen argues, rightly in my view, that it is profitable to move beyond the individual text and look at the genre itself and the social uses to which it is put. His research reveals that television news as genre has several uses or relevances for its viewers, thereby:

> suggesting a contradictory or divided form of everyday consciousness . . . In fact, polysemy may be a characteristic of the reception of news, which bears witness to contradictions at the level of social structures. It is the polysemy of reception, rather than the polysemy of media texts, which must be explored in order to assess concretely the relative power of media and audiences. (Jensen, 1990:58)

In his interviews, Jensen found a clear contradiction within this polysemy: the lip-service paid to the informational uses of TV news was overshadowed by its uses for self-legitimation and diversion, with embarrassment often arising over the latter. He goes on to point out that television news offers a daily exercise in viewers' sense of their own political competence (thus self-legiti-mation) but that news programmes are:

> not conceived of as a point of departure for action in the institutions and organi-zations of political life. The contradictory nature of news reception bears witness, in a wider perspective, to a divided form of everyday consciousness which derives from contradictions at the macro-level of social organization. On the one hand, the news media are potentially a tool for political influence and change; on the other hand, such social uses of news by the audience-public are not institutionalized and do not have a precedent in practical politics. (Jensen, 1990:73)

He concludes that for the viewers, meaning production may potentially chal-lenge dominant definitions of reality, but normally does not, because the processes of sense-making in relation to TV news are overdetermined by both the social definitions of the genre and by macrosocietal structures. The con-sequence is the reproduction of the prevailing hegemony. 'Ultimately', he suggests, 'it is the audience-public that must insist on the substantive uses of media, both within the political system and in other areas of social and cul-tural life, by transcending the ambiguous role of recipient' (Jensen, 1990:74).

Yet, audience-publics cannot transcend the role of recipient while retaining the role of audience: only by departing from that role will they stop being recipients and start being producers – of political talk and action. Viewers must take the step to act as citizens. It is not just an empirical question of viewers turning off their sets, it also has to do with a recontextualization at the conceptual level. We need to theorize actors as citizens and we need to have an analytic understanding of the specific contexts of action which are accessible to them; particular settings need to be identified. When people make talk and take such action, they leave behind their role as audience.

But in acting as citizens, people do not necessarily leave behind all the sense-making they have done as audiences, which, I would argue, speaks for the continued relevance of the reception site and its practices. As Jensen points out, if this reception is at bottom contradictory in the light of the social definitions of the television news genre and of the macrostructures of society, then these contradictions need to be further examined and theorized; for example, how do some people manage to overcome the contradictions and take various forms of action in their roles as citizens? In what contexts does such political activity manifest itself? How does TV news reception proceed for such people, and what relevances should it be accorded?

To approach this ethnographically, we need conceptually to develop a notion of citizen, as an identity-in-process forged out of sets of contradictory social and discursive forces. I explore this in more detail below, but I think a first step, taking off from Jensen's insightful paper, is to delete the hyphen he uses to link audience and public – the latter, as I read it, being his term for the role of citizen. By treating audience and public as distinct, we will be in a bet-ter position to probe social articulations with the site of reception.

I turn now to Morley, who continues the ground-breaking work he has done on reception by taking up the very evocative question of how television mediates the global and the local. By making use of some Meyrowitz's theses of television's contribution to eroding our 'sense of place', Morley suggests that the media relativize our geographic coordinates and that community as such is no longer directly linked to physical locality: '. . . experience is both unified beyond localities and fragmented within them' (1992:280). Morley then points out the central weakness in the view presented by Meyrowitz and others: the abstract generalizations which refuse to confront the question of power. While the electronic media are clearly contributing to a decline in the importance of locality and the emergence of 'psychological neighbour-hoods', these developments are not randomized: certain kinds of media function in particular ways for certain groups of people – with specific consequences which have political character. Differences are by no means levelled and geography retains analytic importance. For Morley, the issue of spaces and places becomes (here he quotes the geographer Soja): 'how relations of power and discipline are inscribed into the apparently innocent spatiality of social life' (1992:271). Further, Morley advocates that: '. . . we must attend to the need to construct a properly postmodern geography of the relations between communication and power and the contemporary transformation of the public and private spheres' (1992:282). The overall goal, at the end, he suggests, is to '. . . connect the domestic, the local, the national, the inter- or trans-national aspects of communication' (1992:289).

To get at this, Morley argues, rightly in my view, that it is '. . . through detailed "domestic" or "local" studies, focused in the first instance, on the "politics of the sitting room" that we will most effectively grasp the processes of the global and the local (or homogenization and fragmentation)' (1992:272). He effectively responds to the critique aimed at such enterprises, which has argued that this concern with micro-processes misses the larger sociopolitical picture. Such critique ignores several points: that sitting rooms are often the site of important political conflicts, not least in gender terms; and that the construction of collective identities such as 'the nation' and the linkage between the domestic and various national, international 'communities' proceeds via television – in the sitting room. Indeed, one of the central roles of broadcasting has been to mediate between public and private life. One of the interesting things about this, Morley notes, is that in this interface, TV 'domesticates' the 'public realm' while at the same time transforming the private; it becomes 'socialized', as it were. The consequence is that the 'space (and experience) created is neither "public" nor private in the traditional senses' (1992:285).

This is tantalizing. The argument about the importance of the reception site is compelling, as is the question of the power relations at work in mediating the sitting room, the local, the national and the global. So how do we conceptualize the links beyond the sitting room? The spatial/geographical aspects of mediated community are suggestive, though we must be alert to the limits of community founded solely on shared media experience, as I discussed in Chapter 4 with regard to globalization processes. However, it would seem that, at the very least, television has a significant impact on the public/private distinction. It scrambles the distinction in such a way that reception as an activity potentially transcends the geography of the private by discursively positioning the viewer as a citizen, as a member of the public.

The specific contexts to which any given instance of reception may relate can of course potentially be defined by viewers in any number of ways. Ang (1994) underscores this point and argues for the ultimate indeterminacy of how any act of reception can be contextualized beyond itself. She highlights the current crisis in audience studies with reference to the postmodern conditions of social change and their accompanying epistemological quandries. She too underscores the embeddedness of television viewing in everyday life and its heterogeneity and complexity. Sense-making from television must be understood in terms of the multidimensional and intersubjective networks in which it takes place; these are always concrete, and it is these specific contexts which shape the meanings people derive from viewing. This emphasis is the key to Ang's notion of radical contextualism: '. . . theoretically, every situation is uniquely characterized by an indefinite multiplicity of contexts that cannot be known in advance. Further, contexts are not mutually exclusive, but interlocking and interacting, superimposed upon one another as well as indefinitely proliferating in time and space' (1992:11).

Acknowledging that reality looks like this is in my view important, and though it may make research still more complicated and messy than it already is, it is difficult to not concur with Ang's point here. What I would add, however, is that to accept this view of the multiplicities of reception's social and discursive ecology does not mean that such contexts by definition always must resist being productively theorized and generalized. We must allow for a distinction between viewers' subjective contextualization and alternative, analytic contexts derived from social analysis. For example, viewers may or may not contextualize their sense-making of a programme in political terms. Whether or not they do is of great interest, but researchers must be free to draw their own conclusions about the political implications of this sense-making, using broader sociopolitical frameworks of analysis. Also, to find patterns of similarity and articulation between contexts need not deny the specificity of each instance. However, carried to its extreme, it would seem that radical contextualism could work against precisely the kind of knowledge necessary to determine political relevance.

Reception studies thus evoke the question of the broader contexts of reception itself. At this juncture, it would be productive to introduce the notion of civil society. This concept could encompass the terrain of reception's social ecology in everyday life, yet could situate it in a framework which puts the accent on the political and the para-political, articulating with the terrain of the public sphere.

The horizon of civil society

If we reject Margaret Thatcher's famous proposition that there is no such thing as society, we must still be able to locate society as something beyond the individual, the market and the state. Of what does it consist? While this can be answered in many ways, the notion of civil society suggestively serves to capture the domain of uncoerced interaction and association within daily life. The history of civil society as a concept meanders through several centuries of European social thought and political philosophy, in particular as a counterpoint to theories of the state (see Keane, 1988a, 1988b). We can view attempts in the eighteenth century to formulate a vision of civil society as an effort to come to terms with the fundamental questions concerning the relationship between the individual and society, between the public and the private – questions, in other words, which are still of central relevance today. In this early modern period, attempted solutions were premised on notions of natural human sympathy and moral sentiments, premises which did not fare well in the writings of Hegel and of Marx. Within liberal political philosophy, the concept of civil society was built upon the idea of the autonomous individual pursuing his or her own interests, but this continues to raise problems of how the individual is to be integrated into any cohesive community.

The term continues to circulate today, even undergoing a certain 'revival' in recent years. We witnessed its re-emergence as an ideal among dissidents in Central and Eastern Europe prior to the collapse of communism, though, as Seligman (1993) ventures, its use there may have been largely as a neutral synonym for the general concept of democracy, rather than representing a new analytic turn. The term 'democracy' itself, having been incorporated into such formulas as 'People's Democracy', may have been seen as too tainted by historical experience. Gellner (1994), in a sober reflection on civil society in post-communist Eastern Europe, wonders if its historical and cultural conditions – among them the habits and attitudes characteristic of liberal democracy – are sufficiently strong after so many decades of totalitarian rule and with no experience of a market economy. Even in the West we see a renewed interest in the concept of civil society. While conceptual and theoretic development here is important, we should not lose sight of the fact that any given society has its own particular history of the evolution of civil society, anchored in its own political, social and cultural circumstances. Tracing the development of civil society in Sweden (see Micheletti, 1994) – with its history of social democracy, corporatism, popular movements and adult education, and, until recently, a very homogenous cultural and ethnic composition – tells a different tale compared to, say, the United States of America.

Seligman (1993) sees two basic understandings of civil society in circulation. One operates on an institutional-organizational level, and is closely akin to prevailing notions of the general institutional and legal requisites for a democratic society with full-fledged citizenship. The other treats civil society more on the level of beliefs and value systems, with a Durkheimian stress on universalistic moral bonds as a foundation of solidarity. While each version has its own problematics, I would argue that both aspects – appropriate institutional conditions and value systems – are necessary, a point I will expand upon below. The double set of requisites does not, of course, make the goal of civil society easier to attain. I would, however, affirm its importance but also indicate that this concept, like democracy, the public sphere, and citizenship, embodies both analytic ideas and normatic ideals. Seligman (1993:159) tells us to keep in mind 'just how fragile an edifice the idea of civil society is – especially in today's world'.

Keane (1988a:33–6) suggests that the political dichotomy of left and right is not very helpful in sorting out this history and developing a modern and progressive understanding of civil society. While we may find in Gramsci something of a useable tripartite model of state, civil society and economy, most of the Marxian tradition has tended to collapse civil society into bourgeois society, thereby dismissing it as the domain of ideology. And as a blueprint for the organization of society, the meshing of social life with political life has not met with much historical success. The right today tries to equate civil society with the space where the private citizen can pursue his or her individualism, free from the interventionism of the state, thereby turning the concept into an argument for neo-liberal market forces. However, other strands of the broader liberal tradition, starting with Mill and de Tocqueville, have put politics before economics and appropriately warned that the state can abuse its powers, engulf and smother civil society, and undo the fragile progress toward democratization.

As I noted in Chapter 1, a productive perspective emerges in the work of Keane (1988a) and Held (1989) whereby civil society and the state are each seen as constituting the conditions for the other's democratization; what emerges is the need for a double democratization. Moreover, if, as Walzer (1992) suggests, civil society is not to be reduced to the political, politics remain a permanent potentiality within civil society; there can be no hard and fast boundary between the political and the sociocultural. The sociality and the discourses of everyday life cannot be a priori defined as excluding the realm of politics – nor resting content with conventional understandings of what precisely constitutes politics – but we should see civil society as something other than a political arena.

Empirically, the separation between state and civil society may not always be very clear-cut, particularly in societies such as Sweden's, which are characterized by a high degree of corporatism. If, for example, as in Sweden's, many groups and associations receive state funding, does this tarnish their civil society status? Despite such classificatory difficulties, I would argue that the conceptual distinction is crucial, since, without a horizon of civil society, the whole project of democracy becomes vacuous. With regard to the funding of associations, it may well be that it is not a question of whether there is such funding or not, but rather the specific circumstances of the funding: for example, who has access to it, what strings are attached, what are the long-term consequences of such funding? Thus, as far as Sweden is concerned, it would seem that the conditions of state financing has in fact largely enhanced that which we would call civil society, and not merely incorporated it into the state. In practice, it is not a question of a water-tight boundary between state and civil society, but instead that there be a relationship between them which fosters the democratization of both.

By far the most ambitious of recent attempts to deal with the concept of civil society is Cohen and Arato's (1992) massive work. Their model is both descriptive and normative. It claims to offer a particular picture of how society – from the angle of citizens' practices – functions in the modern world. At the same time, their work centres on defending and extending those historical gains from the liberal tradition which are worthwhile (such as legal rights of the individual and viable mechanisms for representative democracy), while at the same time trying to expand civil society as a space of uncoerced interaction. The democratic vision of enhanced autonomy and emancipatory practices is relevant, not just with regard to people's relations with the state but even in the culture of their daily lives.

In compressed terms, they see civil society in the West as a domain of social interaction which is situated between market and state (and organized political society). This domain is characterized by a pluralism of forms of social life and by publicity in appropriate institutions of culture and communication. At the same time this domain is characterized by degrees of privacy, allowing for individual development and moral choices. Finally, the domain of civil society is characterized by legal frameworks to guarantee basic rights and to secure pluralism, publicity and privacy from the state, and, at least partially, from the economy. In this regard, they follow Gramsci's three-part model. Civil society, in other words, is distinct from political parties and institutions (such as parliaments) as well as from corporations, co-operatives, firms and other economic organizations. Moreover, Cohen and Arato's orientation is towards the institutional aspects of civil society, though they seldom take detailed organizational considerations into account. In their view, civil society is institutionally composed chiefly of:

(a) the intimate sphere (especially the family);
(b) the sphere of associations (in particular, voluntary associations);
(c) social movements (which point to its political relevance); and
(d) the many forms of public communication.

We should take note here that this rendering departs from the traditional view – found in Hegel – which associates civil society exclusively with public life and situates family and domestic life as its polar opposite. Instead, here the public/private divide runs *through* civil society, which has implications I will come to presently. Otherwise, the first three institutional areas on this list should be fairly clear even if, empirically, problems of boundaries may arise (for example, if the Greens get enough votes to enter parliament, do they cease to be a social movement and part of civil society?). The category of public communication, however, raises conceptual problems, to which I will also return shortly.

Institutionalized lifeworlds

An important feature of these institutional dimensions is that they are stabilized by fundamental legal rights. These have to do with cultural reproduction (freedoms of thought, press, speech and communication), social integration (freedom of association and assembly) and the protection of privacy, intimacy and the inviolability of the person. There are two other complexes of rights: one mediates between civil society and the market economy (rights of property, contract and labour), the other between civil society and the bureaucratic state (political rights of citizens, welfare rights of clients). How these complexes of rights are aligned determines to a great extent the nature of civil society. Thus, they are a fundamental organizing principle, and for any democratic project it is crucial that these rights be vigorously defended and expanded.

From de Tocqueville, Cohen and Arato emphasize the idea that the democratic nature of political culture or social and political organizations cannot be maintained if there is not active participation on the part of citizens in egalitarian institutions and civil associations. Thus, their model of civil society is seen as sociologically furnishing a 'training ground' for a viable democratic culture. Associational, small-scale self-organizational interaction thus helps not only prepare private individuals for political activity and power holding, but also to preserve the connection between 'prepolitical' social networks and political activity. Civil society is thus created through various forms of self-constitution and self-mobilization. At the same time, I would add, the settings of civil society – which encompass the discursive, spatial and communal dimensions of sociocultual interaction – are the sites where perhaps most processes of individual and collective identity formation take place.

For Cohen and Arato, civil society stands in a dialectical relationship to the political; the political role of civil society is seen not as aiming for the direct control of political power, '. . . but to the generation of influence through the life of democratic associations and unconstrained discussion in the cultural public sphere. Such a role is inevitably diffuse and inefficient. Thus the mediating role of political society between civil society and the state is indispensible' (Cohen and Arato, 1992:ix). Ideally, civil society would function in a similar mediating way *vis-à-vis* economic society but, under capitalist relations, this vector is obviously less pronounced. Here the limits of the liberal legacy come into sharp relief. However, they point out that the economy is by no means immune to pressures from civil society. Their larger theoretical point is that under the present historical circumstances there is no revolution in the economic system on the agenda; Marxist socialist revolution is no longer a viable option.

A good deal of Cohen and Arato's line of reasoning takes the form of an encounter with Habermas, including his theory about the public sphere (1989) and his later theories on communicative action (1984, 1987) where he introduces the system/lifeworld model. In this presentation I cannot retrace all the steps they take, or reproduce Habermas' theoretic edifice, but it may be of help to mention a few points around his system/lifeworld dichotomy. This model has understandably gained considerable currency. These two categories are handy labels, but behind them is an enormously complex framework which entails, not least, an attempt theoretically to reconstruct historical materialism. For our purposes here, we can note that in the modern world, according to Habermas, societies must make use of instrumental, goal-oriented rationality in order to reproduce themselves. Specifically, such rationality is embodied in the dual 'system' of state administration and market, which instrumentally functions as a steering mechanism. For Habermas, we recall, it is important to retrieve some element of the Enlightenment's rationality as liberatory; thus he introduces the concept of the communicative rationality of the lifeworld as the conceptual polarity to the strategic rationality of the system.

According to Habermas, communicative rationality, which I discussed in the previous chapter, comprises among other things the open negotiation of norms and the striving for intersubjectivity and consensus. Habermas' thesis is that modernity involves an increasing differentiation between system and lifeworld, between strategic and instrumental rationality, and the colonization of the latter by the former. That is, strategic rationality – instrumental, goal-oriented logic – is increasingly seeping into and replacing what should be communicative rationality between people. The conditions of intersubjectivity are being eroded by the steering mechanisms. To just convey a sense of the complexity involved here, we must understand, for example, that there are tensions between the political and economic subsystems (for example, the crisis of the welfare state) and that strategic rationality is not merely a creeping cancer to be combated in all instances, but is also a requisite for the lifeworld to function in modern society; the problem is that it is expanding beyond its 'suitable' boundaries. Further, Habermas specifies within the lifeworld Kantian subdomains of science, morality and aesthetics, which implies a contextual differentiation of communicative rationality – different modes in different settings.

For all its theoretic utility and dramatic flair, this modernized version of a theory of reification is not without its difficulties and should not in turn be reified and engraved in granite. It is a theoretically useful construct, but not without its inner problems. Baxter (1987), for instance, points out that the notion of the system colonizing the lifeworld gives rise to the somewhat odd picture that 'formal organizations in state and economy are independent of norms, values and personal motivations' (Baxter 1987:72). This in turn makes the category of the lifeworld somewhat slippery. On the one hand it points to culture, society and personality as *resources* that function as a backdrop, a horizon, to all social action. It thus has to do with problematics of all action, of all human communication: the mutual negotiation of intersubjectivity. On the other hand, it is easy to read the concept as signifying specific *settings* or spheres of action, such as the family, neighbourhood, associations, and so on. We begin to think of the lifeworld as a vague synonym for the microworlds of everyday life in general, when in fact it should be seen as a resource anchored in these settings.

Such a train of thought may also lead us to erroneously dismiss Habermas' 'system' as a realm beyond human subjectivity and intervention. Thus, from the standpoint of civil society, one may too readily ignore the possibilities for democratization (and enhanced communication) within the political and economic subspheres. One may, perhaps unnecessarily, assume a defensive stance which in essence surrenders the political and economic steering systems to instrumental rationality, ignoring the fact that these institutions are populated by people who operate within *their* specific lifeworlds and are not, by definition, beyond communicative reach. In short: even the state and the economy are reproduced daily by the people who embody those multiplicities of social relations, and this reproduction is carried out to a great extent via discourse, that is, people talking and writing to each other – though, of course, it is never a question of *mere* discourse: institutionalized power (using strategic rationality) figures prominently. We must not lose sight of the larger interplay between system and lifeworld, between public and private, or – phrased in the vocabulary of Keane and Held – of the interplay and double democratization of state and civil society. (Enhanced democratization of the state may well have a 'spill-over effect' on the market as well.)

I take up this discussion of Habermas' system and lifeworld categories as a sort of preamble to Cohen and Arato's use of them. They underscore the duality of the system – state administration and market – and further expand on the notion of the lifeworld. Their major move is to treat civil society as the *institutionalized* lifeworld. I take institutionalization to proceed socioculturally and/or legally. Thus, whether we are talking about the lifeworld as communicative horizons and resources, or as concrete social settings, the implication becomes the same: civil society becomes the societal terrain where communicative rationality is to flourish. But it is a terrain which needs to be socioculturally and legally defined and defended. Moreover – and this becomes another important step in their reasoning – the institutionalized dimensions of the lifeworld (that is, civil society) can in turn be seen as comprising both public and private dimensions. The resulting four-cell table (Cohen and Arato, 1992:431) has an important implication for a revised distinction between the categories of public and private. Both public and private now have system and lifeworld dimensions. What emerges is a perspective which allows for both making distinctions *and* charting articulations across the divisions.

	Public	**Private**
System:	political subsystem	economic subsystem
Lifeworld:	public sphere	private sphere

Thus, we can distinguish within the private that which pertains to the economic subsystem and that which pertains to the intimate sphere. For example, issues of ownership in the market have no ideological corollary with the 'private' domain of the intimate sphere; there is no coherent justification for transposing arguments about freedom in one area over to the other. At the same time, the intimate relations of the lifeworld's domestic settings can, depending on circumstances, be contextualized as part of the private sphere or the public sphere. The significance of such fluidity is evident when we link this with the notion of citizenship as an identity which is actualized in some but not all settings, as I discuss below.

From another angle, the category of 'public' can also now be seen as an aspect of both system and lifeworld. The formal political subsystem belongs to the system level, but the *public sphere* as such is now treated as part of the lifeworld, amenable to analysis and evaluation in terms of the norms of communicative rationality. Interaction, as one of the four dimensions of the public sphere (Chapter 1), can now also be seen as the key element of civil society. The links *between* the system and lifeworld can be critically framed in terms of communicative action within the public sphere.

Yet, public communication, one of Cohen and Arato's four institutional areas of civil society, is a somewhat odd category. It would seem to include everything from soap box oratory, through billboards, to mass media. Thus, some forms of public communication reside neatly in the institutional lifeworld (that is, civil society), while others, particularly the mass media, straddle the system/lifeworld boundary (and thereby function as linkages between them). Cohen and Arato actually have very little to say about the media, which is to be regretted. In terms of their model, then, the mass media certainly do not constitute all of the public sphere (which is in keeping with my discussion in Chapter 1), since the public sphere is also built upon social interaction. However, given that the media originate within the level of the two subsystems (corporate and state power) and permeate the lifeworld, their contribution to colonization or liberation can be framed within the terms of Habermas' model. But with regard to the media, Cohen and Arato do not take us much further than that. Indeed, in a follow-up article summarizing the state of our conceptual understanding of civil society, Arato (1994) lists a number of areas which are in need of further research, including the problem of democratic legitimacy, the relationship of political and civil society, and the question of the media's organization, output and publics.

Though both civil society and the public sphere presuppose social interaction, it is important conceptually not to conflate the two categories. In Cohen and Arato's model, civil society, as the institutionalized lifeworld, includes the public and private dimensions, as seen in the table above. Civil society points to patterns of interaction and social organization, including their institutional and legal aspects. The public sphere has to do with societal discourse and dialogue of political relevance. Clearly they can impact on each other. As Calhoun (1993:276) puts it: 'a public sphere depends on a favorable organization of civil society. It is not enough that there simply be a civil society or even a civil society more or less autonomous from the state'. A 'favorable organization of civil society', the site of everyday social interaction, in other words, is an essential prerequisite for a viable public sphere.

At the same time, a democratically functioning public sphere can give shape to civil society. Not only does it potentially allow for the airing of views, the shaping of political will and the resolution of conflict, it also permits people to develop and alter both their individual and collective identities.

Identity formation is not something which is completed in the private sphere and then simply applied to public life:

> It is . . . a matter of how the public sphere incorporates and recognizes the diversity of identities people bring to it from their manifold involvements in civil society . . . Even the very identity of the political community is a product, not simply a precondition, of the activity of the public sphere of civil society. (Calhoun, 1993:279–80)

Yet, we should be wary of implying too neat a picture here. Let us recall the discussion in Chapter 4 on the destabilized microworlds of late modernity. They are pluralized and disembedded; the boundary between public and private, deriving from several historical developments, becomes in practice a permeable – at times contested – border.

Constructive talk and social bonds

The concept of civil society can be seen as a way of contextualizing reception and social interaction more broadly in a manner which emphasizes their centrality for democratic processes. I want here to pick up some items that I introduced earlier and develop them further. In Chapter 1 I presented the idea of sociocultural interaction as a key dimension of the public sphere and, as a parallel, in Chapter 2, I took up the idea of television as a sociocultural experience. I emphasized the constructivist dimension of talk with regard to social relations, and also discussed how talk can generate the unforeseen. I have suggested that interaction encompasses three analytic concerns: the spatial, the discursive and the communal. I have already touched upon the spatial in looking at Morley's (1992) text, and to pursue it further here would take us rather far afield, into considerations of social geography and its interfaces with television. So I will restrict myself to some points about the discursive and the communal aspects of talk.

Writing from within a discourse-based social psychology, Shotter offers some propositions about social constructionism:

> Common to all versions of social constructionism is the central assumption that – instead of the inner dynamics of the individual . . . or the already determined characteristics of the external world . . . – it is the contingent, really vague (that is, lacking any completely determinate character) flow of continuous communicative activity between human beings that we must study. Thus, the assumption of an already stable and well-formed reality 'behind appearances', full of 'things' identifiable independently of language, must be replaced by that of a vague, only partially specified, unstable world, open to further specification as a result of human, communicative activity . . . It is from within this not wholly ordered flow of relational, background activities and practices . . . that all our other socially significant dimensions of interaction – with each other and with our 'reality' – originate and are constructed in 'joint action'. (1993a:179)

Shotter, building on Garfinkel's ethnomethodology, Berger and Luckmann's phenomenological sociology and other social interactionist traditions, situates conversational reality in a particular manner: in a zone between on the one hand actions – what individuals 'do' – and events – that which simply happens 'to, in or around' us, seemingly outside our capacity as individual agents to control. Interaction, what Shotter calls joint action, can generate outcomes which are both unintended and unpredictable. Such an outcome constitutes a 'situation' or an 'organized practical-moral setting', which exists between the participants.

> Although such a setting is unintended by any of the individuals within it, it nonetheless has an *intentional* quality about it . . . that is, participants find themselves both immersed 'in' an already given situation but one with a horizon to it, that makes it 'open' to their actions. Indeed, its 'organization' is such that the practical-moral constraints (and enablement) it makes available to them influence, that is, 'invite' and 'motivate', their next possible actions . . . (Shotter, 1993a:39)

For Shotter, interaction – joint action – is the kind of notion which will help us to see the constructivist dynamics of civil society, of the institutionalized lifeworld, rather than treating them as a finished framework which simply delimits our interaction. Unintended consequences – constructions – come to constitute the new conditions for further actions and interactions. In the flux and flow of interaction, people can generate, largely unconsciously, 'a changing sea of moral enablements and constraints, of privileges and entitlements, and obligations and sanctions – in short, an ethos.' (Shotter, 1993a:39). Moreover, identity, a sense of self and belonging to the social network, is built up and/or hindered in the process. To be taken seriously as a participant, to be treated as a 'co-author', together with others, of one's immediate social reality, becomes an important factor for both the sense of self as well as for the character of the specific social milieu. Here especially we see that the democratization of civil society cannot merely be a task for the state: it must also emerge in the socially-constructed ethos of the micro-levels of the lifeworld.

I highlighted, at the end of Chapter 5, the importance of the notion of the imaginary, particularly in its relationship to emancipatory projects. The imaginary occupies a space between the actual and the non-existent; it is prospective, contestable, yet informs social practices and discourse. The imaginary, in a sense, keeps meaning from becoming rigidified; it acts as a potential counterpoint to the reification of sense-making (and social relations). To go beyond Habermas' position: the imaginary helps the lifeworld to resist colonization by systems logic.

Paraphrasing a famous dictum: we create our social worlds through talk with others, though not under historical circumstances we have ourselves chosen. As I said earlier with regard to the public sphere, social structure impinges on sociocultural interaction. Clearly, we cannot via discursive activity simply create any social reality we choose; talk cannot negate the extra discursive features of historical materiality. To assert that it can would be to regress to old-fashioned idealism. Yet we must bear in mind that 'social reality' comprises an irreducible component of subjectivity: the *social* world is always at least partially 'within us', intersubjectively shared, negotiated, contested. The indeterminate flow of communication to which Shotter refers means that not only is the social world ultimately without foundation in the philosophical sense, but also that it is a world derived in part via argumentation, rhetoric. Thus, we can see civil society as the myriad of sites where the social world is interactively produced and reproduced – keeping in mind, of course, that legal, material and other conditions have their impact. (Indeed, Shotter, from his own perspective, devotes a chapter to 'Rhetoric and the Recovery of Civil Society'.) And it is in that social world, often where it intersects with the media, that we find the public sphere.

The communal aspect of interaction has to do with the nature of the social bonds between those who interact. Neumann et al. (1992), in appropriating the constructivist model for political communication research, also see meaning arising in the interaction between people, and between people and the media:

> Constructionism focuses on 'common knowledge' as opposed to 'public opinion': what people think and how they think about public issues rather than narrowly defined valence-oriented 'opinions' concerning an issue or candidate. The use of 'knowledge' rather than 'opinion' emphasizes the need to organize information into meaningful structures. The phrase 'common knowledge' emphasizes that the structuring and framing of information is not unique to each individual but aggregates into the cultural phenomenon of shared perspectives and issue frames. (Neumann et al., 1992:18)

The underscoring of 'common knowledge' raises the question: common to whom? We must be restrictive in making claims for the concept of 'community', a type of social bond which has not fared so well under modernity. Yet there is a large variety of forms of collectivity, there are modes of cultural commonality and shared interests. The more modest term of 'interpretive community' captures some of this – and at the same time frees the notion of community from its traditional anchoring to a geographic place. Let us recall also the discussion from the previous chapter on the multiplicity of identities that we all embody. Common knowledge is relative to collectivities sharing similar interpretive frameworks. Thus, within civil society, there are innumerable sets of common knowledge, many of them partially overlapping and constituting concentric circles of ever-larger (and more generalized) common knowledge. From the perspective of the public sphere, it becomes a question of politically relevant knowledge becoming common for collectivities of appropriate scale, for example, specific groups, associations, interests, and social movements have their own shared frameworks, but what is the nature of that common knowledge which we might call universal within society as a whole? What identities correlate with such knowledge? This begins to pull us in the direction of citizenship as a form of identity.

The social bonds within a collectivity reflect and reinforce shared frameworks of relevance. Rosen (1986), writing from a Dewey-inspired perspective, makes the point that the less compelling the social bond and shared relevances are within a public, the more the media have to work to hold the public together:

> When there is nothing substantial holding the audience together, anything and everything can become 'news', if it succeeds in gaining the attention of a sufficiently large circle of readers ... Another name for this development is

sensationalism. Sensationalism is not a quality inherent in certain publishers or newspapers, nor is it a reflection of the audiences' 'true' desires. It arises from the ability to link through media of communication people who would not otherwise perceive themselves as a group. Sensationalism is what happens when communication outruns the sense of community. (Rosen, 1986: 391–2)

Thus, a viable public sphere cannot exist solely as a media phenomenon, but must go via the interaction of civil society. If the 'publicness' of media discourses is inadequate for addressing and capturing the attention of people as a public – if it is lacking in shared relevances – the discourses can always fall back on a privatization and personalization (as we well know), thereby addressing people as individuals, but not as members of collectivities with shared frames of relevance and frames of action.

Operating within civil society are people – individuals who belong, in a variety of ways, to the society. At the same time they also stand in complex relationship to the state. Across the terrain of both civil society and the state we find the political. The ways of belonging to society, and the inscribed relations with the state, take us into the (political) question of how citizenship is to be conceptualized, which is the theme of the following sections. Citizenship, like civil society, has relevance for the public sphere, particularly with regard to its dimensions of social structure and sociocultural interaction. In the sections which follow, I will briefly take up the historical evolution of citizenship as a category of belonging to and participating in society. I then look at some debates regarding aspects of universality and community as elements of citizenship. I conclude with a sketch of citizenship as a form of identity.

The evolution of citizenship

Central to any understanding of citizenship is an awareness that as a phenomenon it has not been static, nor is it consistent across societies in the modern world today. Deriving in its modern formulations from the ideals of the Enlightenment, citizenship in practice varies considerably with historical circumstances, and thus is always potentially contestable. A second important point is that citizenship is not merely an ensemble of legal stipulations, a manifestation of macrosocial and political circumstances. Citizenship must also be seen as a feature of culture, operative as a dimension of individual and collective identity.

Over the past years, the concept of citizenship has lost the image of quaintness that it long had. During the last decade or so, the decline in socio-economic conditions in many countries and the political attacks which have seriously weakened the welfare state, have no doubt played a role in putting citizenship back on the political and intellectual agenda (see, for example, Roche, 1992; Turner, 1993a; van Steenbergen, 1994; Twine, 1994). So too has the establishment of new states and the transformation of old ones in the wake of the disintegration of communism, as well as the attention focused on multistate organizations, in particular the European Union. While proponents of a market-steered societal development espouse a delimited notion of citizenship and wish to frame it in consumerist perspectives, the collectivist-oriented left tends to argue for a more inclusive understanding. These lines are by no means neatly drawn, as the traditional political axis of left and right becomes blurred, but we should not lose sight of the political stakes involved in how citizenship is formulated.

Citizenship is a more complicated and contested matter than may at first be apparent. It has to do with belonging, with inclusion; to be a citizen is to be a member of something we (metaphorically) call a community. It also has to do with participation in that community, while community as such has become a highly problematic notion in the contemporary world. Throughout modern history, the membership and participation of various categories of people in their communities have been restricted and even denied. Thus, as Held (1991:20) says, 'citizenship requires us to think about the very nature of the conditions of membership and political participation'. These conditions of membership and participation, the processes which determine inclusion/exclusion, and which accord or deny participation, must be understood broadly. They are not just questions of political life, but of public life more generally. To be a citizen means to be included civically and socially, not just politically. This in turn points to issues of the material foundations of that inclusion, the economic prerequisites for participation. Moreover, citizenship touches on the allocation of cultural as well as material resources. To unravel this complexity, it can be helpful to frame citizenship in an historical narrative.

In the English-speaking world it seems impossible to discuss the evolution of the concept of citizenship without passing through the work of T.H. Marshall (1950). As many have noted, his post-war studies of citizenship can be understood as a progressive liberal response to the question of how to reconcile the formal system of political democracy with the social dislocations deriving from the capitalist economy. Basically, Marshall saw the welfare state as the chief mechanism for countering the worst consequences of capitalism. If the economic system gave rise to the disparities of social class, and if it even resulted in unemployment and/or extreme deprivation, these negative social conditions could be modified, though not eliminated, via the interventions of the welfare state, thereby stabilizing the entire social system. Marshall deemed the inequalities of social class to be acceptable if equality of citizenship is attained. A similar, though politically more left-liberal line of thought regarding the welfare state can be found in the evolution of social democracy in the Nordic countries.

Marshall traced the historical evolution of citizenship in Britain by conceptualizing three dimensions, which point to three sets of rights: civil, political and social. Civil citizenship has to do with the legal rights protecting the individual's freedom. It began to emerge in the seventeenth century, as the absolute state began to wane and basic rights guaranteeing such things as a fair trial were institutionalized. Political citizenship, which addresses the individual's rights to participate in politics and the exercise of political power, began to take hold in the eighteenth and nineteenth centuries. It was during these centuries that the rights to assemble, to associate freely, to participate in government, and to exercise freedom of speech began to be secured. Political citizenship became fully embodied in the institutions of parliamentary political systems. Social citizenship has to do with a whole range of rights which include the right to minimal economic security and welfare, so that one can, in Marshalls's words, 'live the life of a civilised being according to the standards prevailing in the society' (quoted in Turner, 1993b:20).

There has been some debate in recent years over Marshall's interpretation of capitalism, the welfare state, and citizenship. Without going into all the issues, I can comment that from today's perspective, his interpretation that the contradictions have basically been resolved is seen as bit hasty, to say the least. While it may be argued that the current status of civil and political citizenship in the West shows a successful development, social citizenship is in deep trouble, as economic devastation hits large portions of the population and the welfare state itself is both defensive and contracting. Other voices, particularly those espousing a politics of identity, call for an expansion of rights to include cultural citizenship. Also, as Turner (1993b) observes, in Marshall's scheme there is no theoretic dimension which can help explain *how* citizenship develops (or dissolves) historically. Marshall simply charted its evolution in conjunction with capitalist development, and there is little which helps clarify the relationship between the three depicted dimensions of citizenship.

Despite the unresolved tensions in Marshall's work, it has the merit of solidifying a fuller, more multidimensional view of citizenship. He affirmed that for individuals to belong to and to participate within the communities in which they live, there are certain legal, political and social requisites. We can readily understand that we participate in the public sphere as citizens, yet we perhaps do not as readily see that our very belonging and participation in civil society is also an expression of citizenship. Moreover, belonging and participating at this level requires specifically *social* rights, social entitlements. Such entitlements, a product of the struggle to create the welfare state, are in some ways more radical than even the civil and political rights, since they raise questions about the limits of market mechanisms and about the redistribution of wealth. Thus, it is not surprising that throughout the 1980s, with economic slumps prevalent, an ideological climate emerged to restrict such redistribution, that is, to reduce the scope of the welfare state. Once again the tension between capitalism and democracy, between the market and (social) citizenship, came to the fore. In Hobsbawm's words (1994; quoted in the *Independent on Sunday*, 'The Sunday Review', 16 Oct. 1994, p. 9): 'To put it brutally, if the global economy could discard a minority of poor countries as economically uninteresting and irrelevant, it could also do so with the very poor within the borders of all its countries, so long as the number of potentially interesting consumers was sufficiently large.'

Thus, the decline in social welfare must be seen as detrimental to citizenship. The notion of social citizenship implies, in essence, that poverty itself is antithetical to citizenship. However, the eradication of poverty in western society, let alone on the planet, is not on the immediate horizon. Also, it would be too simplistic merely to blame corporate economic logic for the dilemmas within social citizenship. Roche (1992), in tracing the evolution of social citizenship, argues that there are some deep moral/political problems, which have become recognized by both the left and the right. Social citizenship, with its emphasis on entitlements, tends to promote a 'duty free' understanding of citizenship within political culture, severed not only from notions of obligation or responsibility, but also from the civil and political dimensions of citizenship. The duties of citizenship, in effect, are not deeply felt; citizenship, unwittingly, becomes depoliticized and consumerist. Moreover, social citizenship, as embodied in welfare politics, has obviously been linked to the nation-state, to national politics, to national industrial capitalism. These, as we saw in Chapter 4, are being modified by the global contingencies of modernity. The era in which citizenship, in particular social citizenship, could be conceptualized exclusively in national and welfare state terms has passed. This does not signal the end of citizenship, either in fact or as an ideal, but rather a renewal and pluralization of the concept.

Community, difference, universality

Within contemporary debates around political and moral philosophy, a number of positions have crystallized which are of direct relevance for the notion of citizenship. (See Benhabib, 1992, Chapter 2, and Mouffe, 1992b, for entry ports into the literature of these debates.) In cursory terms, liberalism, as exemplified by Rawl's theory of justice, emphasizes that citizens should be free to pursue their own conceptions of the good, though with respect and consideration for others. To do this, they need equal rights and opportunities, as well as an equal material base. The just society is one which strives to realize this vision of equality. In the rationalist morality at work here, the guiding vision is what is right and just, rather than what is good or virtuous. This liberal view is premised on an abstracted notion of the individual, who emerges seemingly out of nowhere, fully socialized and acculturated, with mature cognitive and moral facilities. This individual is treated as epistemologically 'free' to take an Archimedean view of things – a sort of Olympian rationalism – while at the same time pursuing his or her own self-interests. The individual in the liberal view is not implicated in any necessary social bonds, but seemingly floats above them. The intersubjective constitution of individuals via social interaction is not on the horizon.

Two versions of critical response to this liberal ideal have recently emerged. One is communitarian (though at times the label civic republicanism can be used); the other can be typified as postmodern. 'Communitarianism' is a label which has come to be applied to a number of writers, such as Charles Taylor and Michael Walzer, who, despite differences among themselves, share a critical perspective on this liberal political philosophy. While accepting a number of liberalism's elements, these writers strongly reject what they see as the poverty of such an atomized view of society. Communitarians underscore the concept of public good, and promote the idea of the socioculturally situated and constructed individual. Further, communitarians respond negatively to what they see as liberalism's compliance with the anomie and fragmentation of modernity, and they therefore privilege the idea of shared values which help to constitute the identity of individuals. In short, citizenship in this view presupposes and promotes some sense of community.

As Benhabib (1992) suggests, this communitarian political thinking contains within it two divergent strands; one she terms 'integrationist', the other 'participatory'. Integrationist thinking strives for a coherent value framework, often to be achieved via revival movements and/or religious zeal. The notion of the common good which is to prevail is distressingly unitary. Thus, integrationist thought can readily assume an antimodern posture, and manifest strains of authoritarianism and patriarchalism; community can become a smothering and repressive social order. We witness such tendencies today not least among Christian and Islamic fundamentalists, as well as among some nation-states with deep ethnically-based identities. Liberals are of course right to warn of the totalitarian dangers of trying to formulate 'the common good'.

The participatory strand of communitarian thought places less importance on questions of belonging, instead promoting the centrality of political agency and efficacy. Citizenship, which is not intended to encompass the person in his or her entirety, is learned by doing, by participating in a multifaceted civil and political society. In this regard, communitarianism tends to see the welfare state as a means for enhancing participation generally – civically, socially, politically, culturally. The participatory view assumes social pluralism; in the modern world no single overwhelming vision of the good can dominate large and heterogeneous societies or serve as the foundation for political community. Social difference *per se* is not seen as something to be eradicated. Only if difference coincides with domination need it become a general political question.

Generally, if liberal and communitarian views of democracy differ on the question of the individual and community, they share an understanding that citizenship is or should be, a non-exclusionary category. Citizenship is something for everybody, where everybody is rendered equal within the framework of a society's universal citizenship. Liberals too would be in agreement on this point. However, in response to both liberal and communitarian/civic republican positions, we can now also see the contours of a postmodern position – understood as a critical, dialogic encounter with Enlightenment thought, as discussed in Chapter 4.

This postmodern intervention is expressed by a number of writers; Young (1987, 1990a, 1990b) gives it a particularly explicit voice in a series of papers. First, with regard to community, she takes a general position which argues that community, as an ideal, tends to promote unity at the expense of difference. She is by no means against community, or close relationships of friendship. Her point is that those who are politically motivated by the ideal of community:

> ... will tend to suppress differences among themselves or implicitly exclude from their political groups persons with whom they do not identify. The vision of small, face-to-face, decentralized units that this ideal promotes, moreover, is an unrealistic vision for transformative politics in mass urban society. (Young, 1990b:300)

She argues instead for a politics which includes an 'openness to unassimilated others' (Young, 1990b:319). A politics which assumes difference strives for political representation of various groups; it also accords legitimation and indeed celebrates the distinctive cultural differences. We must assume, however, that within various group constellations some sense of community is at work. Her point, however, is that the polity as a whole cannot and should not be conceived in communal terms.

Turning to the related theme of universal citizenship, Young (1990a) problematizes this conception, arguing that the seeming universality of citizenship in fact works against particular groups who are in a subordinate position. In a postmodern move, she notes that:

> The assumed link between citizenship for everyone, on the one hand, and the two other senses of citizenship – having a common life with and being treated in the same way as the other citizens – on the other, is itself a problem. Contemporary social movements of the oppressed have weakened the link. They assert a positivity and pride in group specificity against ideals of assimilation. They have also questioned whether justice means that law and policy should enforce equal treatment for all groups. Embryonic in these challenges lies a concept of differentiated citizenship as the best way to realize the inclusion and participation of everyone in full citizenship. (Young, 1990a:118)

Young is arguing first of all that the ideal of universality carries with it imperatives for a homogeneous citizenry, which continues to give support to the historical mechanisms of exclusion. She observes that in modern political thought, the universality of citizenship implies a status which transcends the particular, and defines everyone as political peers, regardless of other social differences. Equality here means sameness, and citizenship thus expresses what people have in common, rather than how they differ. Secondly, Young makes the point that universality implies that laws and other rules are to be applied equally, with no consideration of individual or group differences. She counters this by saying that certain groups, because of their disadvantaged or oppressed status, require preferential treatment; equal treatment will not help them alter their circumstances. She advocates that we must first identify groups which are marginalized, disadvantaged or oppressed. The voices and experiences of such groups must be given representation and recognition in a democratic public, in explicit juxtaposition to those groups who are more socially, economically and communicatively privileged. Politically, she sees various groups embodying their interests in social movements, and advocates the building of 'rainbow coalitions' where possible.

Young herself readily admits to the many practical difficulties involved in such a political vision. What is not clear in her proposal is the extent legal measures should be taken to guarantee the group representation and recognition she wants to attain. To what degree should we alter the civic, political and social mechanisms of citizenship, and how do we continue with such modification as groups evolve historically? I would be cautious about tampering with these. However, one can read Young's argument as not aiming at any alteration of formal citizenship as such, but rather addressing the question of how to organize the public sphere. For our purposes here, the principle of a heterogeneous polity, and a public sphere explicitly organized to accommodate difference is central.

Seen in this light, Young is arguing that if genuine inclusion and participation is to be achieved there, we must leave behind the notion of a unified public sphere. We must free ourselves from the idea that a common, overarching will can be achieved and given expression, that a general, collective perspective among the polity of modern societies can be taken. There is no 'common perspective' from which all other perspectives can be understood, but only situated ones, based on specific sets of experiences and perceptions. The point of a political arena is not to merge all of these into some artificial synthesis, but rather to enact as much communication as possible between them, acknowledging difference and striving for agreement. Instead of a Habermasian consensus grounded in intersubjectivity, Young opts for a less ambitious practical compromise where people may not necessarily achieve mutual understanding.

Yet the question remains: on what grounds does such communication take place if not on fully attained intersubjectivity, consensus and community which binds together the interaction within modern political life? If we concede, realistically, that in multicultural and hyper-pluralistic societies we may not always really understand each other, what is to be the basis for communication between citizens? There still must be some minimal commonality within a polity if it is to function. How can we conceptualize it?

Citizens and identity

As ideals, the civil, political and social aspects of citizenship require formal institutional anchoring; there must be legal guarantees. These are crucial, and especially in times of instability such guarantees can become politically challenged, requiring a vigorous response. In many settings it would still have radical consequences if these liberal ideals were in fact socially realized; hence the importance of not relinquishing these norms and their legal foundations, and, indeed, expanding upon them where possible. However, for citizenship to be a living force within a democratic society, it must be internalized – as a value system, as a horizon, as *a form of identity* – and anchored within the lifeworld of civil society. Citizenship must be a part of the democratic culture of civil society.

Even if a strong vision of an all-encompassing community is not essential to modern citizenship, a minimal common civil and political culture is. In today's world, as I discussed in Chapter 4, we are seeing considerable fragmentation and differentiation within culture. Such a common culture of citizenship, however defined, would seemingly become more remote as cultural differentiation proceeds. This is apparently all the more so when the dominant horizontal, unifying identity is that of consumer. (Turner, 1994, explores the tensions between citizenship and postmodernism.) Yet such tendencies must be seen as partly in tension with some of the processes of globalization and the newer forms of citizenship which they engender – identities of belonging and participation, which look beyond the nation-state to see the planet, or collectivities of nation-states, as the appropriate 'home' of citizenship. Falk (1994) names several of these, including the global reformer, normally somebody situated in élite circles; the transnational activist, often engaged in environmental politics; and the regional multinational citizen. The institutional underpinnings of genuinely global citizenship are still fragile, and it is perhaps a matter of temperament if one chooses to be pessimistic or optimistic about their future development; one can mobilize evidence for both attitudes. Undeniably, the identity as citizen, legal nationality and national identity fuse together in the minds of many people, curtailing identities of transnational citizenship. At the regional level, however, we do see developments which suggest to some people that at least some of their interests transcend the boundaries of national states. The European Union is a paradigmatic example, with its increasingly developed transborder citizen rights, not least in regard to social entitlements (see Meehan, 1993).

In theorizing citizenship as a form of identity, Young and others draw attention to one of the central problems in democracy today, namely reconciling the principle of *universal* needs and interests with the many legitimate forms of *difference* which do not violate generalized needs. These differences are expressed not least in the associations, movements and interest groups within civil society. Communities based on gender or ethnicity, for example, raise the issue of the status of citizenship; how can citizenship incorporate both the universal and the particular? One important line of thought is to reject any staunch unitary conception of citizenship at the level of identity. With the social and cultural transformations under way in the modern world, people continually have to work out what it means to belong to and participate within the communities and polities in which they live. To argue for a 'one size fits all' citizenship would be counterproductive.

Another line of thought is the attempt to specify the minimalist democratic culture and identity necessary for a democratic society. One version, advocated by Mouffe (1988b, 1992b, 1993) in a framework she calls radical democracy, tries to define a societal vector which assumes the shifting multiplicities of various political groups and yet strives for a 'hegemony of democratic values'. This perspective, with its roots in civic republicanism and post-empiricist philosophy, looks towards a maximal degree of diversity in a society which is at the same time held together by a unifying 'cultural glue' of democratic values and identities as citizens. Her view, in brief, takes as its point of departure the multiple and situated subject; each citizen/person can assume many – and at times contradictory – subject positions. Which identity is 'activated' or promoted is contingent and contextual, and can never be fully fixed and stabilized. No one position is a priori privileged, although we should add that some are more likely to play a central role than others, and that we would be wise not to exaggerate the transitory quality of subject positions. If not pushed to the extreme, this line of reasoning is fruitful. In a sense, it is an extention of the traditional insight that any individual embodies a number of varying and, at times, conflicting interests. Mouffe and similar theorists extend the argument to include the deepest levels of our subjectivity. Yet, as I argued in the previous chapter, this does not make us totally dispersed as individuals; we construct coherence in our lives and our identities.

Such a view could be usefully applied to the civil society model in terms of individual and collective identity processes. The contingency or the multi-dimensionality of the subject can be made fundamental to the very understanding of democracy and of citizenship. Democratic citizenship has to do with a form of identity constructed by the social practices of agents; it is not simply a legal status. This is an argument for a common political identity, acknowledging that political involvement must always be dualistic, advocating *both* the particular interest and defending/promoting the universal democratic interest. What this amounts to is a programmatic call for creating alliances, whereby all active groups and interests who share a loyalty to genuine democratic procedures should make manifest this solidarity. Such a perspective contends that democratic citizenship 'consists in identifying with the ethico-political principles of modern democracy' (Mouffe, 1992b: 237); in other words, identifying with a shared *res publica*.

The radical democracy programme embodies a strong articulation between the imaginary and the emancipatory. The contribution of this Utopian vector is that it helps us to link the civil society model with this vision of citizenship and its emphasis on a shared democratic culture, taking our vision of the public sphere a few steps further. It certainly begs a number of big questions, such as just how are shared democratic values and the identification as democratic citizens to be achieved and maintained? How are such political/civic cultures generated? How do we transcend Sennett's (1977) diagnosis of public culture implying a dead end for the interactional dimension of the public sphere? Obviously there are no simple answers, but hopefully this attempt to establish the theoretical linkages will aid us in better grasping the conditions, the requisites, for a functioning public sphere.

Mouffe explicitly distances herself from Habermas, but I see an obvious parallel: though using a different vocabulary, Mouffe appears to be arguing for a 'weak' or 'minimalist' version of communicative rationality and inter-subjectivity. Like Young, she does not see consensus or a common perspective as attainable, but posits, at least implicitly, a sense of qualified community within groups, and a minimal intersubjectivity – a sharing of democratic values as *res publica* – between groups who build democratic alliances. Without minimal collective support for democratic procedures and norms, without a self-understanding among citizens that differences of interest and orientation must at some point be accepted as secondary to the overall rules of the democratic game, without a visible democratic culture within civil society, the public sphere will not be viable. Indeed, the notion of *res publica*, which evokes the cultural requisites for democracy, is a distant cousin of such conceptions as 'the civic culture' (Almond and Verba, 1963), though it is politically very distant from such legacies of the Cold War.

Indeed, despite Mouffe's political radicalism, her understanding of citizenship shares features with views emanating from more traditional quarters. Heater (1990), from a more liberal orientation, presents a three-dimensional model of citizenship with clear parallels to Mouffe. One dimension has to do with the geographical scope of citizenship: he cites levels ranging from the global down to the provincial/local. A second dimension takes up what he calls the 'elements' of citizenship. He names the legal/civil, political and social, but also virtue and identity. Virtue captures the normative aspect, the sense of responsibility and duty. Identity of course means that citizenship must be integrated with our definitions of self. The third he terms education, which includes knowledge, attitude and skills. This dimension should not be treated as merely something done in schools. It has to do with socialization and acculturation, with competencies and values learned via the multiple interactions within civil society. Despite their probable political differences, Heater would not be opposed to Mouffe's view of *res publica* and its requisites.

A second body of literature which addresses the question of citizenship as a form of identity, and partly overlaps with the radical democracy project, is feminist in origin. Though emerging out of feminist thought, this literature is not aiming for a feminist theory of politics. Rather, it is trying to develop a general, progressive understanding of democracy by theorizing citizenship, democracy and identity from feminist perspectives. A good number of the these contributions have found valuable elements in the work of Arendt (1958), at first glance a somewhat surprising figure (for example, Canovan, 1994; Honig, 1992; Dietz, 1991, 1992; Passerin d'Entrèves, 1992; see also McClure, 1992. Benhabib, 1992, takes a more critical view of Arendt). Many questions about Arendt's perspective are aired in this literature. All the commentators underscore the limitations of Arendt's Hellenic views for feminist politics; in her work there is no acknowledgement of gender politics. Many see as problematic Arendt's distinction between labour, work and action, as well as her idiosyncratic definition of 'the social'. I will not embark on a review of all the issues raised, but will restrict myself to two themes which these authors have found fruitful in Arendt's work and which have a bearing on the present discussion, namely the notion of citizenship as an identity and the distinction between public and private which these authors derive from Arendt.

Just to sketch briefly the contours of the perspective these authors develop: in contrast to earlier formulations of the individual agency and radical politics, this literature, following Arendt, displays a marked shift away from conceptions of 'truth' and 'authenticity' as the bedrock of politics. In a way which foregrounds some postmodern thought, politics is rather the 'space of appearances', where people ('men', in Arendt's prefeminist formulation) encounter each other in speech and action. Communication is not strictly rationalist, however; passion, drama and the visual are all assumed to be features of public discourse. Further, the constructed 'artificial' quality of public life and politics (and the 'truth' it may generate) is affirmed. Politics is a performative activity, and intimacy, warmth and sentiment have no real place in the public arena. At the same time, this literature underscores the qualities of solidarity and pluralism. Citizens cannot be expected to share the same values, but they must share the same public space and have a common language.

With some further specification, most of these propositions can be integrated with the orientation which I have been developing thus far. Among other things, we have here a reading of Arendt which sees identity as a performative production; we create ourselves, not least as citizens, by the things we do and say. There is no inner essence being expressed in our actions. Such a view is compatible with the notion of a multiple, contingent and even contradictory subjectivity: the subject creates him or herself and is created in concrete contexts, in continual processes of becoming. Though there are profound differences in theoretical premises, this view also connects with the anti-essentialist interactionist tradition of Goffman, whose approach has been applied to the area of citizens and politics (Eliasoph, 1990). From a feminist view, the catch with Arendt is that she could only acknowledge this within the public realm. She did not see the private, domestic setting as a context for the generation of identity. Therefore, the feminist position is, of course, to emphasize the intimate realm both as a social terrain of identity formation *and* politics. However – and this is the interesting move here – a distinction is still retained between acting as a citizen and acting in the capacity of our other identities. This line of feminist thought underscores the importance of *not* grounding the concept of citizen – morally or epistemologically – on any 'womanist' platform. Biological sex and cultural gender are clearly of fundamental importance to all individuals, male and female, but cannot be taken as privileged positions from which to act as citizens. Rather, they can serve as the point of departure for political activity – as defining sets of interests and identities. When entering the realm of *politics*, however, one does so with the identity of a citizen, which means one is pursuing specific collective interests, but abiding by the assumption of equality among all citizens and following the accepted procedures of democracy.

Parallel to this view is an understanding of the distinction between public and private contexts. These spaces have historically been defined in sexist terms, as I discussed in Chapter 4. 'Arendtian feminism', if one may use such a label, however, does not aim for the total eradication of the boundaries, as do such slogans as 'the personal is political'. Rather, where appropriate, it strives for a redefining of the boundaries, and above all, a combating of sexism on both sides of the public/private divide. As Dietz (1991:247) says: 'The point is not to accept these gendered realms as fixed and immutable, but rather to undermine the gendering of public and private and move on to a more visionary and liberating conception of human practices, including those that constitute politics.' Phillips (1993:85–6) illustrates this affirmation of the boundaries with two illustrations: first, we all have the right to keep the details of our intimate lives private, yet we also have the right to engage politically in sexual issues, and no issue should a priori be defined as unsuitable for public discussion. Secondly, we would be acting in the role of citizens if we were politically involved in an issue relating to the sharing of household work, but we would not be doing so we were attempting to sort out the division of labour within our own household. There is, in other words, a distinction between public and private discourse, as well as between private and public space.

Pulling together the themes I have addressed with regard to citizenship, we must acknowledge and continue to struggle for its institutional requisites. The Marshallian model of civil, political and social citizenship is still valid, though incomplete and as yet historically not fully achieved. In terms of political philosophy, participatory communitarianism, civic republicanism and various postmodern trajectories all have contributions to make regarding our understanding of pluralism, belonging and participation. In particular, the postmodern horizon underscores the heterogeneity of modern society and the challenges this presents to our conception of citizenship. Indeed, we would do well to shy away from a singular conception of citizenship and allow for the play of multiple versions, at least as far as it has to do with a form of identity. The postmodern notion of plural and contingent subjects provides a useful link to understanding citizenship as a specific form of identity, while at the same time opening the door, theoretically, to the idea of a common, minimalist *res publica*. Parallel with this, the distinction between public and private is retained as a set of coordinates defining discursive spaces which can serve to contextualize the identity and practices of citizenship.

PART III

FLICKERING HOPES

7

Democratic mediations?

To return to a theme I introduced at the outset, the democratic character of the public sphere cannot simply be assumed, but must be continually achieved. It is an intricate and multiply contingent set of social spaces and practices whose boundaries always remain negotiable – and thus potentially renewable. What I have tried to convey is a sense of this complexity and to illuminate the major issues involved. In so doing I have also been emphasizing the importance of conceptually situating the public sphere and the questions which surround it within larger social theoretic contexts. Easy recipes for progressive policies or political interventions are wanting. While focused attention on the public sphere is essential, it is also imperative that efforts at enhancing democracy – from micro-situations to macrosocial structures – incorporate a public sphere perspective, as an indispensable and inseparable component of all democratic striving.

Trying to elucidate the conditions for the public sphere at this historic juncture becomes all the more difficult when, as I pointed out in Chapter 4, the grounds for knowledge of society, of others, of ourselves, are reflexively being problematized. Analyses of the historical present, including the public sphere, cannot avoid being somewhat equivocal. This does not mean capitulating in the struggle to understand our present circumstances, nor does it suggest the a priori futility of politics. Rather it implies modesty in the face of the recognized situatedness of our knowing. With that reminder (not least to myself), my aim in this final discussion is to highlight some of the key points from the previous chapters and carry them forward, in a speculative manner, within three areas of concern. I will take up television journalism and its possibilities, citizens and the political possibilities of civil society, and lastly – to engage in some policy sketching – the contours of a model of the public sphere in light of the arguments I have presented.

Television in its place

As I discussed in Chapter 4, under the capitalism of late modernity, societal contrasts – clearly recognizable from earlier industrial capitalism – become all the more staggering as they juxtapose themselves with contemporary cultural developments: social devastation versus Utopian visions, pockets of sedate affluence versus unmanageable 'wild zones', pluralization and disembedding of social relations versus new forms of collective identity, the dismembering of class cultures and neighbourhood cohesion versus new social movements. The semiotic environment envelopes the globe in images of consumerist redemption, while huge populations are excluded from participating and many other groups and individuals challenge and reject such images of fulfilment. One of the major negative features of consumerism as an ideological force is that it mitigates against collective identities and actions: solutions are always individualistic. Thus, the tension between consumer and citizen as identities is fundamental. Their incompatibility and conflictual character become increasingly visible in the context of the crisis of the welfare state and the political promotion of market forces as the ideological bedrock for societal relations. Any gains in the identity of citizenship will, to a large extent, have to be won at the expense of consumerist identities.

Television operates in this late modern setting as an industry, as an incessant producer of audio-visual discourses which have a central position in the semiotic environment. As an industry, television has to follow the precepts of audience maximization and profits; moreover, it is the paramount vehicle of consumer culture. While television is the dominant medium of the public sphere, 'public sphering' is clearly not television's dominant purpose, and its institutional logic of course greatly conditions its role within the public sphere.

As a sociocultural experience, television provides symbolic 'raw materials' which are experienced and reflected upon in varying degrees. People make their own sense of television, though such meaning-making tends to follow established sociocultural patterns. Television's discourses are juxtaposed with other experiences of everyday life – sometimes confirming them, sometimes framing them in a mythic way, sometimes challenging and contradicting them. Television fragments and unites, it clarifies and occludes, it informs and distracts. It contributes to a ubiquitous doxa at the same time that it can give some voice to critical sentiment from various sectors of the population. All this is true of television journalism as well. In terms of television's role in the public sphere, we would be foolish to exaggerate its contribution to critical reason and progressive affect. Television journalism does remain laden with ideology – not just in the traditional sense of fostering ways of seeing and understanding which serve to reproduce relations of domination, but also in its very obstruction of understanding and even meaning itself. Yet it would also be a serious mistake to simply write off all its journalistic efforts as basically meaningless or exclusively ideological.

We understand how, in television, the journalistic profession is poised in an increasing tension around its goals and ideals. The sociology of journalism has given us insights into the processes by which television journalism is constructed, and understanding the constructed nature of television's representations of social reality is immensely important. The significant dose

of relativism which follows from this is a healthy antidote to lingering objectivist notions of journalism's representations. However, absolute relativism is
not how this story ends. Our knowledge of the social world via television does
not become entirely up for grabs, nor are we left without criteria for judging
the validity of television's representations. We can still speak of the informational, factual dimensions of television journalism, the thematic dimension of
its 'messages', as it were, without at the same time having to buy into an
exclusively rational, information model of communication. Some accounts
are simply more valid and have more practical implications than others.
Information can still be evaluated according to criteria of importance, relevance, comprehensiveness, accuracy, and so on without one having to accede
to the dominant journalistic conceptions of objectivity and impartiality, and
the empiricist epistemology from which they derive.

It may seem a bit silly to emphasize such a commonplace notion – that the
factual dimension of journalism is crucial – but recent developments in television analysis in some quarters have been strong on formal or structural
qualities, while they have tended to downplay the question of information, as
if it were only of concern to journalists themselves. From a sturdy realist
position, Philo (1990) argues against the 'misty relativism' emanating from
some sectors of Cultural Studies and for the view that social reality is not just
the discursive constructs of subcultural sense-making. While he perhaps
ignores some of the subtleties of the constructivist arguments, his intervention
is a helpful reminder that there are indeed features in the real world out there
which are important to know, and that how they are represented makes a
difference.

Obviously the same set of facts can be discursively framed in various ways
to address and position the viewer differently and to invite different conclusions. Different versions are congruent with different ways of seeing and
different interests – an insight which prepares the way for the still very relevant analysis of ideological dimensions in journalism. This ongoing critical
evaluation of television journalism is an important one. Those who have been
doing it for years may, understandably, feel that they risk repeating themselves, but with every new important issue and event being covered, there
remains the task of putting forth critical counter-interpretations to a wider
audience, most of whom may not previously have seen such deconstructions.
And, since these analyses are usually presented in esoteric academic discourse, it would be nice if we could see more 'popular' interventions and
their greater dissemination within the larger public sphere beyond academic
journals and books.

I can only concur with Gitlin's (1991b) complaint about the esoteric mode
of expression of much media studies. If this book is guilty in perpetuating it,
I must plead that there are various contexts – specific public spheres – which
require various discursive modes (which, of course, is still no justification for
bad writing, which he criticizes). The relatively detailed, conceptual fine-
honing in this text is clearly inappropriate for reaching out to a larger
audience but, from teaching and other writing, I know that the important

points can be made accessible to non-specialists. The task is also one of renewing the popular language of critique, writing in idioms which can resonate with larger audiences and the current semiotic environment. (The problem is not least one of finding the time to work on several fronts at once.) But to return to the basic point here: there is still an important role for ongoing critical analysis of television journalism, to try to make the situatedness of its representations a part of public knowledge, to develop and introduce new critical discourses on the media into the public sphere in compelling ways.

Yet, as should be clear by now, there is no road to representational information (or critique, for that matter) which does not, at least in part, pass through the terrain of the affective and the arational. The passage can be a fleeting one, or a deep and lingering one, depending on the communicative mode, yet it ushers us, at the level of theory, into the realm of the unconscious. The unconscious resonates with the arational, figural regimes of signification in our semiotic environment, not least within television. The rhetorical, mythic, narrative and symbolic features of television journalism's communicative modes cannot be eliminated, nor should they be. How they are used is another question. As I indicated in Chapter 5, the unconscious processes of figural communication can cut both ways. They may potentially mobilize fear, hatred and subordination just as readily as they may induce reflection, empathy, solidarity and critique.

It is especially the arational which is mobilized in the popularization of television journalism. The equivocal character of television journalism is not perfectly symmetrical – I weigh the pitfalls as being greater than the promises – and while some tendencies are encouraging, others are clearly disheartening, even alarming. Yet we would be wise to avoid an 'all-or-nothing' dead end position: given the transitions currently at play within television journalism, and given the openings for experimentation in its popularization, it is not unrealistic to assume that some innovative journalists and producers will continue to develop the promises and avoid the worst of the pitfalls. I harbour the idea that there still are other, unexplored or underutilized ways of using television's forms of representation and expression to enhance the public sphere. But such possibilities will not be realized unless some journalists and producers – armed with reconstructed notions of professionalism – can develop some new practices which work against the established institutional grain. Such a development is predicated on many factors, not least on being supported by new patterns of demands and expectations among viewers. The two sets of conditions, on the production side and among the audiences, are mutually conditioning, yet may not be on the horizon in the absence of other major, critical social developments.

Until then, we will probably have to live with a television which is continually following a logic of development in which public sphere criteria play a minimal role. Yet, demoralizing as this might be, it does not signal the end of the public sphere. For the public sphere does not rest exclusively on television or the mass media generally.

Citizens and politics

In the first chapter of this book I suggested that we could fruitfully conceptualize the public sphere in terms of four dimensions. These dimensions
include, along with media representation and media institutions, social structure and sociocultural interaction. I observed that the social structural
dimension of the public sphere shades into the structural features of society
as a whole, and that these latter features impinge on the other dimensions of
the public sphere in a variety of ways. Social structural factors are not easily
grasped as a totality. For our purposes, the aspects of social structure which
are most visible (though incompletely) and most amenable to intervention
(though only partially), are those refracted through the lens of civil society. I
argued that not only is civil society the terrain of sociocultural interaction –
crucial for the public sphere – but, more to the point here, it is also to be
understood as an institutionalized, though contested, domain. Thus, it presents itself as a vast array of contexts which – from the standpoint of
democratic politics – are to be secured (and expanded) by legal guarantees via
the state. Civil society thus is both a setting for, and an object of, collective
action of political import. There may well be limits as to the structural
alterations which can be attained via civil society; however, in the present historical situation, the potential still far outweighs theoretical limits.

In keeping with Habermas' – and also Dewey's – understanding of what
constitutes a public, I emphasized the crucial component of interaction: without discussion among citizens, the label 'public' becomes meaningless. I
mentioned the spatial, discursive and communal aspects of such interaction,
and suggested these too are shaped in innumerable ways, often negatively, by
the contingencies of modernity. For example, the social geography of modern
urban life and the nature of the social bonds between citizens tends to reduce
interaction with strangers. From Habermas' perspective, the logic of the system and its instrumental rationality subvert the communicative rationality of
the lifeworld. Indeed, in my discussion of civil society – understood as the
institutionalized lifeworld – I underscored the importance of not only its
democratization generally, but also of its practical facilitation of interaction,
of the conditions which shape communicative encounters. Institutional safe-
guards and protections, including the rights, means and logistics of
interaction, become paramount. This orientation in turn leads us to the various dimensions of citizenship – civic, political, and social – without which
citizens are hampered in their membership and potential participation.

All of civil society is not equivalent to the public sphere, but civil society
constitutes the setting for the interactional dimension of the public sphere. As
Cohen and Arato (1992:502) argue, even if people have political goals with
regard to the state and the economy, civil society is the 'indispensable terrain
on which social actors assemble, organize, and mobilize'. Civil society
becomes, therefore, not just a goal in itself, but also the vehicle for keeping
alive a public sphere in the face of unfavourable media circumstances.

Moreover, I suggested that it is via interaction that we generate not only our socially constructed realities and intersubjectivities, but our identities as well. Thus, we cannot mark a boundary between the generation and maintenance of our identities within civil society on the one hand, and the public sphere on the other. We do not enter the public sphere as fully formed individual citizens; our self conceptions and their collective affinities are perpetual processes which continue to be formed even as we participate within the public sphere itself. Thus, the public sphere is also a terrain of socialization and acculturation, a setting for the shaping of who we are as citizens, and what citizenship itself means to us as part of our identities. Both civil society and the public sphere are in part *constituted by* the sociocultural interaction of citizens; the social world, in short, derives from collective action and interaction.

If television and other media output manifest elements of the arational, likewise so does sociocultural interaction – that is, both media reception and face-to-face encounters with other people. The arational points to modes of reasoning and forms of subjectivity which lie outside the criteria established by Habermas in his theory of communicative rationality. That is to say, non-oppressive intersubjectivity can be established even if communicative rationality is not as fully rational as Habermas' terms would have it. In Chapter 5 I tried to show that we cannot avoid the various arational characteristics of communication; these derive not least from the pre-linguistic modes of signification within the primary processes of the unconscious, and they are especially actualized in the figural signifying regime of the semiotic environment. Habermas is right to warn of the dangers of 'unreason'; the arational embodies a potentially dark and dangerous side – the irrational. Yet so does the rational, as Horkheimer and Adorno, Foucault, and others have argued. At the same time, the arational can give rise to the imaginary, the innovative, the creative; communication between people can generate the unexpected, as can even the sense-making processes of reception among media audiences.

The constructivist approach advocated here implies a view of political subjectivity which is at variance in many ways with the prevailing conceptions of what is called public opinion (see Price, 1992, for a recent overview of the theoretical and methodological issues around opinion research). Without pursuing the many differences in detail, it is worth noting that the tradition of public opinion analysis tends to ignore the context in which the interviews take place – normally a stranger asking questions of an individual out of the blue. While the social processes of opinion generation are often acknowledged, they largely do not figure in the actual survey research. 'Opinion' becomes that which is already present in the respondent's head and is given in reply to questions in a setting which deviates profoundly from the normal interaction within his or her microworlds. Not least, the issue of the choice of questions, their formulations, the alternative answers provided, and their phrasing, all become problematic, as many commentators have observed.

Control over the settings and contexts of discursive interaction can of course shape the nature of what emerges in discourse. For example, within the traditional research field of political communication, the measurement of political knowledge and competence within the general populace has largely been carried out in ways identical to public opinion polling, that is, via large survey data, gathered with the aid of terse questionnaires. The picture which emerges from such studies is generally neither flattering nor encouraging: political ignorance and incompetence appear rampant. On the other hand, when use is made of depth and group interviews, a somewhat different picture emerges. Such methods, which explicitly align themselves with a constructivist stance, capture the capacity among ordinary citizens for discursive creativity, an ability to uncover the connections between private circumstances and public affairs, and critically to analyse current issues within the context of group interaction – even if important factual information may be missing. This capacity is often invisible in the communicatively constrained situation of survey data collection (see Gamson, 1992; Neumann et al., 1992, for examples of such alternative approaches). The talk in such interactional research settings becomes an occasion for manifesting production, rather than for recording something assumed to be already existing and finished, inside people's heads.

In this ongoing generation of social reality, the place of social movements takes on special significance. At the end of Chapter 4 I touched upon contemporary social movements as an expression of the new political milieu of late modernity, as manifestations of political subjectivity which cannot be contained within the limits of established, official politics. We can see social movements as the ever-present political potential of civil society, a witness to the tensions between lifeworld and system. Contemporary movements address an array of issues, and challenge the prevailing social order from various political and cultural positions, outside the institutionalized mechanisms for the mediation of interests. In most movements one can identify a core membership, but there is often a larger, more diffuse membership as well. There are often large groups of sympathizers outside whatever organizational framework may exist.

Collective action has long had a bad press; ever since the first studies of crowd psychology, such action has been coloured by images of irrationality. Alternatively, within functionalist sociology, it has been viewed as an expression of social strain – a problem to be resolved for a more harmonious social system. More recently, especially in the USA, social movements, as a particular form of collective action, have been analysed as rational efforts to enact change based on strategic thinking. Competing with this view is an alternative perspective, largely European in origin, which underscores such themes as collective identity and the role of culture in shaping 'imagined communities', shared values, life styles and political goals, as well as social action generally, as the basis of society. (There is an enormous literature on social movements, which I cannot pursue here; a useful starting point can be found in Morris and Mueller, 1992.) For the purposes of the discussion here, I would just emphasize two aspects: identity and knowledge production.

It is the work of Melucci (1989, 1992) which has argued most compellingly for the understanding of contemporary social movements in terms of identity; participation is not just a means of achieving certain goals but becomes itself a form of fulfilment. The link between social, cultural and political processes on the one hand, and individual subjectivity on the other, is made explicit in such research. Movements are often reflexive in the sense that they are concerned about their own 'usness', about who they are. Their collective identity is part of their overall project, their achievement, a view which ties in with what Giddens terms 'life politics'. This is not to say that strategic goals are absent from such movements, only that strategic goals presuppose a dimension of collective identity. This emphasis on identity is complemented by another perspective developed by Eyerman and Jamison (1991). They emphasize social movements as 'cognitive praxis'. They argue that such movements can be seen as part of society's generation of itself, particularly in terms of the production of knowledge:

> The forms of consciousness that are articulated in social movements provide something crucial in the constitution of modern societies: public spaces for thinking new thoughts, activating new actors, generating new ideas, in short, constructing new intellectual 'projects'. The cognitive praxis of social movements is an important, and all too neglected, source of social innovation. (Eyerman and Jamison, 1991:161)

We can begin to see, at the theoretical level, the coming together of social interaction, the social construction of reality, civil society as a terrain, and the theme of the public sphere. Social movements signify social renewal. As the most explicitly self-conscious and normatively driven activist elements within civil society, they straddle the boundary between culture and politics. Their impact can be quasi-political and political. They can be viewed as highly significant from the standpoint of the public sphere. Through the social interaction which they embody, they carry forward the societal dialogue we associate with the public sphere. In fact, we can see social movements in part as constituting alternative public spheres. In their function of providing collective identities for their members, they are also defining and socializing their participants to new understandings of citizenship. I must hasten to warn against romanticizing social movements (some are quite reactionary), and exaggerating their extent and significance. Only a small minority of the populations of western society belong to social movements. However, indications are that in the current juncture of late modernity, they will continue to grow; and this becomes important not only for society generally, but for the public sphere specifically – their impact can proportionally far exceed the actual extent of their memberships:

> The success of social movements on the level of civil society should be conceived not in terms of the achievement of certain substantive goals or the perpetuation of the movement, but rather in terms of the democratization of values, norms, and institutions that are rooted ultimately in a political culture. Such a development cannot make a given organization or movement permanent, but it can secure the movement form as a normal component of self-democratizing civil societies . . . The rights achieved by movements stabilize the boundaries between lifeworld, state, and economy; but they are also the reflection of newly achieved collective identities, and they constitute the condition of possibility of the emergence of new

institutional arrangements, associations, assemblies, and movements. (Cohen and Arato, 1992:562)

If social movements can be seen as alternative public spheres, we must still specify what public sphere or spheres they are an alternative to, and also try to say something about the relationship between them. In other words, we still need a sketch of the contours of a possible overall public sphere for today's society, one which might address our democratic imaginary, yet still retain an anchoring in present historical circumstances. What follows, and concludes my discussion, is not so much a full-scale, full-blown blueprint as some speculations on possible directions.

Common domain, advocacy domain

Cohen and Arato (1992), as I noted in Chapter 6, include the various forms of public communication, both mediated and face to face, as one of the institutional elements of civil society. This, however, does not imply a simple equation between the public communication of civil society and the public sphere. Much public communication has been institutionally subsumed under the mass media, which in turn – as institutions – straddle the boundaries between the system levels of state/power and economy/money on the one hand, and civil society on the other. The media permeate – and are experienced as part of – the daily life of civil society, but, as often large corporate complexes which are in varying degrees subject to state power, they also reside within the steering systems of modern society. While we must distinguish between a neighbourhood weekly newspaper and a transnational conglomerate, those media institutions which are of most significance for the majority of citizens are, in other words, to a great extent beyond the reach of citizen practices and interventions. That is the rub: this duality is a central source of tension within the public sphere – and, to all possible extent, needs to be democratically modified in media policy considerations.

The more centralized and the more 'massive' the mass media, the more remote and immune they remain to input from civil society. In recent decades there have been many attempts, with modest degrees of success, to decentralize the media, and make them more accessible and responsive to citizens. Many European countries have experienced a growth in local media, such as community radio. The 'minimedia' of various social movements have also played a small but important role, not least in the feminist movement (see C.S. Smith, 1993). At the same time, of course, the major trend within media industries has been towards concentration, and powerful interest groups can make use of their own minimedia.

A way of looking at the public sphere which may cast it in more dynamic and interventionist terms might be to make an explicit analytic distinction between what I call the common domain and the advocacy domain. This distinction already has empirical grounding in that both tendencies are quite evident in western society, but the conceptualization has not gone very far. In this functional differentiation, the common domain is the arena which strives for universalism. It is here we find for the most part the dominant media, which ideally provide information, debate and opinion for all members of society. This is done through a variety of media, formats and representational modes, taking into account the sociocultural segmentation of society. The common domain basically reflects the liberal tradition of the media serving citizens in an impartial manner, even if today we readily understand that such notions of 'objectivity' are always relative, and that 'truth' itself is contingent on discursive reason.

This domain also has the responsibility of trying to maintain the cultural experience of *res publica*, addressing all citizens in their common identity as members of sociopolitical entities. These entities can range, spatially, from local neighbourhoods, through provinces, regions and nation-states, up to the 'global community', but all of them embody the 'society' to which citizens belong. An important criterion and assumption here is a relative goodness of fit between the geographic boundaries of political entities and the reach of the media to which they correspond.

Within any society, prevailing conventional wisdom, not least political wisdom, must be continually revised if the system is to avoid stagnation and remain responsive to changes in its environment. Yet the media of the common domain tend to remain remote from experiences within civil society, and ideologically wedded to the powerful. Thus, this common domain needs to be complemented by what I term an advocacy domain. (This distinction between common and advocacy domains corresponds roughly with the essential features in Curran's (1991) ambitious model of a democratic media system. My emphasis, however, is different and this presentation does not make claims to present a full-scale model for how the media are to be organized, only to demonstrate some conceptual points.)

The advocacy domain consists partly of time and space made available within the dominant media (though I will not pursue the mechanics of this complicated aspect here), and partly of a plurality of smaller 'civic media' from political parties, interest groups, movements, organizations and networks. Civic media encompass a broad and diverse realm of communication channels, including newsletters, electronic bulletin boards, neighbourhood radio stations, magazines and the organizational press. This advocacy domain would be the setting for all citizens who wish to pursue special interests, and generate group-based cultural and political interpretations of society. Ideally, marginalized and oppressed groups would be assisted with financial and technical means to enable their participation in the advocacy domain. The advocacy domain would serve partly as alternative and oppositional public spheres for different groups, as Fraser (1992) and others have urged, allowing them not only to air and shape their own views, but also to develop their group identities. This domain would also function as an organized source, providing dialogic, contesting voices for the common domain. The net result would be what Gans (1979) calls multiperspective journalism, which would help counter the prevailing understanding that there is only one version of what constitutes truth or reality and only one way to talk about it.

In general it is no doubt true, as Chaney (1993:118) remarks, that it is 'impossible for ruling élites to contain the proliferation of more specialist publics who may develop radically alternative interpretive frameworks'. However, the issue is to what extent these alternative frameworks can proliferate and what political impact they can have. We must understand that the growth of the advocacy domain would no doubt also entail an opening for reactionary as well as progressive ideas. How are alternative and oppositional ideas to be promoted and/or contained; what kinds of limit do we need? How much pluralism can political entities manage without unravelling? Such questions will not be settled merely by the rational exercise of policy, they are also 'resolved' in part by the exercise of power. Yet, even the liberal goal of a marketplace of ideas gives credence and legitimacy to the concept of an advocacy domain. It is not far-fetched to think that the qualified institutionalization which we already see in this regard in most liberal democracies could be expanded, given favourable political strategies and circumstances. The assumption is that the common domain would represent the 'lowest common denominator' with regard to shared assumptions, and would struggle centripetally to hold together dominant perceptions, much like the major media do today. The advocacy domain would allow alternative perceptions to flourish, generating adversarial interpretations and cultural practices.

Civic media are better anchored within the contexts of civil society – the everyday lives of their audiences, members and supporters – and are thus theoretically more responsive to them. Civic media are often an expression of members' and supporters' 'identity work' within the respective collectivities, giving voice to these citizens as partisans with special interests. Moreover, civic media (again, ideally) often function as information sources and critical dialogic partners with the major media of the common domain. In other words, a continual and dynamic interface, with a tier-like structure, between the common domain and elements in the advocacy domain is a way of maintaining a pluralism of perspectives in the public sphere. The relationship, the interfaces between common and advocacy domains, is crucial for the success of such a public sphere.

Within the advocacy domain we find a spectrum of media, ranging from slick opinion magazines to the investigative journalism of political activists, from the electronic bulletin boards of high-tech subcultures to desk-top published newsletters of special interest groups and business-oriented think-tanks. Social movements figure importantly here; while some are well established and organized and have their own organizational media which link them together and interface with the dominant media of the common domain, others are less well situated. Most alternative or oppositional civic media have difficulties in their contacts with the media of the common domain. The case of social movements, though perhaps somewhat extreme in this context, illustrates the general problem. While some movements are well established and have civic media output, others are only semi-organized, with occasional press releases being the height of their media activities.

If movements constitute alternative public spheres for their members, their relations with the dominant media at present are far from unproblematic. In an insightful article, Gamson and Wolfsfeld (1993) offer a framework for examining the interaction between the media and social movements. Among the things they observe are that these interactions are highly complex. The media have their own varying organizational conditions and operating procedures, their journalistic cultures and values. The movements have their own. The transactions between them are structured by the asymmetry of power. The movements need the media for mobilizing new members, for validating the movement, and for enlarging the scope of its activities. The media need news, but movements must compete with many other newsmakers for media coverage.

Also, how the movement and its initiatives are framed is an important and contested aspect: the struggle over the meaning of events and issues is crucial, and movements, at least initially, are the underdogs on this score. The tendency towards entertainment slants, mainstream values, dominant modes of discourse, and other factors which characterize the dominant media's ways of operating serve to put social movements at a disadvantage. They are forced into communication strategies which in many cases are culturally remote from them. Yet, as movements become established and begin to develop their own civic media, some of these problems diminish, even if it is at the cost of 'cooptation' and assimilation, the blunting of the movement's radical edge. The point about social movements, however, is that they are dynamic. Over time, some fade, others grow, new ones emerge. The public sphere must be able to adjust to this process. With time and with the development of established practices and policy, it may be possible to develop a better communicative structure between movements and dominant media.

Of course, the policy problems here are immense, and this discussion is not aimed at tackling them. The social anchoring within civil society which groups, associations and movements have is precisely one of the definitive assets of the advocacy domain, enhancing interaction. Structurally, ways must be found to ensure some degree of equity, stability and diversity (political and cultural) within the advocacy domain – both with regard to access to the dominant media as well as to civic media. In the common domain, the dominant media, to safeguard their universality, must be protected to some degree from the state, from capital, and from forms of domination based on class, gender, race and cultural affinities. This is – and must be – an ongoing political struggle. Yet in the advocacy domain, it is precisely this particularity of interests and ways of seeing which must be given expression. Policy-wise, it is no easy task.

Questions abound: for example: how does society ensure viable legal, economic and technical conditions for the advocacy domain without letting capital be the sole criteria for participation? Should civic media be subsidized? How can market mechanisms be structured in ways which foster, rather than hinder, diversity? How can we ensure that the civic media of powerful vested interest groups do not drive out those of weaker movements? Quick reflection will readily bring to mind some of the many other kinds of problem to be dealt with: for example, which individuals/groups are to be deemed the 'legitimate' representatives of a particular movement/interest group? Yet these kinds of structural issues must be confronted if the advocacy domain is to flourish.

In terms of representation, the advocacy status of civic media means that they will be portraying the world in ways which may differ from the canons of professional journalism. To what extent this may require the establishment of alternative sets of guidelines or even legal frameworks is an open question. On the other hand, the ongoing development of newer forms of expression and newer modes of subjectivity can be seen as a strategic asset, particularly within the advocacy domain. The smaller scale of operations and the closer links with civil society's daily life may well permit more experimentation and generate more diversity of cultural expression, which can 'seep' into and modify the common domain, transforming – in the longer perspective – the dominant culture itself.

This returns us to the issue of a centralized versus pluralistic public sphere and the question of a universally valid mode of discourse. Some argue that no one idiom can lay claim to a monopoly of communicative rationality, yet, I would suggest, there is a practical need for a commonly accepted lingua/cultural franca. In blunt terms, money and power tend to be indifferent with respect to cultural diversity. Those who lack the competence to use the communicative idioms prevalent among dominant groups, and who are unable to participate effectively within the political units to which they belong, are at a disadvantage. Particularly in the very explicit case of multilingual and/or multicultural societies, the best strategy seems to be to ensure that as many have access to the dominant idiom as possible, while fostering, multi- rather than mono-registers within the citizenry (see Taylor, 1991).

Within the advocacy domain, however, a wide variety of subcultural, alternative modes of communication may bloom. Apter (1992), in a suggestive essay, writes about the utility of 'inversionary discourse' as a postmodern political strategy aimed at the power centres. Allowing for settings where 'unruly' discourse may manifest itself may in certain circumstances promote 'rational' results. Whatever the mode which flourishes within any particular sector of the advocacy domain, an all-important feature is the 'translation mechanism', that there are people who are multicodal and competent in facilitating communication between the two domains. Without this component, the whole structure comes apart and the adversarial domain becomes reduced to a constellation of discursive ghettos, uncoupled from the common domain and thus politically neutralized.

The possibilities for, and the impact of, the advocacy domain must be seen with a dose of modest realism. Today it is in a rudimentary condition and needs a good deal of nourishment; in the long term, we should treat it as a vital component of the public sphere as a whole. The public sphere, with its two domains, cannot be seen as a *fait accompli*, but remains an ongoing political accomplishment, inseparable from the task of the double democratization of civil society and the state.

References

(Note: In the cases of translation into English, I have restricted myself to providing only the dates of English publication and not noting original publications in other languages.)

Abercrombie, N., Lash, S. and Longhurst, B. (1992) 'Popular representation: recasting realism' in S. Lash and J. Friedman (eds), *Modernity and Identity*. Oxford: Blackwell.

Achille, Y. and Bueno, J.I. (1994) *Les télévisions publiques en quête d'avenir*. Grenoble: Presses Universitaires de Grenoble.

Adbusters Quarterly: Journal of the Mental Environment (1992–) (Vancouver, BC).

d'Agostino, P. and Tafler, D. (eds) (1995) *Transmission: Toward a Post-Television Culture*. 2nd edn. London: Sage.

Alcoff, L. (1988) 'Cultural feminism versus post-structuralism'. *Signs* 13(31).

Alejandro, R. (1993) *Hermeneutics, Citizenship, and the Public Sphere*. Albany: State University of New York Press.

Alexander, J. (1991) 'Habermas and critical theory: beyond the marxian dilemma?' in A. Honneth and H. Joas (eds), *Communicative Action*. Cambridge: Polity Press.

Allen, R.C. (ed.) (1992) *Channels of Discourse, Reassembled*. London: Routledge.

Altheide, D. (1985) *Media Power*. London: Sage.

Altheide, D. and Snow, R. (1991) *Media Worlds in the Post-Journalism Era*. New York: Aldine de Gruyter.

Almond, G. and Verba, S. (eds) (1963) *The Civic Culture*. Princeton, NJ: Princeton University Press.

Ang, I. (1991) *Desperately Seeking the Audience*. London: Routledge.

Ang, I. (1994) 'Ethnography and radical contextualism in audience studies' in L. Grossberg (ed.), *Towards a Comprehensive Theory of the Audience*. Boulder/Oxford: Westview Press.

Apter, D. (1992) 'Democracy and emancipatory movements: notes for a theory of inversionary discourse' in J.N. Pieterse (ed.), *Emancipations, Modern and Postmodern*. London: Sage.

Arato, A. (1994) 'The rise, decline and reconstruction of the concept of civil society and the directions for future research'. *The Public (Javnost)* 1(1–2) (Ljubljana).

Arendt, H. (1958) *The Human Condition*. Chicago: University of Chicago Press.

Arnason, J.P. (1990) 'The theory of modernity and the problematic of democracy' in P. Beilharz, G. Robinson and J. Rundell (eds), *Between Totalitarianism and Postmodernism: A Thesis Eleven Reader*. London: MIT Press.

Baldi, P. (1994) 'New trends in European programmes'. Diffusion EBU: Summer.

Barker, D. (1988) '"It's been real": forms of television representation'. *Critical Studies in Mass Communication* 5:42–56.

Barrett, M. (1991) *The Politics of Truth*. Cambridge: Polity Press.

Barry, A. (1993) 'Television, truth and democracy'. *Media, Culture and Society* 15:487–96.

Baudrillard, J. (1983) *Simulations*. New York: Semiotext(e).

Bauman, Z. (1991) *Modernity and Ambivalence*. Cambridge: Polity Press.

Bauman, Z. (1992) *Intimations of Postmodernity*. London: Routledge.

Baxter, H. (1987) 'System and life-world in Habermas' *Theory of Communicative Action*'. *Theory and Society* 16:39–86.

Beaud, P. (1994) '"Medium without message? Public opinion, in spite of all"'. *Réseaux: The French Journal of Communication* 2(2).

Beck, U. (1992) *Risk Society*. London: Sage.

Beck, U., Giddens, A. and Lash, S. (1994) *Reflexive Modernization*. Cambridge: Polity Press.

Benhabib, S. (1986) *Critique, Norm and Utopia*. New York: Columbia University Press.

Benhabib, S. (1992) *Situating the Self*. Cambridge: Polity Press.

Benhabib, S. and Cornell, D. (eds) (1987) *Feminism as Critique*. Cambridge: Polity Press.

Benjamin, A. (ed.) (1989) *The Lyotard Reader*. Oxford: Blackwell.

Bennett, L. (1988) *News: The Politics of Illusion*. New York: Longman.

Bennett, L. and Edelman, M. (1985) 'Toward a new political narrative'. *Journal of Communication* 35(3).

Bennington, G. (1988) *Lyotard: Writing the Event*. Manchester: Manchester University Press.

Berger, P. and Luckmann, T. (1967) *The Social Construction of Reality*. London: Penguin.

Berman, M. (1982) *All That is Solid Melts into Air*. London: Penguin.

Berman, R. (1991) 'Popular culture and populist culture'. *Telos* 87: Spring.

Bernstein, R. (1983) *Beyond Objectivism and Relativism*. London: Blackwell.

Best, S. and Kellner, D. (1987) '(Re)watching television: notes toward a political criticism'. *Diacritics*: Summer.

Best, S. and Kellner, D. (1991) *Postmodern Theory*. London: Macmillan.

Björkegren, D. (1994) 'Turbo TV'. Stockholm School of Economics: *MTC Annual Report*.

Bock, G. and James, S. (eds) (1992) *Beyond Equality and Difference: Citizenship, Feminist Politics and Female Subjectivity*. London: Routledge.

Bourdieu, P. (1977) *Outline of a Theory of Practice*. Cambridge: Cambridge University Press.

Brenkman, J. (1987) *Culture and Domination*. Ithaca, NY: Cornell University Press.

Brown, Wendy (1988) *Manhood and Politics: A Feminist Reading in Political Theory*. Totowa, NJ: Rowman and Littlefield.

Brown, M.E. (ed.) (1990) *Television and Women's Culture*. London: Sage.

Bruner, J. (1986) *Actual Minds, Possible Worlds*. Cambridge, MA: Harvard University Press.

Burkitt, I. (1991) *Social Selves*. London: Sage.

Butler, J. and Scott, J.W. (eds) (1992) *Feminists Theorize the Political*. London: Routledge.

Calhoun, C. (ed.) (1992) *Habermas and the Public Sphere*. London: MIT Press.

Calhoun, C. (1993) 'Civil society and the public sphere'. *Public Culture* 5(2): Winter.

Camauër, Leonor (1993) 'Populär TV-journalistik och offentlighetsteori: en fallstudie av Ikväll: Robert Aschberg' in Peter Dahlgren (ed.), *Den mångtydiga rutan: nordisk forskning om TV*. Stockholm: Department of Journalism, Media and Communication, Stockholm University.

Canovan, M. (1994) 'Politics as culture: Hannah Arendt and the public realm' in L.P. Hinchman and S.K. Hinchman (eds), *Hannah Arendt: Critical Essays*. Albany: State University of New York Press.

Carey, J.W. (1989) *Communication as Culture*. London: Unwin.

Carpignano, P., Anderson, R., Aronowitz, S. and Difazio, W. (1990) 'Chatter in the age of electronic reproduction: talk television and the "public mind"'. *Social Text* 25/26:33–55.

Castoriadis, C. (1987) *The Imaginary Institution of Society*. Cambridge: Polity Press.

Castoriadis, C. (1994) 'Radical imagination and the social instituting imaginary' in G. Robinson and J. Rundell (eds), *Rethinking Imagination*. London: Routledge.

Caughie, J. (1991) 'Adorno's reproach: repetition, difference and television genre'. *Screen* 32(2).

Chaney, D. (1993) *Fictions of Collective Life: Public Drama in Late Modern Culture*. London: Routledge.

Charon, J.-M. (1994) 'The fragmentation of journalism'. *Réseaux: the French Journal of Communication* 2(1).

Cohen, A., Levy, M., Gurevitch, M. and Roeh, I. (1995) *Eurovision and the Globalization of Television News*. London: John Libby.

Cohen, J. and Arato, A. (1992) *Civil Society and Political Theory*. London: MIT Press.

Cohen, S. and Taylor, L. (1992) *Escape Attempts*. 2nd edn. London: Routledge.

Collins, J. (1992) 'Television and postmodernism' in R.C. Allen (ed.), *Channels of Discourse, Reassembled*. London: Routledge.

Collins, R. (1992) *Satellite Television in Western Europe*. Rev. edn. London: John Libby.

Collins, R. (1993) 'Public service versus the market ten years on: reflections on Critical Theory and the debate on broadcasting policy in the UK'. *Screen* 34(3).

Coole, D. (1992) 'Modernity and its Other(s)'. *History of the Human Sciences* 5(3).

Corner, J. (1991) 'Meaning, genre and context: the problematics of "public knowledge" in the new audience studies' in J. Curran and M. Gurevitch (eds), *Mass Media and Society*. London: Edward Arnold.

Corner, J. (1992) 'Presumption as theory: "realism" in television studies'. *Screen* 33(1).

Corner, J. (1995) *Television Form and Public Address*. London: Edward Arnold.

Curran, J. (1990) 'The new revisionism in mass communication research: a reappraisal'. *European Journal of Communication* 5: 135–64.

Curran, J. (1991) 'Mass media and democracy: a reappraisal' in J. Curran and M. Gurevitch (eds), *Mass Media and Society*. London: Edward Arnold.

Dahlgren, P. (forthcoming) 'Cultural Studies and media research' in J. Corner, P. Schlesinger and R. Silverstone (eds), *The International Handbook of Media Research*. London: Routledge.

Dahlgren, Peter and Sparks, Colin (eds) (1991) *Communication and Citizenship*. London: Routledge.

Dahlgren, Peter and Sparks, Colin (eds) (1992) *Journalism and Popular Culture*. London: Sage.

Davis, D.K. (1990) 'News and politics' in D.L. Swanson and D. Nimmo (eds) *New Directions in Political Communication*. London: Sage.

Deming, R.H. (1985) 'Discourse/talk/television'. *Screen* 26(6).

Dewey, J. (1954/1923) *The Public and its Problems*. Chicago: Swallow Press.

Dews, P. (1987) *Logics of Disintegration: Post-structuralist Thought and the Claims of Critical Theory*. London: Verso.

Dews, P. (1989) 'The return of the subject in late Foucault'. *Radical Philosophy* 51: Spring.

Diamond, E. and Bates, S. (1988) *The Spot: The Rise of Political Advertising on Television*. 3rd edn. London: MIT Press.

Dietz, M. (1991) 'Hannah Arendt and feminist politics' in M. Lyndon and C. Pateman (eds), *Feminist Interpretations and Political Theory*. Cambridge: Polity Press. Also in: L.P. Hinchman and S.K. Hinchman (eds) (1994), *Hannah Arendt: Critical Essays*. Albany: State University of New York Press.

Dietz, M. (1992) 'Context is all: feminism and theories of citizenship' in C. Mouffe (ed.), *Dimensions of Radical Democracy*. London: Verso.

Eder, K. (1993) *The New Politics of Class: Social Movements and Cultural Dynamics in Advanced Societies*. London: Sage.

Eduards, M. (1991) 'Toward a third way: women's politics and welfare policies in Sweden'. *Social Research* 58(3).

Eliasoph, N. (1990) 'Political culture and the presentation of political self'. *Theory and Society* 19(4).

Elliott, A. (1992) *Social Theory and Psychoanalysis in Transition*. London: Blackwell.

Elliott, P. (1972) *The Making of a Television Series*. London: Constable.

Elshtain, J.B. (1993) *Public Man, Private Woman: Women in Social and Political Thought*. 2nd edn. Princeton, NJ: Princeton University Press.

Enzensberger, H.M. (1993) *Inbördes krig*. Stockholm: Norstedts. ('De vill skicka sig själva till den absoluta botten'. *Dagens Nyheter*, 23 June, p. B3).

Ericson, R.V., Baranek, B.M. and Chan, J.B.L. (1987) *Visualizing Deviance: A Study of News Organization*. Milton Keynes: Open University Press.

Ericson, R.V., Baranek, B.M. and Chan, J.B.L. (1989) *Negotiating Control: A Study of News Sources*. Milton Keynes: Open University Press.

Eyerman, R. and Jamison, A. (1991) *Social Movements: A Cognitive Approach*. Cambridge: Polity Press.

Falk, R. (1994) 'The making of global citizenship' in B. van Steenbergen (ed.), *The Condition of Citizenship*. London: Sage.

Fay, B. (1987) *Critical Social Science*. Cambridge: Polity Press.

Featherstone, M. (ed.) (1990) *Global Culture*. London: Sage.

Featherstone, M. (1991) *Consumer Culture and Postmodernism*. London: Sage.

Featherstone, M. (1992) 'Postmodernization and the aestheticization of everyday life' in S. Lash and J. Friedman (eds), *Modernity and Identity*. Oxford: Blackwell.

Featherstone, M. (1993) 'Global and local cultures' in J. Bird, B. Curtis, T. Putnum, G. Robertson and L. Tickner (eds), *Mapping the Futures*. London: Routledge.

Ferguson, M. (1992) 'The mythology about globalization'. *European Journal of Communication* 7:69–93.

Feuer, J. (1992) 'Genre study and television' in R.C. Allen (ed.), *Channels of Discourse, Reassembled*. London: Routledge.

Findahl, O. (1988) *Televisionen möjligheter och begränsningar*. Stockholm: Swedish Broadcasting.

Findahl, O. and Höijer, B. (1981) 'Media content and human comprehension' in K.E. Rosengren (ed.), *Advances in Content Analysis*. London: Sage.

Findahl, O. and Höijer, B. (1985) 'Some characteristics of news viewing and comprehension'. *Journal of Broadcasting and Electronic Media* 29(49).

Fiske, J. (1987) *Television Culture*. London: Routledge

Fiske, John (1989) 'Popular news' in J. Fiske (ed.), *Reading the Popular*. London: Unwin Hyman.

Flax, J. (1990) 'Postmodernism and gender relations in feminist theory' in Linda J. Nicholson (ed.), *Feminism/Postmodernism*. London: Routledge.

Fornäs, J. (1995) *Cultural Theory and Late Modernity*. London: Sage.

Foucault, M. (1984) 'What is Enlightenment?' in P. Rabinow (ed.), *The Foucault Reader*. New York: Pantheon.

Fraser, N. (1987) 'What's critical about critical theory? The case of Habermas and gender' in S. Benhabib and D. Cornell (eds), *Feminism as Critique*. Cambridge: Polity Press.

Fraser, N. (1990) 'Talking about needs: interpretive contests as political conflicts in welfare state societies' in C.R. Sunstein (ed.), *Feminism and Political Theory*. Chicago/London: University of Chicago Press.

Fraser, N. (1992) 'Rethinking the public sphere: a contribution to the critique of actually existing democracy' in C. Calhoun, (ed.), *Habermas and the Public Sphere*. London: MIT Press.

Frosh, S. (1991) *Identity Crisis: Modernity, Psychoanalysis and the Self*. London: Macmillan.

Gamson, W.A. (1992) *Talking Politics*. Cambridge: Cambridge University Press.

Gamson, W.A. and Wolfsfeld, G. (1993) 'Movements and media as interacting systems'. *Annals, AASSS* 528: July.

Gandy, O. (1993) *The Panoptic Sort: A Political Economy of Personal Information*. San Francisco/Oxford: Westview Press.

Gans, H. (1979) *Deciding What's News*. New York: Random House.

Garnham, N. (1983) 'Public service versus the market'. *Screen* 5(1).

Garnham, N. (1992) 'The media and the public sphere' in C. Calhoun (ed.), *Habermas and the Public Sphere*. Cambridge, MA and London: MIT Press.

Gellner, E. (1994) *Conditions of Liberty: Civil Society and its Rivals*. New York: Allen Lane/Penguin Press.

Giddens, A. (1990) *The Consequences of Modernity*. Cambridge: Polity Press.

Giddens, A. (1991) *Modernity and Self-Identity*. Cambridge: Polity Press.

Gitlin, T. (1985) *Inside Prime Time*. New York: Pantheon.

Gitlin, T. (1991a) 'Bites and blips: chunk news, savvy talk and the bifurcation of American politics' in P. Dahlgren and C. Sparks (eds), *Communication and Citizenship*. London: Routledge.

Gitlin, T. (1991b) 'The politics of communication and the communication of politics' in J. Curran and M. Gurevitch (eds), *Mass Media and Society*. London: Edward Arnold.

Golding, P. (1990) 'Political communication and citizenship: the media and democracy in an inegalitarian social order' in M. Ferguson (ed.), *Public Communication: The New Imperatives*. London: Sage.

Golding, P. and Elliott, P. (1979) *Making the News*. London: Longman.

Golding, P. and Murdock, G. (1991) 'Culture, communication and political economy' in J. Curran and M. Gurevitch (eds), *Mass Media and Society*. London: Edward Arnold.

Graber, D. (1987) *Processing the News*. 2nd edn. New York: Longman.

Griffin, M. (1992) 'Looking at TV news: strategies for research'. *Communication* 13:121–41.

Gunter, B. (1987) *Poor Reception: Misunderstanding and Forgetting Broadcast News*. Hillsdale, NJ: Lawrence Erlbaum.

Habermas, J. (1984, 1987/1981) *The Theory of Communicative Action*. 2 vols. Cambridge: Polity Press.

Habermas, J. (1989/1962) *Structural Transformation of the Public Sphere*. Cambridge: Polity Press.

Habermas, J. (1992a) 'Further reflections on the public sphere' in C. Calhoun (ed.), *Habermas and the Public Sphere*. London: MIT Press.

Habermas, J. (1992b) *Postmetaphysical Thinking*. Cambridge, MA and London: MIT Press.

Hackett, R.A. (1984) 'Decline of a paradigm? Bias and objectivity in news media studies'. *Critical Studies in Mass Communication* 1(3).

Hagen, I. (1994) 'The ambivalence of TV news viewing: between ideals and everyday practices'. *European Journal of Communication* 9:193–220.

Hall. S. (1974) 'Media power: the double bind'. *Journal of Communication*: Autumn.

Hall, S. (1984) 'The narrative construction of reality' (Interview). *The Southern Review*: 17 March.

Hall, S. (1992) 'The question of cultural identity' in S. Hall, D. Held and T. McGrew (eds), *Modernity and its Futures*. Milton Keynes: Open University Press.

Hall, S., Held, D., and McGrew, T. (eds) (1992) *Modernity and its Futures*. Milton Keynes: Open University Press.

Hallin, D.C. (1994) *We Keep America on Top of the World: Television Journalism and the Public Sphere*. London: Routledge.

Hannerz, U. (1992) *Cultural Complexity: Studies in the Social Organization of Meaning*. New York: Columbia University Press.

Hansen, K. (1987) 'Feminist conceptions of public and private'. *Berkeley Journal of Sociology* 32.

Hansen, M. (1993) 'Unstable mixtures, dilated spheres: Negt and Kluge's *The Public Sphere and Experience*, twenty years later'. *Public Culture* 5:179–212.

Harris, D. (1992) *From Class Politics to the Politics of Pleasure*. London: Routledge.

Hart, A. (1988) *Making The Real World: A Study of a Television Series*. Cambridge: Cambridge University Press.

Hartley, J. (1992a) 'Heliography: journalism and the visualization of truth' in J. Hartley (ed.), *The Politics of Pictures*. London: Routledge.

Hartley, J. (1992b) *Tele-ology: Studies in Television*. London: Routledge.

Harvey, D. (1989) *The Condition of Postmodernity*. Oxford: Blackwell.

Harvey, D. (1993) 'From space to place and back again: reflections on the condition of postmodernity' in J. Bird, B. Curtis, T. Putnam, G. Robertson and L. Tickner (eds), *Mapping the Futures*. London: Routledge.

Heater, D. (1990) *Citizenship: The Civic Ideal in World History, Politics and Education*. London and New York: Longman.

Heath, S. (1990) 'Representing television' in P. Mellancamp (ed.), *Logics of Television*. Bloomington: University of Indiana Press.

Hebdige, D. (1988) *Hiding in the Light*. London: Routledge.

Hekman, S.J. (1990) *Gender and Knowledge: Elements of a Postmodern Feminism*. Cambridge: Polity Press.

Held, D. (1989) *Political Theory and the Modern State*. Cambridge: Polity Press.

Held, D. (1991) 'Between state and civil society: citizenship' in G. Andrews (ed.), *Citizenship*. London: Lawrence and Wishart.

Held, D. (1993) 'Democracy: from city states to a cosmopolitan order?' in D. Held (ed.), *Prospects for Democracy*. Cambridge: Polity Press.

Heller, A. and Fehér, F. (1988) *The Postmodern Political Condition*. Cambridge: Polity Press.

Herbst, S. (1993) 'The meaning of public opinion: citizens' constructions of political reality'. *Media, Culture and Society* 15(3).

Hermes, J. (1993) 'Meaning, media and everyday life'. *Cultural Studies* 7(3).

Hirdman, Y. (1991) 'The gender system' in T. Andreasen (ed.), *Moving On: New Perspectives on the Women's Movement*. Aarhus: Aarhus University Press.

Hjarvard, S. (1993) 'Pan-European television news: towards a European political public sphere?' in P. Drummond, et al., (eds), *National Identity and Europe: The Television Revolution.* London: British Film Institute.

Hobsbawm, E. (1994) *Age of Extremes: the Short Twentieth Century 1914–1991.* London: Michael Joseph. (Quoted in *The Independent on Sunday,* 'The Sunday Review', 16 Oct., 1994, pp. 9–11).

Hohendahl, P. (1992) 'The public sphere: models and boundaries' in C. Calhoun (ed.), *Habermas and the Public Sphere.* London: MIT Press.

Honig, B. (1992) 'Toward an agonistic feminism: Hannah Arendt and the politics of identity' in J. Butler and J.W. Scott (eds), *Feminists Theorize the Political.* London: Routledge

Hoy, D.C. and McCarthy, T. (1994) *Critical Theory.* Oxford: Blackwell.

Hoynes, W. (1994) *Public Television for Sale: Media, the Market and the Public Sphere.* Oxford: Westview Press.

Hvitfelt, H. (1994) 'The commercialization of the evening news: changes in narrative techniques in Swedish TV news'. *The Nordicom Review* 2:33–41.

Höijer, B. (1992) 'Socio-cognitive structures and television reception'. *Media, Culture and Society* 14:583–603.

Ingram, D. (1987) *Habermas and the Dialectic of Reason.* New Haven, CT and London: Yale University Press.

Jameson, F. (1983) 'Pleasure: a political issue' in *Formations of Pleasure.* London: Routledge and Kegan Paul.

Jameson, F. (1991) *Postmodernism: or, the Cultural Logic of Late Capitalism.* London: Verso.

Jensen, K.B. (1990) 'The politics of polysemy: television news, everyday consciousness and political action'. *Media, Culture and Society* 12:57–77.

Jónasdóttir, A.G. (1991) *Love, Power and Political Interests.* Örebro, Sweden: University of Örebro Press.

Joyrich, L. (1991–92) 'Going through the e/motions: gender, postmodernism, and affect in television studies'. *Discourse* 14(1).

Katz, E. and Lazarsfeld, P. (1955) *Personal Influence.* Glencoe, IL: Free Press.

Keane, J. (1984) *Public Life and Late Capitalism.* New York: Cambridge University Press.

Keane, J. (1988a) *Democracy and Civil Society.* London: Verso.

Keane, J. (ed.) (1988b) *Civil Society and the State.* London: Verso.

Keane, J. (1991) *The Media and Democracy.* Cambridge: Polity Press.

Kearney, R. (1991) *The Poetics of Imagining.* London: HarperCollins Academic.

Kellner, D. (1990) *Television and the Crisis of Democracy.* Boulder/Oxford: Westview Press.

Kelly, M. (ed.) (1994) *Critique and Power: Recasting the Foucault/Habermas Debate.* Cambridge, MA and London: MIT Press.

Kepplinger, H.M. and Köcher, R. (1990) 'Professionalism in the media world?'. *European Journal of Communication* 5:285–311.

Kilborn, R. (1994) '"How real can you get?": recent developments in "reality" television'. *European Journal of Communication* 9:421–39.

Knight, G. (1989) 'The reality effects of tabloid television news' in M. Raboy and P.A. Bruck (eds), *Communication For and Against Democracy.* Montreal: Black Rose Books.

Knight, G. and Dean, T. (1982) 'Myth and the structure of news'. *Journal of Communication* 32(2).

Kress, G. (1986) 'Language in the media: the construction of the domains of public and private'. *Media, Culture and Society* 8:395–419.

Kristeva, J. (1984) *Revolution in Poetic Language.* New York: Columbia University Press.

Laclau, E. and Mouffe, C. (1985) *Hegemony and Socialist Strategy.* London: Verso.

Langer, J. (1992) 'Truly awful news on television' in P. Dahlgren and C. Sparks (eds), *Journalism and Popular Culture.* London: Sage.

Larsen, P. (1992) 'More than just images: the whole picture. News in the multi-channel universe' in N. Skovmand and K.C. Schrøder (eds), *Media Cultures.* London: Routledge.

Lash, S. (1990) *The Sociology of Postmodernism.* London: Routledge.

Lash, S. (1994) 'Reflexivity and its doubles: structure, aesthetics, community' in U. Beck, A. Giddens and S. Lash, *Reflexive Modernization.* Cambridge: Polity Press.

Lash, S. and Urry, J. (1987) *Disorganized Capitalism.* Cambridge: Polity Press.

Lash, S. and Urry, J. (1994) *Economies of Signs and Space*. London: Sage.

Lavoinne, Y. (1994) 'Journalists, history and historians'. *Réseaux: the French Journal of Communication* 2(2).

Lawson, H. (1985) *Reflexivity: The Postmodern Predicament*. London: Hutchinson.

Lee, B. (1993) 'Going public'. *Public Culture* 5:165–78.

Lenart, S. (1994) *Shaping Political Attitudes: The Impact of Interpersonal Communication and Mass Media*. London: Sage.

Lindell, K. (1992) 'Den 4.e dimensionen'. *Pressens Tidning* 20:12–13, 20.

Livingstone, S. and Lunt, P. (1994) *Talk on Television*. London: Routledge.

Lodziak, C. (1986) *The Power of Television*. London: Frances Pinter.

Luke, T.W. (1989) *Screens of Power*. Urbana and Chicago: University of Illinois Press.

Lull, J. (1990) *Inside Family Viewing*. London: Routledge.

Lundqvist, Å. (1992) 'Politiker som "opolitisk underhållning"'. *Dagens Nyheter*, 29 Nov., section C, p. 7.

McCarthy, T. (1991) *Ideals and Illusions*. Boston, MA: MIT Press.

McClure, K. (1992) 'On the subject of rights: pluralism, plurality and political identity' in C. Mouffe (ed.), *Dimensions of Radical Democracy*. London: Verso.

McGrew, A. (1992) 'A global society?' in S. Hall, D. Hall and T. McGrew (eds), *Modernity and its Futures*. Cambridge: Polity Press/Open University.

McGuigan, J. (1992) *Cultural Populism*. London: Routledge.

McIntyre, J.S. (1987) 'Repositioning a landmark: the Hutchins Commission and freedom of the press'. *Critical Studies in Mass Communication* 4:136–60.

McLaughlin, L. (1993a) 'Feminism, the public sphere, media and democracy'. *Media, Culture and Society* 15:599–620.

McLaughlin, L. (1993b) 'Chastity criminals in the age of electronic reproduction: reviewing talk television and the public sphere'. *Journal of Communication Inquiry* 17(1).

McLennan, G. (1992) 'The enlightenment project revisited' in S. Hall, D. Held and T. McGrew (eds), *Modernity and its Futures*. Cambridge: Polity Press/Open University.

McManus, J.H. (1994) *Market-Driven Journalism: Let the Citizen Beware?* London: Sage.

Madison, G.B. (1988) *The Hermeneutics of Postmodernity*. Bloomington: Indiana University Press.

Mander, M. (1987) 'Narrative dimensions of the news: omniscience, prophesy and morality'. *Communication* 10:51–70.

Marshall, B.L. (1994) *Engendering Modernity: Feminism, Social Theory and Social Change*. Cambridge: Polity Press.

Marshall, T.H. (1950) *Citizenship and Social Class*. Cambridge: Cambridge University Press.

Meehan, E. (1993) *Citizenship and the European Community*. London: Sage.

Melucci, A. (1989) *Nomads of the Present*. London: Hutchinson.

Melucci A. (1992) 'Liberation or meaning? Social movements, culture and democracy' in J. Nederveen Pieterse (ed.), *Emancipations, Modern and Postmodern*. London: Sage.

Meyrowitz, J. (1985) *No Sense of Place*. New York: Oxford University Press.

Micheletti, M. (1994) *Det civila samhället och staten*. Stockholm: Fritzes.

Milner, A. (1993) *Cultural Materialism*. Melbourne: Melbourne University Press.

Molander, B. (1993) *Kunskap i handling*. Göteborg: Daidalos.

Moores, S. (1993a) *Interpreting Audiences*. London: Sage.

Moores, S, (1993b) 'Television, geography and "mobile privatization"'. *European Journal of Communication* 8:365–79.

Morley, D. (1992) *Television, Audiences and Cultural Studies*. London: Routledge.

Morley, D. and Silverstone, R. (1990) 'Domestic communication – technologies and meanings'. *Media Culture and Society* 12:31–55.

Morris, A.D. and Mueller, C.M. (eds) (1992) *Frontiers in Social Movement Theory*. New Haven, CT and London: Yale University Press.

Morse, M. (1985) 'Talk, talk, talk'. *Screen* 26(2).

Mouffe, C. (1988a) 'Hegemony and new political subjects: toward a new concept of democracy' in C. Nelson and L. Grossberg (eds), *Marxism and the Interpretation of Culture*. Urbana: University of Illinois Press.

Mouffe, C. (1988b) 'Radical democracy: modern or postmodern?' in A. Ross (ed.), *Universal Abandon? The Politics of Postmodernism*. Edinburgh: Edinburgh University Press.

Mouffe C. (ed.) (1992a) *Dimensions of Radical Democracy*. London: Verso.

Mouffe, C. (1992b) 'Democratic citizenship and the political community' in C. Mouffe (ed.), *Dimensions of Radical Democracy*. London: Verso.

Mouffe, C. (1992c) 'Feminism, citizenship and radical democratic politics' in J. Butler and J.W. Scott (eds), *Feminists Theorize the Political*. London: Routledge.

Mouffe, C. (1993) *The Return of the Political*. London: Verso.

Mulgan, G. (1991) *Communication and Control: Networks and the New Economies of Control*. Cambridge: Polity Press.

Mulgan, G. (1994) *Politics in an Antipolitical Age*. Cambridge: Polity Press.

Murdock, G. (1990) 'Television and citizenship: in defence of public broadcasting' in A. Tomlinson (ed.), *Consumption, Identity and Style*. London: Routledge.

Murdock, G. (1992) 'Citizens, consumers, and public culture' in M. Skovmand and K.C. Schrøder (eds), *Media Cultures*. London: Routledge.

Murdock, G. (1993) 'Communication and the constitution of modernity'. *Media, Culture and Society* 15:521–39.

Murdock, G. and Golding, P. (1989) 'Information poverty and political inequality: citizenship in the age of privatized communications'. *Journal of Communication* 39(3).

Negt, O. and Kluge, A. (1993/1972) *The Public Sphere and Experience*. Minneapolis: University of Minnesota Press.

Neumann, R.W., Just, M.R. and Crigler, A.N. (1992) *Common Knowledge*. Chicago: University of Chicago Press.

Newcomb, H. and Hirsch, P.M. (1984) 'Television as a cultural forum' in W.D. Rowland and B. Watkins (eds), *Interpreting Television*. London: Sage.

Nicholson, L. (ed.) (1991) *Feminism/Postmodernism*. London: Routledge.

Nicholson, L. (1992) 'Feminist theory: the private and the public' in L. McDowell and R. Pringle (eds), *Defining Women*. Cambridge: Polity Press/Open University.

Olson, S.R. (1987) 'Meta-television: popular postmodernism'. *Critical Studies in Mass Communication* 4:284–300.

Passerin d'Entrèves, M. (1992) 'Hannah Arendt and the idea of citizenship' in C. Mouffe (ed.), *Dimensions of Radical Democracy*. London: Verso.

Pateman, C. (1987) 'Feminist critiques of the public/private dichotomy' in A. Phillips (ed.), *Feminism and Equality*. Oxford: Blackwell.

Pateman, C. (1988) 'The fraternal social contract' in J. Keane (ed.), *Civil Society and the State*. London: Verso.

Pateman, C. (1992) 'The patriarchal welfare state' in L. McDowell and R. Pringle (eds), *Defining Women*. Cambridge: Polity Press/Open University Press.

Peck, J. (1995) 'Talk shows as therapeutic discourse: the ideological labor of the televised talking cure'. *Communication Theory* 5(1):58–81.

Peters, J.D. (1993) 'Distrust of representation: Habermas on the public sphere'. *Media, Culture and Society* 15(4).

Phillips, A. (1991) *Engendering Democracy*. Cambridge: Polity Press.

Phillips, A. (1993) *Democracy and Difference*. Cambridge: Polity Press.

Philo, G. (1990) *Seeing and Believing: The Influence of Television*. London: Routledge.

Pieterse, J.N. (ed.) (1992) *Emancipations, Modern and Postmodern*. London: Sage.

Poole, R. (1991) *Morality and Modernity*. London: Routledge.

Porter, E.J. (1991) *Women and Moral Identity*. North Sydney: Allen and Unwin.

Porter, V. (1993) 'The consumer and transfrontier television'. *Consumer Policy Review* 3(3).

Poster, M. (1989) *Critical Theory and Poststructuralism*. Ithaca, NY: Cornell University Press.

Postman, N. (1985) *Amusing Ourselves to Death*. New York: Viking.

Powers, R. (1977) *The Newscasters: The News Business as Show Business*. New York: St. Martin's Press.

Price, V. (1992) *Public Opinion*. London: Sage.

Raboy, M. (1991) 'L'économie politique des médias et le nouvel espace public de la communication' in M. Beauchamp (ed.), *Communication Publique et Société*. Boucherville, Québec: Gaëtan Morin.

Raboy, M. (1994) 'The role of the public in broadcast policy-making and regulation: lessons for Europe from Canada'. *European Journal of Communication* 9:5–23.

Raboy, M. and Dagenais, B. (eds) (1992) *Media, Crisis and Democracy*. London: Sage

Rajchman, J. (1988) 'Habermas's complaint'. *New German Critique* 46: Fall.

Readings, B. (1991) *Introducing Lyotard: Art and Politics*. London: Routledge.

Reimer, B. (1994) *The Most Common of Practices: On Mass Media Use in Late Modernity*. Stockholm: Almqvist & Wiksell International.

Reimer, B. (1995) 'The media in public and private spheres' in J. Fornäs and G. Bolin (eds), *Youth Culture in Late Modernity*. London: Sage.

Rheingold, H. (1994) *Virtual Community: Homesteading on the Electronic Frontier*. New York: Harper Perennial.

Richardson, L. (1990) 'Narrative and sociology'. *Journal of Contemporary Ethnography* 19(1).

Ricoeur, P. (1974) 'Consciousness and the unconscious' in P. Ricoeur (ed.), *The Conflict of Interpretations*. Evanston, IL: Northwestern University Press.

Ricoeur, P. (1981) *Hermeneutics and the Human Sciences*. J.B. Thompson (ed. and trans.). Cambridge: Cambridge University Press.

Ricoeur, P. (1984, 1986) *Time and Narrative*. 2 vols. Chicago: University of Chicago Press.

Ricoeur, P. (1986) *Ideology and Utopia*. New York: Columbia University Press.

Ricoeur, P. (1994) 'Imagination in discourse and action' in G. Robinson and J. Rundell (eds), *Rethinking Imagination*. London: Routledge.

Robertson, R. (1992) *Globalization*. London: Sage.

Robins, K. (1993) 'The war, the screen, the crazy dog and poor mankind'. *Media, Culture and Society* 15:321–7.

Robinson, J.P. and Levy, M.R. (1986) *The Main Source: Learning from Television News*. Beverley Hills, CA: Sage.

Roche, M. (1992) *Rethinking Citizenship: Welfare, Ideology and Change in Modern Society*. Cambridge: Polity Press.

Rosen, J. (1986) 'The impossible press: American journalism and the decline of public life'. PhD dissertation, New York University.

Rosenstiel, T.B. (1992) 'Talk-show journalism' in P.S. Cook, D. Gomery and L.W. Lichty (eds), *The Future of News*. London: Johns Hopkins University Press.

Ruellan, D. (1993) 'An undefined profession: the issue of professionalism in the journalistic milieu'. *Réseaux: the French Journal of Communication* 1(2).

Rundell, J. (1994) 'Creativity and judgement: Kant on reason and imagination' in G. Robinson and J. Rundell (eds), *Rethinking Imagination*. London: Routledge.

Saenz, M. (1992) 'Television viewing as a cultural practice'. *Journal of Communication Inquiry* 16(2).

Scannell, P. (1989) 'Public service broadcasting and modern public life'. *Media, Culture and Society* 11:135–66.

Scannell, P. (ed.) (1991) *Broadcast Talk*. London: Sage.

Schiller, H. (1991) 'Not yet the post-imperialist era'. *Critical Studies in Mass Communication* 8:13–28.

Schlesinger, P. (1987) *Putting Reality Together*. 2nd edn. London: Methuen.

Schlesinger, P. (1993) 'Wishful thinking: cultural politics, media and collective identities in Europe'. *Journal of Communication* 43(2).

Schlesinger, P. (1994) 'Europe's contradictory communicative space'. *Dædalus*: Spring.

Schudson. M. (1978) *Discovering the News*. New York: Basic Books.

Schudson. M. (1991) 'The sociology of news production revisited' in J. Curran and M. Gurevitch (eds), *Mass media and Society*. London: Edward Arnold.

Schutz, A. (1970) *On Phenomenology and Social Relations*. Chicago: University of Chicago Press.

Schwoch, J. (1993) 'Cold war, hegemony, postmodernism: American television and the world-system, 1945–92'. *Quarterly Review of Film & Video* 14(3).

Seidman, S. (1990) 'Substantive debates: moral order and social crises – perspectives on modern culture' in J.C. Alexander and S. Seidman (eds), *Culture and Society*. Cambridge: Cambridge University Press.

Seligman, A.B. (1993) 'The fragile ethical vision of civil society' in B. Turner (ed.), *Citizenship and Social Theory*. London: Sage.

Sennett, R. (1977) *The Fall of Public Man*. New York: Knopf.

Sholle, D. (1993) 'Buy our news: tabloid television and commodification'. *Journal of Communication Inquiry* 17(1).

Shotter, J. (1993a) *Conversational Realities*. London: Sage.

Shotter, J. (1993b) 'Psychology and citizenship: identity and belonging' in B. Turner (ed.), *Citizenship and Social Theory*. London: Sage.

Silverstone, R. (1981) *The Message of Television*. London: Heinemann.

Silverstone, R. (1988) 'Television, myth and narrative' in J. Carey (ed.), *Media, Myth and Narrative*. London: Sage.

Silverstone, R. (1990) 'Towards an anthropology of the television audience' in M. Ferguson (ed.), *Political Communication: the New Imperatives*. London: Sage.

Silverstone, R. (1994) *Television and Everyday Life*. London: Routledge.

Silverstone, R., Hirsch, E. and Morley, D. (1992) 'Information and communication technologies and the moral economy of the household' in R. Silverstone and E. Hirsch (eds), *Consuming Technologies*. London: Routledge.

Simonds, A. (1989) 'Ideological domination and the political information market'. *Theory and Society* 18:181–211.

Smart, B. (1993) *Postmodernity*. London: Routledge.

Smith, C.S. (1993) 'Feminist media and cultural politics' in P. Creedon (ed.), *Women in Mass Communication*. 2nd edn. London: Sage.

Smith, D.E. (1988) *The Everyday World as Problematic: A Feminist Sociology*. Milton Keynes: Open University Press.

Smith, D. E. (1990) 'Femininity as discourse' in D.E. Smith (ed.), *Texts, Facts and Femininity*. London: Routledge.

Smith, P. (1991) 'Laclau's and Mouffe's secret agent' in Miami Theory Collective (eds), *Community at Loose Ends*. Minneapolis: University of Minnesota Press.

Smith, R.R. (1979) 'Mythic elements in television news'. *Journal of Communication* Winter: 75–82.

Smythe, D. (1994) *Counterclockwise: Perspectives in Communication*. Boulder/Oxford: Westview Press.

Soloski, J. (1989) 'News reporting and professionalism'. *Media, Culture and Society* 11:207–28.

Soper, K. (1990) '*Constructa ergo sum*?' in K. Soper (ed.), *Troubled Pleasures*. London: Verso

Sparks, C. (1991) 'Goodbye Hildy Johnson: the vanishing "serious press"' in P. Dahlgren and C. Sparks (eds), *Communication and Citizenship*. London: Routledge.

Splichal, S. and Wasko, J. (eds) (1993) *Communication and Democracy*. Norwood, NJ: Ablex.

Stam, R. (1983) 'Television news and its spectator' in E.A. Kaplan (ed.), *Regarding Television*. Los Angeles: The American Film Institute.

van Steenbergen, B. (ed.) (1994) *The Condition of Citizenship*. London: Sage.

Steiner, L. (ed.) (1994) 'Review and criticism: public opinion paradigms'. *Critical Studies in Mass Communication* 11:274–306.

Stoehrel, V. (1994) 'Berättelsestraegier, kunskap och reflektion'. PhD dissertation, Department of Journalism, Media and Communication, Stockholm University.

van Tassel, J. (1994) 'Yakety-yak, do talk back!'. *Wired*: January.

Taylor, C. (1985) 'Theories of meaning' in C. Taylor (ed.), *Philosophical Papers 1*. Cambridge: Cambridge University Press.

Taylor, C. (1991) *Multiculturalism and 'The Politics of Recognition'*. Princeton, NJ: Princeton University Press.

Taylor, C. (1992) *The Ethics of Authenticity*. Cambridge, MA: Harvard University Press.

Tester, K. (1992) *Civil Society*. London: Routledge.

Tester, K. (1993) *Media, Culture and Morality*. London: Routledge.

Thompson, J.P. (1990) *Ideology and Modern Culture*. Cambridge: Polity Press.

Tolson, A. (1985) 'Anecdotal television'. *Screen* 26(2).

Tolson, A. (1991) 'Televised chat and the synthetic personality' in P. Scannell (ed.), *Broadcast Talk*. London: Sage.

Tomlinson, A. (1991) *Cultural Imperialism*. London: Pinter Publishers.

Tomlinson, A. (1994) 'A phenomenology of globalization?: Giddens on global modernity'. *European Journal of Communication* 9:149–72.

Tuchman, G. (1978) *Making News*. New York: Free Press.

Tulloch, J. (1990) *Television Drama: Agency, Audience and Myth*. London: Routledge.

Turner, B. (ed.) (1993a) *Citizenship and Social Theory*. London: Sage.

Turner, B. (1993b) 'Contemporary problems in the theory of citizenship' in B. Turner (ed.), *Citizenship and Social Theory*. London: Sage.

Turner, B. (1994) 'Postmodern culture/modern citizens' in B. van Steenbergen (ed.), *The Condition of Citizenship*. London: Sage.

Twine, F. (1994) *Citizenship and Social Rights*. London: Sage.

Venturelli. S.S. (1993) 'The imagined transnational public sphere in the European Community's broadcast philosophy: implications for democracy'. *European Journal of Communication* 8:491–518.

Verstraeten, H. (1994) 'The media and the transformation of the public sphere'. Unpublished paper, Centre for Media Sociology, Free University Brussels.

Wagner, P. (1994) *A Sociology of Modernity: Liberty and Discipline*. London: Routledge.

Wallis, R. and Baran, Stanley (1990) *The Known World of Broadcast News*. London: Routledge.

Walzer, M. (1992) 'The civil society argument' in C. Mouffe (ed.), *Dimensions of Radical Democracy*. London: Verso.

Wasko, J. and Mosco, V. (eds) (1992) *Democratic Communications in the Information Age*. Toronto: Garamond Press and Norwood, NJ: Ablex.

Weibull, L. (ed.) (1991) *Svenska Journalister*. Stockholm: Tiden.

White, M. (1992) *Tele-Advising: Therapeutic Discourse in American Television*. Chapel Hill, NC and London: University of North Carolina Press.

White, S. (1988) *The Recent Work of Jürgen Habermas*. Cambridge: Cambridge University Press.

Williams, R. (1974) *Television: Technology and Cultural Form*. London: Fontana.

Willis, S. (1991) *A Primer for Daily Life*. London: Routledge.

Wilson, T. (1993) *Watching Television: Hermeneutics, Reception and Popular Culture*. Cambridge: Polity Press.

Yeatman, A. (1994) *Postmodern Revisioning of the Political*. London: Routledge.

Young, I.M. (1987) 'Impartiality and the civic public' in S. Benhabib and D. Cornell (eds), *Feminism as Critique*. Cambridge: Polity Press.

Young, I.M. (1990a) 'Polity and group difference: a critique of the ideal of universal citizenship' in C.R. Sunstein (ed.), *Feminism and Political Theory*. London: University of Chicago Press.

Young, I.M. (1990b) 'The ideal of community and the politics of difference' in L.J. Nicholson (ed.), *Feminism/Postmodernism*. London: Routledge.

Index

Printed in the United States
759300001B